St. Louis Community College

Library

5801 Wilson Avenue
St. Louis, Missouri 63110

D1256771

INDIAN TREATIES:

Two Centuries
of Dishonor

Rupert Costo
Jeannette Henry

The Indian Historian Press
San Francisco

i

LC Card catalog #72-86875
ISBN No. 0-913436-23-2

Printed in the United States of America

The Indian Historian Press

CONTENTS

Preface v

Introduction ix

Chapter 1
Indian Treaties: Supreme Law of the Land 1

Chapter 2
The New War Against the Indians 41

Chapter 3
Friend Into Foe: The Meeds Dissent 71

Chapter 4
The Big Lie: A Nightmare in the Northwest 117

Chapter 5
The Tribes Today: An Overview 149

Chapter 6
A Discussion of Solutions 181

Appendices:

Establishment of the American Indian
Policy Review Commission by Joint Resolution 198

A Chronology of Indian Treaties 208

Major Laws Which Apply to Indians of All Tribes 219

A Moment of Truth for the American Indian 229

Council of State Governments Resolution 235

Sources of Information 238

ARTICLE VI, SEC. 2
of the
UNITED STATES CONSTITUTION

"This Constitution, and the Laws of the United States which shall be made in Pursuance thereof; and all Treaties made; or which shall be made, under the Authority of the United States, shall be the supreme Law of the Land; and the Judges in every State shall be bound thereby, any Thing in the Constitution or Laws of any State to the Contrary notwithstanding.

ARTICLE II, SEC. 2
of the
UNITED STATES CONSTITUTION

"He (the President) shall have Power, by and with the Advice and Consent of the Senate to make Treaties, provided two-thirds of the Senators present concur; . . ."

ARTICLE I, SEC. 10
of the
UNITED STATES CONSTITUTION

(Limitation of Powers of the States) "No State shall enter into any Treaty, Alliance, or Confederation . . . "

PREFACE

Four books have been published in a series titled *The American Indian Reader*. These four readers deal with: Anthropology, History, Education, and Literature. All have been very well received. The fifth reader is a late offering, entirely because of the vastly changing events in the Indian world.

Originally, the fifth volume was to encompass major aspects of Indian affairs, such as education, tribal organization, economic development, legislation, and major issues such as water and fishing rights.

This plan proved to be too great a task to handle in a single volume.

The editors decided, therefore, to publish a Current Affairs volume devoted to the Indian treaties, the overriding issue affecting every aspect of Indian affairs. Such questions as self-determination, economy, tribal jurisdiction, taxation, water and resources rights are all profoundly affected by issues raised through the Indian treaties.

There is little or no understanding generally, about the treaties, just as there is no understanding about the relationship of the tribes with the federal government. There is no knowledge on the part of the general public, and little understanding on the part of the educational community, of the treaties, what they say, the circumstances under which they were signed, the role of the Senate in either ratifying or refusing to ratify the treaties. This is due to the wretched poverty of this nation's educational system, a state of illiteracy frightening to behold.

This country is changing; its people are changing; the problems are severe, and the issues concerned with the American Indians loom larger than ever before.

During the past year a new Indian war has been launched. There are no guns or cannon in evidence. There are no defenseless Indians to be massacred, such as occurred at Wounded Knee and other places. And there are no blockaded concentration camps where Indians were herded while their land was being taken. But, just as it was expedient at various stages of United States history, to push the Indians westward while settlers crowded in upon their land, so is it now expedient to question and attack Indian rights, because there is a water shortage, an energy shortage, and a need for natural resources. It is a strange twist of fate that while Indian tribes were herded onto reservations that nobody else wanted, on land that was arid, rocky "good for nothing but Indians," the conditions have vastly changed.

A great part of the natural resources of this country lie within Indian reservations. Land that is largely unspoiled, with areas deemed desirable for homes and recreation, for parks and sports, are in the hands of the Indian tribes. It is the last frontier. Every new frontier that has been romanticized as a westward adventure, has fallen to the greed of land developers, gold hunters, and settlers hungry for land. This westward movement, far from being the Great American Adventure, filled with the lore of a courageous people who "faced the wilderness," was a movement to suppress the Native Americans, to take their land, all the while invoking the Christian God for His help in exterminating the Indians.

But the Native endured, and this is perhaps the greatest wonder of all. The Native endured, and now confronts America with the fact of his existence, a flourishing population, sophistication in the political arena, and an educated cadre of specialists.

This new Indian war has as its main target the destruction of the Indian treaties, and thus the destruction of the Native Americans as a people, as a race, as the original owners of the land and the source of its democratic thought.

Ideas are being disseminated which the general public is not prepared to deal with. Certainly the school system has not provided the people with accurate information about American history. Neither has the mass media provided information concerning the true history of the American Indian. The electronic media has performed even worse. The stereotypes and misconceptions about the American Indian have been the rule rather than the exception, and it is only recently that some television programs have attempted to present the Native American as he truly was in history, and as he is today.

It becomes the welcome obligation of this all-Indian publishing house to present the facts, and help develop an objective ideology suitable for preparing all the people of this country with the capacity to block this most recent Indian war.

It is for these reasons that the last volume in the *American Indian Reader* series has been devoted to the Indian treaties. Through such a discussion other current issues in Native American affairs can be understood.

CITIZENSHIP

Indians acquired citizenship nationally by statute passed by the United States Congress June 2, 1924 (43 Stat. 253, 8 U.S.C. 3).

The Act provides:

"That all non-citizen Indians born within the territorial limits of the United States be, and they are hereby declared to be citizens of the United States; Provided, That the granting of such citizenship shall not in any manner, affect the right of an Indian to tribal or other property."

Until 1924, when by this statute Indians were naturalized, "non-citizen" Indians were barred from the ordinary processes of naturalization available to foreigners. Indians born in Canada, Mexico, or other foreign lands and living in the United States were barred from citizenship, since the 1924 Act applied only to Indians "born within the territorial limits of the United States."

This was eliminated by the naturalization act of 1940 (P.L. 853, 76th Congress), which declared that "The right to become a naturalized citizen under the provisions of this Act shall extend only to white persons, persons of African nativity or descent and descendants of races indigenous to the Western Hemisphere."

The 1924 statute naturalized about 125,000 Indians. However, even before the act was passed, nearly two-thirds of the Native Americans had become citizens by various means, including these: by treaties with the tribes; by special statutes naturalizing named tribes or individuals; by general statutes naturalizing Indians who took allotments under the Dawes General Allotment Act of 1887; and by general statutes naturalizing other special classes of Native Americans.

For example, by the Act of March 3, 1873, Sec. 3 17 Stat. 631, 632, provision was made for the naturalization of adult members of any of the Miami Tribe of Kansas and their minor children.

INTRODUCTION

The United States made 394 treaties with Indian nations and tribes between the years 1778 and 1868.[1] Congress ended treaty making with the Indians through the device of the Indian Appropriations Act, in 1871.[2] But the federal government continued to deal with Indian tribes as recognized governments. The process then became one in which agreements were signed, which had to be ratified by both houses of Congress. There are 17 such Agreements on record, some of which were ratified by the Congress, and some that were refused ratification. Executive orders and statutes were enacted as well, the entire process being experienced by no other sector of American society.

No responsible person today disputes the fact that the Native Americans, before European contact, owned the entire North American continent. The nature of this "ownership" was different from that known by the property-holding, feudal regimes of Europe, but it was recognized by the foreign nations in one way or another, that the Natives had prior rights to their lands. Thus, the Indian tribes and nations were dealt with by the Dutch, the French, Great Britain, and later the United States, as foreign governments with whom treaties were made. In the case of Spain, relations with the tribes took the form of ordinances passed by the crown recognizing the rights of the Indian nations, and attempting to protect those rights.

As the continent filled up with populations from European countries, and conflict developed between the differing forms of economy, the tribes and nations were dealt with as domestic independent governments. Finally, as the economic conflict grew into a political and social struggle for control of the continent, the tribes were treated with as domestic dependent nations.

With the emergence of the United States as an independent nation, the tribes were dealt with in a manner that was additional to the treaty making process. Thus, the Trade and Intercourse Acts regulated trade with the tribes and attempted to control the liquor traffic.[3] The Northwest Ordinance of 1787 included a strong statement of good faith and justice towards the Indians.[4] Statutes were enacted throughout the history of the United States governing the federal relations with the Indian tribes and nations.[5] No other sector of American society has had nor does it have, this unique relationship with the United States.

Laws were enacted further acknowledging this unique relationship with the federal government, tightening the control of the government over Indian affairs, and continuing the position of the two political entities as governments dealing, on important issues, one with the other. When the War Department was established in 1789 by the first Congress of the United States, Indian affairs were placed under its jurisdiction.[6] In 1834, a Department of Indian Affairs was organized, which remained under the jurisdiction of the War Department.[7] When the Department of the Interior was established in 1849, the Bureau of Indian Affairs was placed within that jurisdiction.[8] Thus, the United States continued the unique relationship with the Indian tribes and nations, one in which it is recognized without contradiction that the tribes and nations are governments, a different part of the population, one which had rights owned by no other part of the population.

From time to time, attempts were made to blend the Indian people into the general population. In this way, it was hoped that the special relationship with the federal government would be "vacuumed out." Religious groups, educational programs, and schemes to individualize Indian land holdings were attempted, all in an effort to assimilate the Indian into the American melting pot, thereby ending the "Indian Problem." The only result of all these movements was to sink the Indian further into poverty, deprive him of his land, and create a class of people within the heart of the country who remained steadfast in their determination to protect their racial integrity and position as a sovereign people, original owners of the land with rights granted to them by treaties and statutes, acknowledged as heirs (not merely descendants) of those original owners.

The Indian treaties, moreover, provide the clearest evidence of the sovereign nature of Native American tribal governments. A careful examination of the treaties themselves supports this position. These documents of national and international law are legally binding contracts and solemn agreements and stand as canons of federal law, in which the tribes ceded or granted *their* lands to the federal government, for which they were to receive certain services, funds, protection against invasion or trespass, and self-government. But the treaties are not the only instruments of law binding the United States to the protection of Indian rights. With the ending of the treaty making process, the government continued to treat with the tribes and nations through executive orders, agreements, and statutes. Negotiations with the tribes, from historic times to the present, took place under the highest authority of the federal government.

No other sector of the American population has this unique relationship, and these historic rights.

Opposition to the continuing federal-Indian relationship, and conflict over what came to be considered as "special" Indian rights held by none other in the nation, began in the early days of the nation's history. This opposition took the form of genocide during the gold rush, an attempt to exterminate the Indian when secularization of the Spanish missions took place, and the infamous Removal era, in which the tribes and nations were herded like cattle to distant lands, compelled to give up their own land and property in actions that violated the laws of the nation.

When settlers demanded land in the process of westward expansion, the Indians were the victims. Forced to cede still more land, they were pushed further and further towards the Pacific Ocean. When gold was discovered in the Black Hills, the sacred place was desecrated and stolen from the Indian tribes. When railroads were planned, the tribes were made to give up huge parcels of land to provide the country with this modern development. The list of illegal taking of Indian land, the unconscionable destruction of Indian rights, makes a litany of the cruelest injustice, comprising centuries of dishonor practiced by the federal government, the states, corporate entities, and even powerful private individuals.

There is today still another wave of dishonor sweeping the land. Under the guise of "equal rights," quoting the 14th Amendment to the Constitution,[9] a national movement has been organized, with chapters in states having Indian populations with rights that are only now being brought to the attention of the United States. In other historic years, the issue was the demand for land, rights of way for railroads, gold and minerals, the establishment of military facilities on Indian reserved land. These issues arose at times when the powerful forces that control this nation demanded expansion, desired the precious metals, and plotted to gain more profits. There were many, in those past years, who followed the leadership of these powerful forces, and the good old American philosophy, "get rich quick," induced many to speculate with their lives to mine the gold, lay claim to Indian land, and begin the process of "conquering the wilderness."

Certainly there were others who were seeking a new and better life, who wanted sincerely to settle on the land, and make it their home. It was not their fault that the government encouraged them in the belief that the land was "vacant." Indeed it was not vacant, but was owned by the Indian people, most of whom would have welcomed farmers and husbandmen to come and live among them in peace.

It is once more in this vein that the offensive against Indian rights is being organized. People who are illiterate about Indian affairs, about Indian rights both historic and current, are being exploited and convinced they ought to join a movement that is not in their interests, and most assuredly will result in a conflict between Indian and nonIndian such as has not been seen before.

What is the issue this time? These are the facts: American expansion has turned upon the people and confronted them with social and economic crises never before experienced. The country has been over-exploited. The land has been over-exploited. The air is polluted. In many sections of the country, particularly the southwest, there is a shortage of water. Indians are claiming their lawful rights to fishing, hunting, and ricing, and the commercial fishermen, together with the sportsmen's organized groups, see their activities considerably narrowed. They will have to share with the Indians now. The state of Washington has become the center for the attack against the Indian tribes and nations.

The Northwest has produced two ideologists for the position that demands the abrogation of Indian treaties, and the ending of the special relationship with the original owners of the land. These ideologists have published a book of sorts, titled *Indian Treaties: American Nightmare*. United with the ideologists (who have, by the way, written the crassest inaccuracies, the most flagrant errors, into their book), are some members of Congress such as Rep. Lloyd Meeds and Jack Cunningham. These individuals, together with organized groups that claim membership from the state of Washington, through Montana and Wyoming, on to Maine and Massachusetts, have united in a general assault upon the Indian people.

The principal weapon of these people and those groups, is misrepresentation, misconception, inaccuracy, and outright falsification.

Perhaps this book will serve to allay the fears of some, and provide the truth to many, about the goals of the Indian tribes, the actual nature of their rights, and the manner in which the tribes can live peacefully and more successfully than at present, with all the people of this land.

In past years, when the Indian people were confronted by other offensives, other assaults upon their rights and liberties, strong elements of humanitarianism were felt. Reformers took up the cause of the Taos Indians (Blue Lake), the Southwest Indians (religious freedom), educational and economic conditions (the Meriam Report), and various Indian claims for compensation for land taken from them, of which the California claim is one of the best known. Talented and prominent people took up the cause of the American Indian, bringing the light of public scrutiny to bear upon Indian conditions. This help was fruitful. Conditions improved. Of even more importance was the fact that a united front was made possible between the tribes and other parts of the population. But with the blessing of public support came the curse of some well-intentioned proposals, made by people who, through their organizations, sought to influence Indian affairs and legislation, without consulting the tribes. Laws proposed by some of these groups served only to burden the Indian with more acute problems. Such, as only one example, was the Indian Rights Association, which worked for passage of the Dawes Allotment Act. This legislation deprived the American Indian of most of his land. Only many years later was the legislation abandoned as an unsuccessful experiment at best.

The Native Americans face the new war against the tribes with the same fortitude and hope that has been their reaction in other desperate days. A united program of action has been developed with the "other Americans." A united front has been developed on the international level with indigenous peoples of other lands. These are the first stirrings of a movement for Indian rights that will bring to light the struggle of all people for human rights and self-determination.

A word must be said about major sources of documentation that will be cited here.

A basic legal source, containing historic evidence, citations from legal cases, and concepts accepted by the best legal minds of the world, is the *Handbook of Federal Indian Law*, by Felix Cohen. Most Indians know this work as well as many others know their Bible. The *Handbook* was produced as an official document of the United States Federal Government. It contains a preface by the

Secretary of the Interior, and was distributed as a basic text in Indian law. Now out of date, (published 1941, with at least six additional printings), it is being revised to include additional material and legal decisions not available to Cohen in the 1930s and 1940s.

Of equal importance are the *Reports and Hearings* of *the American Indian Policy Review Commission*, established by the United States Congress in 1975[10] "to conduct a comprehensive review of the historical and legal developments underlying the Indians' unique relationship with the Federal Government in order to determine the nature and scope of necessary revisions in the formulation of policies and programs for the benefit of Indians."

The Commission was established with a membership of both Indians and Members of Congress from the Senate and the House. Task forces were set up for investigating the many complex aspects of the Indian condition. Hearings were held on reservations and in urban centers. Data was assembled concerning economic conditions, legislation, legal decisions, jurisdiction, education, the federal trust responsibility, and criminal justice, among other aspects of Indian affairs. Only two years of work accomplished a remarkable task. The data and information assembled in these reports are profoundly important, and will serve as a basis for future investigation for many years to come. Two hundred and six recommendations for change evolved from the work of the Commission. Both Houses of Congress will be considering these recommendations during the next few years. Meanwhile, a Senate Select Committee on Indian Affairs has been set up, to hold hearings, consider legislation, make specific recommendations on proposed legislation, and offer its help to the Congress in an attempt to bring some order out of the federal Indian policy, in line with the Policy Review Commission's recommendations. It is to be hoped that this committee will heed the advice of the Indian people.

This work leans heavily on the data developed by the Commission, and joins with other scholars and investigators, as well as with the concerned public, in lauding the work of the Commission as an outstanding contribution to American thought and Indian welfare. The wording of the legislation establishing the Commission is itself a historic document and is published in full in the Appendices.

For the actual wording, signatories, and other pertinent information about stipulations in the Indian treaties, *Indian Affairs: Laws and Treaties*, Vol. 2 (Treaties), published by the U.S. Government Printing Office in 1904 and since reprinted, is the authority. More intensive research is possible through the National Archives which has documentation from the Indian Office, reports of the Indian Commissioners, and data relating to treaties that failed to obtain ratification.

A chronological listing of the 394 Indian treaties and 17 Agreements is provided also in the appendix.

A bibliography of recommended reading is included. It would be impossible to list all the available literature, either on general Indian affairs, or the treaties themselves.

Rupert Costo

San Francisco
October, 1977

Jeannette Henry

INTRODUCTION
References

1. *U.S. Laws and Statutes*. Indian Treaties, Vol. 2. Compiled and edited by Charles J. Kappler, LL. M., Clerk to the Senate Committee on Indian Affairs. Washington, Government Printing Office, 1904. (Reprint available from AMS Press, N.Y.)

2. U.S. Statutes at Large, 16:566, (1871). *An Act making Appropriations for the current and contingent Expenses of the Indian Department.* The Act stated, in part ". . . Yankton Tribe of Sioux . . . For insurance and transportation of goods for the Yanktons, one thousand five hundred dollars: Provided, That *hereafter no Indian nation or tribe within the territory of the United States shall be acknowledged or recognized as an independent nation, tribe, or power with whom the United States may contract by treaty;* Provided further, That *nothing herein contained* shall be construed to invalidate or impair the obligation of any treaty heretofore lawfully made and ratified with any such Indian nation or tribe . . ." (Emphasis supplied.)

3. *U.S. Statutes at Large*, 1:137-38, (1790); U.S. Statutes at Large, 2:139-46 (1802); U.S. Statutes at Large, 4:729-35 (1834).

4. *Journals of the Continental Congress*, 32:340-41, provided that ". . . The utmost good faith shall always be observed towards the Indians, their lands and property shall never be taken from them without their consent; and in their property, rights and liberty, they never shall be invaded or disturbed unless in just and lawful wars authorized by Congress, but laws founded in justice and humanity shall from time to time be made, for preventing wrongs being done to them, and for preserving peace and friendship with them . . ."

5. *See Handbook of Federal Indian Law*, Felix Cohen, Chairman, Board of Appeals, Department of the Interior. Foreword by Harold L. Ickes, Secretary of the Interior; introduction by Nathan R. Margold, Solicitor for the Department of the Interior. Published by the U.S. Government Printing Office 1941, reprinted issue utilized herein, 1945, 662 pages, index, bibliography, maps, reference tables, citations and notes.

6. *U.S. Statutes at Large*, 1:49-50.

7. *U.S. Statutes at Large*, 4:735-38.

8. *U.S. Statutes at Large*, 9:395. See Sec. 5. "And it is further enacted, That the Secretary of the Interior shall exercise the supervisory and appellate powers now exercised by the Secretary of the War Depart-

ment, in relation to all the acts of the Commissioner of Indian Affairs; and shall sign all requisitions for the advance or payment of money out of the treasury; on estimates or accounts, subject to the same adjustment or control now exercised on similar estimates or accounts by the Second Auditor and Second Comptroller of the Treasury . . ."

9. *U.S. Constitution*, Article XIV. Ratification announced by Secretary of State, July 28, 1868. "Section 1. All persons born or naturalized in the United States, and subject to the jurisdiction thereof, are citizens of the United States and of the State wherein they reside. *No State shall make or enforce* any law which shall abridge the privileges or immunities of citizens of the United States; nor shall any State deprive any person of life, liberty, or property, without due process of law; nor deny to any person within its jurisdiction the equal protection of the laws." (Emphasis supplied.)

10. *Public Law* 93-580, 1975. See Appendix for further information and personnel of the American Indian Policy Review Commission.

"It makes little difference where one opens the record of the history of the Indians; every page and every year has its dark stain.

"The story of one tribe is the story of all, varied only by differences of time and place; but neither time nor place makes any difference in the main facts.

"Colorado is as greedy and unjust in 1880 as was Georgia in 1830, and Ohio in 1795; and the United States Government breaks promises now as deftly as then, and with an added ingenuity from long practice."

A Century of Dishonor
Helen Hunt Jackson
1881

INDIAN TREATIES: SUPREME LAW OF THE LAND

In 1880, Helen Hunt Jackson, a noted author and social reformer, conducted an exhaustive investigation of Indian conditions. Her survey included an examination of documentary sources and a personal inspection of Indian reservations. The findings were published in 1881. In that report, Mrs. Jackson described the treatment of the American Indians by the United States as "a century of dishonor." The book was published under that title.

A Century of Dishonor aroused the nation to the deplorable conditions of the native people and the systematic violations of Indian treaties. The dishonesty practiced against the Indians by the federal government, the states, the settlers and miners, and the corporations, was documented. The actions of the United States Government in making treaties with the tribes, then cynically violating them, were traced methodically. And the fact that these conditions had persisted for an entire century was dramatically described by Mrs. Jackson, one of the foremost literary figures of her time.

Another century has passed, and the evidence provided by the American Indian Policy Review Commission reveals conditions amounting to *two centuries* of dishonor. It is a different kind of horror story that is revealed, but equally horrifying as an example of injustice and contempt for law. The Commission's Report shows continuing unconscionable violations of Indian treaty rights, the failure of the federal government to fulfill its responsibilities to the Indian tribes, and the deliberate actions of the government in refusing the tribes their rights as political entities having functioning, lawful governments.

That the Indian tribes are nations endowed with sovereignty has never been disputed by the federal government, nor by the Supreme Court of the United States. This doctrine has been affirmed, confirmed and reconfirmed through the years. Whether such tribal sovereignty may be considered of a "quasi" type, or another type after these two centuries of dishonorable actions by the government, is beside the point. The fact is that the tribes exist as nations, living under the protection of the United States. Under whatever type of sovereignty they are considered to have, it provides for the right to self-government.

Self-government includes the right to self-determination and/or jurisdiction over their lands, resources and members, and the right to perform any actions or services a government is capable of performing. These are the pragmatic exercises of self-government. The protection of the United States, under contracts solemnly entered into through treaties and agreements between the sovereign Indian nations and the sovereign United States, is both implicitly and explicitly provided for in the treaties. A formidable body of law supports and confirms this relationship.

The protection undertaken by the United States has come to be known as a "trust responsibility." It involves the obligation to defend the tribes aggressively against assault upon their lands and resources, whether such actions are committed by individuals, by states, or by corporations. In most cases this obligation has been surrendered, because, it is pleaded, a "conflict of interest" exists within those agencies of government whose sworn duty it is to defend and protect the tribes against such incursions as have denied or appreciably limited their powers of government, abrogated their human rights, and led to a considerable loss of their land and natural resources.

Through the years, Indian nations have been compelled to fight for rights that were theirs by law, and should have been at least a matter of common justice. More recently, in the first half of the 1970s, tribes have gone to court in litigation fully exposing two centuries of dishonor, and demanding a redress of grievances that have accumulated through those years, despite repeated efforts on the part of the Indian people to obtain justice. Litigation has been pursued by the Oglala Sioux, the Omahas, the Chippewas, the Colvilles, Quinaults, Yakimas and others of the Northwest, as well as by tribes in the east such as the Passamaquoddy and Penobscot, the Mashpee and Oneida.

Suddenly the fact burst upon the American people that there were indeed Indian nations and tribes existing within the United States.

They had endured. Their culture had been retained, although changed to accomodate their changing social relationships with an alien world. Their languages were largely alive. They had endured such violations of human rights and indignities that the cold statistics must in themselves shock the nation. Unemployment is from 35 to 70 percent. Disease is at least 25 percent higher than that of the general population. The span of life of an Indian is 45 years. Most reservations do not have running water nor sewage systems. Indian reservation land, through the interference of the Bureau of Indian Affairs, with the connivance of the federal government, has been leased to nonIndians, a guarantee of economic impoverishment. These are merely the bare outlines of the Indian condition in the 1970s, after two hundred years of trust responsibility solemnly undertaken by the United States in signing the treaties and agreements with nations and tribes that were eminently capable of resisting the European onslaught at the beginning of white contact and throughout the colonial period.

American society is experiencing vast adverse changes economically as well as in social relationships. This overriding critical situation is the result of a hundred years of exploitation of the natural resources, without consideration for future needs. Pollution, shortages of water and energy-producing materials have suddenly confronted the country with the fact that this rich continent has limitations. The lack of care for the earth, the sky, the waters and the environment generally, has placed an enormous burden upon the people as a whole. It is suddenly discovered that the Indian tribes, which had been permitted to exist peacefully on land that nobody else wanted, were living on reservations that were now highly desirable, filled with minerals and oil, containing water to which the Indian nations have prior and paramount rights.

The Indian reservations are the last American frontier. Except that the frontier is no longer one of expansion and manifest destiny, but of maintaining a way of life that has no care for the needs of future generations. The corporations are particularly pressed. Their profits and realms of influence and power are derived from ready access to all the natural resources.

It is within this sphere, the new needs and demands of the United States, its population and its corporate powers, that the Indians now find themselves encircled with the same type of pressures that forced removal from their homelands, and compelled the cessions of their land so that settlers might have farms and gold miners engage in the pursuit of happiness.

There is an abysmal lack of knowledge about Indian history in all sectors of American society. There is ignorance of the position, status, and role of the Native in his relations with the government and society.

Setting aside for the moment the ignominious treatment accorded the Indians throughout the history of the United States, it is worthwhile to explore the historic and legal justification for the unique position of the tribes, unequalled in any other part of American society.

Evidence has been accumulated in quantity that no European power "discovered" America. The Native peoples had complex civilizations, had developed a high degree of their arts and handicrafts, and lived under recognized, freely functioning governments. There was great variety among the tribes, considerable differences in cultures, languages and economy, as well as in their forms of government. But the Europeans who were met by the Natives saw a land filled with people who had perfected a way of life and an economy that was eminently suited to their needs.

For many years following white contact, the Native population greatly outnumbered the European immigrants. During the early colonial days, and on into the years of the American Revolution and the birth of the United States, all the nations dealt with the Indians as with sovereign, independent nations. The European powers engaging in exploration of the North American continent made treaties with the Indian tribes and nations. England, France, the Netherlands, Spain and Portugal fought for control of the New World and its riches. But all recognized the Indians "right of occupancy." These words recur frequently in treaties between the foreign nations in their relations with each other, as well as in cessions from one foreign nation to another, in ordinances passed by the sovereign heads of government, and in various documents of international law. Also found in the literature is the "right of discovery."

There is a misconception that "right of discovery" means that the European powers had such rights in the context of a vacant continent. But the continent was not vacant. It had been discovered thousands of years before white contact. In fact, the limitations imposed by discovery existed between the European powers in their relations internationally with one another. It was an implicit agreement not to intervene in the control of any area that was claimed by another power. All the foreign powers recognized the original Indian entitlement to the land. When colonial settlement began, the Indians had the right to sell their land, at their own price and conditions, to whomever they desired. As settlement increased and various European powers confirmed their hold on certain regions with the use of arms and settlers, the Indian entitlement to their land changed, so

4

that they could cede their land (thereby extinguishing their title), only to that power which had acquired the right of discovery over all others that might claim it, without interference from other foreign nations.

Thus it was that in ceding land from one foreign power to another, whether by sale or conquest, the international treaties recognized the natives' right of occupancy, or aboriginal title, and stipulated continuing protection of their Indian citizens. The Treaty of Guadalupe Hidalgo between Mexico and the United States confirmed that all rights extended to its Indian citizens would be accepted by the United States.

Spain recognized tribal self-government in the earliest times, and through the Laws of the Indies, protected the natives and their governments.

England granted land through letters patent. It was left to each colony to negotiate with the Indians and institute their own policy. In some cases, negotations were held prior to settlement on Indian land. Roger Williams in 1638, William Penn in 1681, and Lord Baltimore in 1632, negotiated with the Indian tribes before settling on the land.

On October 7, 1763, the king of England signed a Royal Proclamation defining the rights of Indians in their land, as follows:

Indians were entitled to occupy their lands without molestation.

The Appalachian watershed was established as a dividing line between the British settlements and Indian country.

Persons were to be removed who had settled on land not ceded to Britain by the Indian tribes.

Land purchases were unlawful, unless done in a public meeting of government representatives and Indian delegates. (However, in violation of the Proclamation, in December, 1773, settlers were on the Ohio River between Pittsburgh and the river's mouth.)

Uninformed people, suddenly confronted by Indian claims to land, see this as a new phenomenon. Indian tribes have more intelligence than these people are willing to believe, however. They understood the laws of the foreigners who invaded their land, just as they understood and observed their own unwritten laws. (England's Magna Carta is also unwritten.) In this respect, it may be instructive to relate the history of a lawsuit that took forty years to settle.

The Mohegan Indians sued in the British Court against the colony of Connecticut in 1705. Confronted by the illegal invasion of their land by the colonial settlers, the Mohegan Nation petitioned the British Queen, complaining it had been deprived of parcels of land

5

reserved by them in a treaty with the colony of Connecticut.

The Royal Commissions sat in deliberation on three occasions: in 1705, 1738, and 1743. The decision was finally written by Commissioner Horfmander, acting for the majority. It was a major statement describing the legal position of the Indian nations. Part of the text follows:

"The Indians, though living among the king's subjects in these countries, are a separate and distinct people from them, they are treated with as such, they have a policy of their own, they make peace and war with any nation of Indians, when they think fit, without control from the English.

"It is apparent the crown looks upon them not as subjects, but as a distinct people, for they are mentioned as such throughout Queen Anne's and his present majesty's commissions by which we now sit. And it is as plain, in my conception, that the crown looks upon the Indians as having the property and the soil of these countries, and that their lands are not, by his majesty's grant of particular limits of them for a colony, thereby impropriated in his subject till they have made fair and honest purchases of the natives.

"So that from hence I draw this consequence, that a matter of property in lands in dispute between the Indians as a distinct people (for no act has been shown whereby they became subjects) and the English subjects, cannot be determined by the law of our land, but by a law equal to both parties, which is the law of nature and nations; and upon this foundation, as I take it, these commisssions have most properly issued.

"And now to maintain that the tenants in possession of the land in controversy are not bound to answer the complaint before this court, is to endeavor to defeat the very end and design of our commission; for surely it would be a very lame and defective execution of it, to hear only the matter of complaint between the tribe of Indians and this government." The Commissioners found for the Mohegan Nation.[1]

In 1532, the king of Spain directed Franciscus de Victoria to advise him on the rights of Spain in the New World. De Victoria asserted that the aborigines were the true owners of the land. If Spain was to acquire land in the New World, it must be done by treaty with the sovereign Indian nations. The findings of de Victoria were accepted by the European countries, and treaties with the natives were negotiated on the basis of international law. (Spain, however, made no treaties, acting instead through ordinances and proclamations.)

That treaties made by the United States and the Indian nations are of the same dignity as treaties with foreign nations is a view that has been repeatedly held by the federal courts and never successfully challenged, according to Cohen (*Handbook,* page 33.)[2] The contention now being made by those who are attempting to designate the treaties as "stale" is not confirmed in law. Treaties made with the Indians are not of some inferior validity, "or purely antiquarian interest," Cohen declares.

In 1828 Attorney General William Wirt stated, in a letter to the President:

"If it be meant to say that, although capable of treating, their treaties are not to be construed like the treaties of nations absolutely independent, no reason is discerned for this distinction in the circumstances that their independence is of a limited character. If they are independent to the purpose of treating, they have all the independence that is necessary to the argument . . ."[3]

In 1852, the Circuit Court for the Michigan District ruled:

" . . . It is contended that a treaty with Indian tribes has not the same dignity or effect as a treaty with a foreign and independent nation. This distinction is not authorized by the constitution. Since the commencement of the government, treaties have been made with the Indians, and the treaty-making power has been exercised in making them. They are treaties, within the meaning of the constitution, and, as such, are the supreme laws of the land."[4]

Treaties were made with the Indian nations in a number of ways, and for various purposes. They were negotiated and consummated with individual tribes, with bands, with groups of tribes, and with regions in which a number of different tribes resided. The treaty with the Delawares, in 1778, was the first treaty signed by the United States with an Indian nation. Its purpose was to bring the Delawares to the position of allies of the United States in the war with England. This treaty has an interesting condition, one which has never been fulfilled. The two parties to the Delaware treaty agreed that " . . . should it for the future be found conducive for the mutual interest of both parties to invite any other tribes who have been friends to the interest of the United States, to join the present confederation, and to form a state whereof the Delaware nation shall be the head, and have a representative in Congress . . ." This provision (Article 6) made it necessary to receive "the approbation of Congress."

It is now two centuries since that treaty was signed. The Delawares owned territory on the eastern seaboard along the banks of the Delaware River and the areas drained by its tributaries. Their original name was Lenni Lenape, but they were given the name of Lord de la Warr, governor of the English colony at Jamestown, Virginia. They originally lived in New Jersey, Delaware, parts of southeastern Pennsylvania, and parts of southeastern New York State. Their total estimated population at the time of white contact was 12,000. They are distinguished by their *Walum Olum,* the story of their various travels, and a history of their people, which was found on tablets and called the "Red Score" by historians. This Homeric epic has been of exceeding interest to scholars for a hundred years, as an example of extraordinarily beautiful poetry linked with the history of the people.

The Delawares, in many treaties with the United States, were pushed farther and farther from their homeland. Today there are two bands in a reservation in Kansas, a Stockbridge-Munsee band in Wisconsin, and three bands in Canada. Some live with the Six Nations on their reserve in Brant County, Ontario. There is a reservation in Kent County, Ontario; near the town of Melbourne, there are Munsees on a reservation with the Oneida and Chippewa people. Others are in Northeast Oklahoma, and in Anadarko, Oklahoma. These are the remnants of a once proud and powerful nation. The history of their treaties, traced chronologically, clearly describes the dishonor with which they were treated by the United States Government. As the treaty-making process went on, it was clear that railroads and corporations were being given special preference by the federal government in order to acquire Delaware land.

The treaty of May 30, 1860, for example, had the purpose of selling Delaware land to the Leavenworth, Pawnee and Western Railroad Company, the total land amounting to 227,000 acres. In 1861, the attorney for the Delaware Indians then living in the State of Kansas protested that reservation land sold to the railroad was a "fraud on the Indians of the most flagrant character," because the land had been appraised at $1.28 per acre, while it was worth at least $10 an acre.[5]

Treaties with the Indian nations were made for various purposes. There were treaties for mutual protection, for peace, in support and regulation of trade with the Indians, to provide for military posts, to arrange for rights of way so that corporations might build railroads through Indian land, to wrest cessions of land from the natives, to ensure neutrality in the war with England and in the war of 1812, and for the benefit of individuals in order to provide them with Indian land.

As the settlers, railroads and miners moved into the land, Indians were forced into submission. Even then, "conquest" was not considered a means of acquiring title to Indian land. Treaties were negotiated, and signed by the two sovereigns, the United States and the Indian tribes.

There are those who, in an effort to completely wipe out Indian tribal rights, point to the contention that the Indian tribes were conquered by the superior forces of the United States. In the first place, there were no declared wars upon the Indian nations. Conflict that was often armed on the part of the Indians were defensive actions provoked by inhuman and cruel acts against the Indians. A case in point is that of the Apaches, who later became noted for their depredations. Originally a peaceful people, they had come to the United States Army post at Camp Grant in Arizona Territory under a flag of truce. Accepted by the commander, they began to raise crops and established a small colony of nearly seven hundred. On April 30, 1871, according to the report of C.B. Brierley, Acting Assistant Surgeon, U.S.A., they were massacred by a "large party" of white men "who had left Tucson with the avowed purpose of killing all the Indians at this post."

Brierley describes what was found at the Indian camp.

"Their camp was burning, and the ground strewed with their dead and mutilated women and children. I immediately mounted a party of about twenty soldiers and citizens, and sent them with the post surgeon with a wagon to bring in the wounded, if any could be found. The party returned late in the afternoon, having found no wounded, and without having been able to communicate with any of the survivors."

The report stated that the Apaches were "so changed as to not be recognizable from those he had known. Another attack on the Indian camp at the post occurred soon after. The Report of the Board of Indian Commissioners for 1871 contains a description of another massacre against the Apaches, in which one white man by the name of Johnson used a howitzer to massacre a group of Apaches with whom he had been on the most friendly terms, and they with him. His reason for this outrage was the offer of a bounty for Indian scalps.

Killing, massacres, depredations existed on both sides, the whites and the Indians. The whole 19th century was filled with the conflict, the Indians being pushed farther and farther west, regardless of the most solemn treaties made with their nations.

Despite the conflict characterizing the century, the claim of conquest as bestowing an effective title over Indian land has been denied in Court decisions.

Chief Justice Marshall ruled, in 1832, that "It may not be unworthy of remark that it is very unusual, even in the cases of conquest, for the conqueror to do more than to displace the sovereign and assume dominion over the country. The modern usage of nations which has become law, could be violated; that sense of justice and right which is acknowledged and felt by the whole civilized world would be outraged, if private property should be generally confiscated, and private rights assailed."

Cohen (*Handbook,* page 123), adequately responds to the theory of conquest in these words: "Conquest renders the tribe subject to the legislative power of the United States and, in substance, terminates the external powers of sovereignty of the tribe, namely, its power to enter into treaties with foreign nations, but does not by itself affect the internal sovereignty of the tribe, that is, its powers of self-government."

A historical overview of treaty-making with the Indian nations would, briefly, show this outline:[6]

From 1532 to 1776, the principle acknowledging the rights of the Indian tribes and nations noted through advice by Franciscus de Victoria, as described above.

The theory of Indian title was generally adopted by the European powers. The Dutch, in a statement drafted about 1630 for the guidance of the Dutch West Indian Company, asserted:

"The Patroons of New Netherland, shall be bound to purchase from the Lords Sachems in New Netherland, the soil where they propose to plant their Colonies, and shall acquire such right thereunto as they will agree for with the said Sachems."

From 1776 to 1783, efforts were made in the early days of the Revolutionary War, to induce the Indians to take a neutral position. As the war continued, there were strong efforts both on the part of England and the United States to force the Indians to become allies. Considerable concern for the Indian tribes was expressed by the Continental Congress, and the treaty with the Delawares was signed in 1778 [7]

From 1783 to 1800, the United States made treaties involving a peaceful relationship with the tribes. Commissioners were appointed in 1784 to negotiate with the Indians. They were instructed to draw boundary lines, conclude peace, and compel recognition of United States sovereignty and dominion over the tribes.

From 1800 to 1817, expansion begins and tribes are removed, their lands further reduced by amended treaties, and some responsibility is taken by the United States for services such as education and the propagation of religious teaching. Substantial cessions of Indian land were made at this time.

From 1817 to 1846, the practice of removal begins in earnest, in which Indian tribes were moved to Indian Territory, later to become the State of Oklahoma. Suggestions for removal as an answer to the "Indian Problem" had been made from the time of George Washington, but had not been actively pursued.

From 1854 to 1861, new efforts to remove Indians, and force more cessions of land from them for the purpose of white settlement. Treaties were negotiated, generally amending previous treaties, and permitting the settlement of Indian land by the whites.

From 1861 to 1865, the years of the Civil War. Some tribes supported the Union forces; others supported the Confederates. Treaty negotiations continued, particularly in Utah and Nevada Territory.

From 1865 to 1871 saw many Indian councils and negotiations in which treaties were signed pledging mutual friendship and peace. The Indians complain of depredations by whites, and conflict breaks out with the Plains tribes. The massacre of Wounded Knee takes place in 1868, and the tribes of the Plains are subdued, only to take up the struggle for their rights at another time, in another way.

The end of treaty making came in 1871, when Congress passed the Indian Appropriations Act and included the termination of treaty-making with the Indian nations.

However, as Cohen relates, "The substance of treaty-making was destined to continue for many decades. For in substance a treaty was an agreement between the Federal Government and an Indian tribe. And so long as the Federal Government and the tribes continue to have common dealings, occasions for agreements are likely to recur. Thus the period of Indian land cessions was marked by the 'agreements' through which such cessions were made."

Discussing the sovereign nature of Indian tribes and their right to self-government, Cohen declares:

"Legislation based upon Indian consent does not come to an end with the close of the period of Indian land cessions and the stoppage of Indian land losses in 1934.

"For in that very year the underlying assumption of the treaty period that the Federal Government's relations with the Indian tribes should rest upon a basis of mutual consent was given new life in the mechanism of federally approved tribal constitutions and tribally approved federal charters established by the Indian Reorganization Act of June 18, 1934."

"Thus," Cohen observes, "while the form of treaty-making no longer obtains, the fact that Indian tribes are governed primarily on

11

a basis established by common agreement remains, and is likely to remain so long as the Indian tribes maintain their existence and the Federal Government maintains the traditional democratic faith that all Government derives its just powers from the consent of the governed.''

It is to be noted that Indian tribes, through the Indian Reorganization Act, adopted constitutions and charters, but with the approval of the Secretary of the Interior. There were many tribes which objected to the continued dominance of the Interior Department, more particularly in the right granted through the 1934 act, making it mandatory for a tribe to obtain the Secretary's approval for laws and ordinances, the leasing of tribal property, the consummation of tribal contracts, and the holding and banking of tribal money (which is generally deposited in the United States Treasury and held ''for the benefit'' of the tribe. Requests for expenditures must be approved by the Secretary.) [8]

During the 1950s, when Dillon S. Myer held office as Commissioner in the Bureau of Indian Affairs, an epidemic of depredations and violations against Indian rights began, following a period of attempts to right certain wrongs. The following information is contained in an article written by Felix Cohen in the Yale Law Journal 1953, (Vol. 62:348-390), titled ''The Erosion of Indian Rights.''

Interference with the right to vote increased through the use of federal funds and direct interference. On the Blackfeet reservation in June, 1950, thirty-six pages of mimeographed materials attacking candidates for tribal office were circulated. The flyers charged tribal officers with unsubstantiated criminal and illegal acts. The misinformation was printed on government mimeograph machines, at government expense, by government employees. Upon a request by an Indian group whether this action had been approved by Interior, the response was affirmative.

During the Blackfeet and Choctaw referendum election of 1950, letters from Interior officials on the merits of the issues were distributed at government expense. It was an effort to influence the voters. This was done on the basis that the voters needed to be ''informed'' on the issues.

When the Blackfeet tribe held another referendum in 1952, on a proposed amendment to their constitution, the Interior Department held a rival election. It was managed by Indian Bureau employees. The Bureau special police was called out, closed some polling places, seized tribal funds without tribal consent, to pay some of the expenses of the Bureau election. In an effort to validate the election, the Bureau attempted to strike more than one thousand Blackfeet names from the list of eligible voters.

At San Ildefonso Pueblo, New Mexico, the Indian Bureau seized control of valuable land, then disposed of the Pueblo resources without statutory authority. The excuse was that the Pueblo had failed to elect a governor. This was untrue.

In 1965, during the course of hearings on the California Indian claims case, the Pit River Indians in central California held an election to decide whether they wished to accept the compromise settlement of 47 cents an acre for their land. The tribal vote was critical, since only one of the dozen cases then at issue would have had to vote against the settlement in order to invalidate it. Either the Pit Rivers or the Mission Indians of Southern California were entitled to this condition. The Pit Rivers voted against the settlement. The Bureau of Indian Affairs then held its own election, called in nearly 700 Indians (the tribe had only about 400 enrolled) and the vote was voided. At hearings held subsequently, it was charged that some of these "Bureau voters" were dead people; others were not of the Pit River tribe, and still others were of other tribes and voted in two elections. Nevertheless, the compromise settlement was approved by the Interior Department.

The Yavapai Indians at Fort McDowell in Arizona have been subjected to interference in their elections throughout the 1970s, in an effort to induce them to vote in favor of construction of the Orme Dam, which would flood their land.

In Arizona, under the direction of Area Director John Artichoker, the tribes have had their elections invalidated, often without explanation. Such incidents were reported as late as 1975.

The Comanche Tribe in Oklahoma in 1977, still had no tribal council, due to the Bureau's rejection of a tribal election, and the failure of the Interior officials to settle the matter.

Such practices have been common in United States Indian affairs. In this way, the Interior Department has subverted the voting rights of the Indian people, the most elementary of all rights.

When Commissioner Myers attempted to control the selection of attorneys by the tribes, hearings were held and the Interior Secretary rejected Myers' regulations. Despite this, Myers continued to deny thousands of Indians the right to employ attorneys of their choice.

Another method was used, and in many cases is still used, to still the voice of the Indian people and deny them the right to speak freely. Here is only one incident that became a celebrated cause:

when the Oglala Sioux tribe in 1950 petitioned Congress to cut the wasteful expenditures of the Indian Bureau in its "extension service" in South Dakota, they were advised that $140,000 of credit funds allocated to the tribe some few months earlier would be frozen until the tribe withdrew its criticisms. Today, if a tribe expresses a position contrary to the desires and interests of the Interior Department, another method is used. If they have a federally funded program, their checks are held up, and the explanations are so dreary it is to wonder they even try to explain. The checks are just "late."

The Indian Bureau has on many occasions testified in congressional hearings against tribal positions. In other cases, the Bureau has not notified tribes that hearings would be held, and thus the tribal position was not known to the congress. In late 1977 the Interior Department published regulations concerning the use of water on reservations as well as in various states. Information about the dates and places of the hearings, (required by law), were sent out after the hearings were held, or too late for the tribes to send representatives. A tribal attorney, asked to appear in Los Angeles on behalf of the All Indian Pueblo Council, had to cancel court appearances in order to be present at the hearing. He was given ten minutes to testify.

In order to discourage Indian tribesmen from remaining on their reservations, Commissioner Myer closed down several small hospitals, and refused to rebuild the burned-down Papago Hospital, the only medical facility on a 2,835,000 acre reservation.

The Commissioner took the trouble to interfere in the religious practices of the Indian tribes, continuing the 16th and 17th centuries' refusal to permit the Indians freedom of religion. At one of the Rio Grande Pueblos, ancient tradition forbids a white person to remain within the Pueblo at certain sacred ceremonials. The Bureau officials insisted that they must remain on the Pueblo grounds, despite the objection of the Pueblo people.

The article written by Felix Cohen reveals other discriminatory practices against Indians. Cohen, who witnessed many of these practices personally, stated:

"Because of discriminatory restrictions, the vast majority of Indian landowners are barred from using their own land. The reasons given for this conclusion vary from acre to acre: On one acre the Indian Bureau acts as a guardian of unknown heirs, as a perpetual administrator of an indivisible inheritance, and as a rent-collector for holders of claims against Indians who have long since passed away; on a second acre, where an Indian wants to graze his ponies, the Indian Bureau appears as a grazing master, securing for outside livestock operators an ever-increasing control of Indian lands by forbidding the use of the range to all Indians who are too poor to construct barbed wire fences (at least 98 percent of the population); on a third acre, the Indian Bureau turns up with a mortgage which enables it to direct almost every movement of the Indian "owner."

"Faced by hundreds of special restrictions which do not apply to their white neighbors, Indians have survived on land where white men would starve to death and under regulations which could drive men of any race to insanity."

The Indian Bureau, under the direction of the Interior Department has for more than a hundred years disposed of Indian tribal lands without the consent of the Indians. This practice, which was revived in the 1950s, had resulted in more than 80 millions of dollars in judgment against the United States.

In 1951, leases were issued by the Interior Department, without Indian consent and over their protest, covering a valuable building materials deposit on the lands of the Pueblo of San Ildefonso. In 1950, leases of valuable Blackfeet tribal grazing lands were issued by the Bureau of Indian Affairs despite the protests of the tribe against the leases. When the tribal secretary appeared at the sale to warn lessees of the tribe's objection, he was ejected from the room by the reservation superintendent.

When an Indian Superintendent at the Pyramid Lake Reservation tried to protect Indian lands against white trespassers whose claims had been rejected by the federal courts, (Depaoli v. United States, 139 F 2nd 225, 9th Cir. 1943) the superintendent was removed at the request of the trespasser's legal advisor, the senior Senator from Nevada, Mr. McCarran. It took the intercession of President Truman to stop the removal. The superintendent, however, found it was impossible to continue in his job because of harassment and lack of support from the Interior Department.

Another system, widely in use during the 1950s, still having some application today, is the jurisdiction over Indian land despite the allotment system, in which an Indian has been given a certain acreage. This sytem, which began with the Dawes General Allotment Act in 1887, was devised so that the Indian might learn to handle his own property, "learn the white man's ways," and eventually develop what the Indian Bureau euphemistically referred to as the "sacred egotism" of the white man.

But when the Indian began to display just these skills and attitudes, the Bureau created a system to roll back all power over Indian allotments into Bureau hands. This "recapture" device is generally called the "unit" or "power of attorney" system.

Under the system, each Indian is persuaded, or if necessary compelled to turn over to the reservation superintendent a power of attorney which gives the official complete authority to dispose of Indian lands for grazing purposes. This began as a voluntary arrangement. It soon became utilized with ruthless force. Between 1950 and 1952, the Bureau had sent notices to Indians telling them they will not be allowed to collect any income from their lands unless they surrender power over these lands to the agency superintendent by signing a power of attorney. Similar notices are sent to livestock operators in the vicinity who might be inclined to contract with Indians for the grazing of stock, warning them that such contracts would not be tolerated.

The statutory authority of the Interior Secretary to approve or disapprove of Indian leases has been and is now being used to centralize the leasing of Indian lands in the Bureau itself. The Interior Department gave lands for free grazing by lambs owned by big out-of-state sheepowners. When the Blackfeet Indians protested, the practice continued. The *Portland Oregonian,* (January 25, 1952) exposed a gigantic fraud in the disposal of Indian timber lands, in which a tract worth $400,000 was sold for two checks, one of $135,000 to the original Indian owners, and one of $25,000 to an agent for interested Bureau employees.

Various Indian tribes earn substantial incomes from such enterprises as cattle raising, stores, and other commercial enterprises. Their funds are deposited by the Interior in the Department of the Treasury, to be used "for them" with the approval of the Interior Secretary. When the tribe decides that a certain project or program is worthy of support, and requests the fund distribution from Interior, they are rejected if the project does not meet with the Secretary's personal judgment, or the desires of the Interior Department officials. For example, when the Jicarilla Apache Indians of New Mexico requested their own funds from the United States Treasury, through petition to the Interior, in order to conduct a hydrological survey of their water rights, they were refused in 1973. Such a survey was required so that they could quantify their water rights, and then have those rights adjudicated.

Tribal constitutions under the Indian Reorganization Act, and even for those who do not come under this Act, must be approved by the Secretary of the Interior. They are actually written by the Interior, as are all amendments and ordinances.

All the vital activities and actions of the tribes go through a maze of bureaucratic officialdom, making a travesty of the most elementary processes of democracy, and guaranteeing the immobility of the tribe's economy. First, the tribe goes through the local superintendents, then the regional area offices, then various other offices of the Bureau of Indian Affairs in Washington, D.C., then finally to the desk of the Secretary of the Interior, for his approval. The process is dreary, frustrating, time consuming and expensive. For such tribes as those geographically isolated in the Northwest, it means the expenditure of days and weeks of travel to and from the regional office, the area office, and even to Washington, D.C.

During the last few years, an effort has been made at the tribes' insistence, to at least permit them to use their own money, deposit in banks of their own choosing, and handle at least part of their funds for purposes of governing themselves. This is a recent development, and not all tribes have won this concession.

During the drought years of the 1930s, the government, as relief to distressed farmers, purchased drought cattle at an average price of $12 a head. Most of the cattle were given away free to relief clients. In the 1950s, Indians who received such drought cattle were charged up to $140 a head or more, for something that was a gift to everyone else.

Also in the 1930s, the Indian Bureau engaged in a program of irrigation on tribal land that was dry and incapable of supporting farming or cattle raising. Without consulting the tribes of Southern California, irrigation ditches were forthwith dug on various reservations, and in some areas where the dryness of the land would soon fill up the ditches. This was the case on the Cahuilla Indian Reservation in Riverside County. The ditches were dug, and then left to fill in. No effort was made to maintain them, if they could be maintained. Nevertheless, the Indians were charged for the irrigation ditches and for nearly thirty years thereafter, interest accumulated on the charges. Protests and petitions were of no avail, until, in the 1960s, Interior issued a regulation voiding the charges.

The statement has been made that certain huge claims of Indian tribes have passed the statute of limitations, due to the Act instituting an Indian Claims Commission. Previously, Indians had been compelled to deal with the Court of Claims, and it was not unusual for twenty years to elapse before a decision was rendered.

The Indian Bureau, however, found a way to institute regulations which practically inhibited the tribes from making use of the Indian Claims Commission for a long time. The Commissioner of Indian Affairs refused to approve attorneys engaged by the Indians. He then blocked the enactment of a bill giving Indians additional time to employ lawyers and file their claims. Then, the Bureau refused access to the tribes of materials vital to their cases and lodged in the Interior Department. As a final insult, the Commissioner adopted the extraordinary practice of promulgating official opinions on questions before the Indian Claims Commission. Every such opinion rendered during 1950-1952 has thus been adverse to the Indians.

Indian tax exemptions are not personal to the Indian but are characteristic of certain forms of property, resting generally on a treaty or agreement promising that a piece of land would remain in Indian ownership forever. Such promises were generally part of the bargains by which most of the land of the United States was sold to the government. Indians are willing to give up their tax exemptions if the federal government will give them back the land. The courts have held that such promises of tax exemption create vested rights which even the congress is constitutionally bound to respect.[9] Beginning in 1950, the Indian Bureau has sponsored a series of bills which unilaterally would end such tax exemptions. Today, this effort has been undertaken by the states and county communities. Thus, the Indian tribes have been struggling against this oppressive proposal for twenty-seven years.

Until recently, the Indian Bureau had taken to itself the power to expend tribal trust funds (the tribes' own money) without authority or even the knowledge of the tribes. There are cases in which tribal land, as well as the land of individual tribal allottees has been sold without their knowledge or consent. An investigation of misuse of tribal funds by the Indian Bureau brought to light a considerable evidence of fraud as well as misuse of tribal assets. A series of Acts was passed in congress establishing a tribal veto power over various activities of the Bureau.[10] The Act of March 4, 1933 authorized modification of timber contracts.[11] The Act of May 31, 1933 gave the Pueblos of New Mexico a veto power over Bureau expenditures of Pueblo funds.[12] There then followed a series of statutes requiring Indian consent to Bureau expenditures.[13]

Recent actions by the states attempting to gain jurisdiction over Indian tribes is merely a continuation of such attempts in earlier times. Bills giving several states the power to extend state criminal laws over Indians on Indian reservations were introduced year after year in congress for nearly a century. Such bills have been opposed by the Indians and generally were defeated. In 1949 President Truman vetoed a bill that would have extended state criminal laws to the Navajo and Hopi Indians without their consent. Truman's grounds for the veto were stated in these words: "This bill violates one of the fundamental principles of Indian law accepted by our Nation, namely, the principle of respect for tribal self-determination in matters of local government."[14]

One of the historic examples of the Interior Department and Bureau of Indian Affairs flagrant violation of the laws concerning Indians is expressed in the Commissioner's reaction to the doctrine of consent. On August 5, 1952, the Commissioner sent a "Withdrawal Memorandum" to the superintendents in all agencies:

" . . . Agreement with the affected Indian groups must be attained if possible. In the absence of such agreement, however, I want our differences to be clearly defined and understood by both the Indians and ourselves. We must proceed even though Indian cooperation may be lacking in certain cases."

The concept of American democracy, that of government by consent of the governed, has been violated so brutally throughout the history of Indian affairs, that it has created virtually insurmountable obstacles to Indian progress, let alone self-determination. The Indian Bureau, on occasion, and when sharply pressed, has instituted a system of "consultation," instead of consent. In practice, consultation means attempting to get the Indians to agree with a Bureau decision or program. If this fails, then the Bureau asks congress to adopt the Bureau program anyway. Most of the time, it works, and the Bureau has its way.

The Bureau of Indian Affairs has been under the jurisdiction of the Department of the Interior since 1849. Decisions of the Bureau are subject to approval by the Secretary of the Interior. Within the Interior there are the Bureau of Reclamation, and a number of other agencies which have interests directly opposed to those of the Indian tribes. As only one example, the Reclamation division wants to construct a dam. The Fort McDowell Indians don't want the dam.

(Note Orme Dam situation, described herein.) The Interior Department is compelled to decide which of the two interests it ought to support. Usually the Interior Department supports Reclamation, because Reclamation presents the case for the states and industries and indeed to all intents and purposes represents the corporate interests, as will be shown here.

There is ample evidence that corporate powers control the Department of the Interior, which controls the Bureau of Indian Affairs, which controls natural resources on Indian reservations. That there has existed and still exists a conflict of interest between Interior and the Indian tribes in their effort to protect their natural resources has long been evident. [15]

Interior has had close connections with the United States petroleum industry for at least thirty years. Interior controls the leasing of federal lands (including Indian lands), for oil and gas drilling and development. The Bureau of Mines and United States Geological Survey have their offices within Interior. During World War II and the Korean War the petroleum industry was mobilized in the war effort, with the Secretary of the Interior at the head of such organizations as the Petroleum Administration for War, in World War II; and the Petroleum Administration for Defense, in the Korean War. These two organizations had the appearance of governmental groups with authority to allocate and ration scarce supplies of crude oil and petroleum products. But the staffs and policy direction were controlled by the major oil companies.

Following these patriotic services of the oil company officials (their salaries were continued by the companies), the Interior Secretary formed a permanent National Petroleum Council, ostensibly to advise him on national oil policy matters. Members of the council are named by the Secretary. But the industry itself, through its trade association, the American Petroleum Institute, presents the Secretary with a list of names recommended by the oil industry. The Secretary assigns the council to make studies and report to him on oil industry issues. Generally, these requests originate within the industry. Thus the oil companies are free from anti-trust suits, and they gain prestige and credibility to the report when it is issued by the National Petroleum Council.

The relationships of congressmen who have served their stint in the nation's highest legislative body, with big corporations, may be shown in these facts: The biggest lobby in the congress is the American Petroleum Institute, by all reports. It is headed by former Congressman Frank N. Ikard of Texas. The Interstate Natural Gas Association of America is headed by Congressman Walter E. Rogers, also from Texas. The National Petroleum Council, a semi-government and industry advisory committee, is headed by Kenneth H. BeLieu, a former member of the administrative officialdom in both the Johnson and Nixon Administrations.

Millions of dollars in corporate funds are expended every year by their lobbying groups, and the hand of corporate power can be seen in legislation and the activities of the congressmen.[15] Added to the lobbying efforts (and successes) of the oil and gas companies, must be the coal mining industry with its huge corporations now eyeing Indian reservation land as the last frontier for energy-producing enterprises, and the enormous profits to be derived thereby.

With corporate representatives in high positions of the United

States Government, residing deep in the heart of the Interior Department, what chance do the tribes have to protect their resources?

What is bound to ensue is a sharp struggle between the Indians, with consumer support, and the federal government through the Interior Department, because of the conflict of interest evident through corporate power which is fully exercised within the Interior Department. Utilization of tribal natural resources is, and will be subject to the Interior's proclivity to protect and support the corporations.

The Bureau of Reclamation, the United States Army Corps of Engineers, and other departments within Interior, all dance to the tune of the corporate powers. There is no other way to explain their persistent attack on Indian natural resources, and their continuing efforts to divert reservation water, obtain coal and mineral leases on reservations, with the greatest benefit to themselves, and the greatest harm to the environment, and bury the Indian tribes in excessive litigation looking towards the mere protection of their remaining resources.

The general public is also endangered through the activities of these government agencies. Water on most streams has been over-appropriated, so that there has been and will continue to be a shortage for all. Corporations such as those using strip mining methods requiring huge quantities of water are favored, thereby sharply reducing the public water supply, even for domestic use. It appears there is no plan, or long range approach to the problems of conservation of the resources of this continent. What happens in such a situation, is that the Indian reservations are being blamed for shortages. Suddenly a "new frontier" emerges, in which the idea is being sold to the public that if only the reservations could be made to be "good boys" and release their claims to water and their demands for protecting their natural resources, everything would be fine in these United States.

This is not a new situation, it should be observed. Throughout American history, the Indian tribes have been victims of corporate interests. In the 1870s, railroad corporations entered the Indian Territory, and the practice of negotiating formal treaties with Indians ended. Coal corporations were established on tribal land, followed in the 1880s by cattle corporations, and in the 1890s by oil corporations. Indian control of their own affairs declined, and the nature of civilization was increasingly determined by gandy dancers, cowboys, and roughnecks, one writer observes.[16]

It was Cherokee Chief Lewis Downing who stated, in a melancholy mood as he saw the direction of events in 1869, that rules must be agreed upon and adhered to, especially since there was such a great difference between the Indian tribes and the American businessman "in that industry, habit and energy of character which is the result of the development of the idea of accumulation."

Without such restraints, Downing warned, "once cut loose from our treaty moorings, we will roll and tumble upon the tempestuous ocean of American politics and congressional legislation, and shipwreck be our inevitable destination."[17]

The Cherokee treaties had written into them provisions for rights of way for railroads, and the Nation looked forward to obtaining stock options in the railroad corporations as one way in which to increase their wealth, and have some decision-making powers over the corporations that inevitably would seek to control their land and destiny.

In 1857, Thaddeus Hyatt went to Indian Territory to find opportunities for constructing a railroad. Government reports described a "hardy, daring and determined pioneer population" moving into Indian country, some motivated by a "restless spirit of adventure," and others by "a feverish spirit of speculation." It was admitted that these individuals could not be restrained. A congressman said, in 1852, that "The Indian is placed between the upper and nether millstones and must be crushed . . . Humanity may forbid but the interest of the white man demands their extinction."[18]

The Cherokees in Indian Territory, later to become the State of Oklahoma, attempted to join the promising industrial movement, as they had emulated the mode and structure of American government and society in Georgia, by buying stock in the corporations. The Cherokee National Council, in 1866, guaranteed a $500,000 stock subscription in the Union Pacific Southern Branch Railroad. They also took an option to buy more stock within three years. The corporation was given the right to take building materials from Cherokee land to be paid for in stock as well as cash. The railroad defaulted on its promises, failed to pay for the materials, and left the Cherokees outside looking in.

In 1870 the Cherokee Nation in Indian Territory had the means and wanted to build its own railroads. Instructions were given to its Washington delegation by the Cherokee National Council:

" . . . the possession and ownership of a most valuable tract of belt of land through the heart of their country by any corporation of citizens of the United States or foreign countries—capitalists and strangers, who have no sympathy for Indians or their peculiarities, who would desire the lands along their road brought into market and opened to immigration as speedily as possible—who would only look upon their Nation and perhaps their existence and presence in any form as an encumbrance and a nuisance—could only result in the disruption of their Nationality and the ruin of their people."[19]

The tribal leaders said they wanted to build their own railroads "for reasons above all pecuniary consideration." They wanted a continual progress toward "Christian civilization" but also they wanted to maintain the best of their Indian culture and tribal rights. It was Ely Parker, a mixed blood Seneca, Commissioner of Indian Affairs in 1870, who recommended denying the Cherokee request. They were not sufficiently "qualified," he thought. The institution of the tribe should be destroyed, he said, and its members become United States citizens.

The Creeks also applied for permission to build their own railroad. It was denied. Parker, a hero to the white establishment, was a Quisling to his people.

Indian trust funds have been a source of capital for American industrialists. United States bonds, in which the Cherokee National Fund and the Cherokee Orphan Fund were invested by the United States to support the Union Pacific Eastern Division Railway, is a case in point. The corporation was at that very time illegally cutting timber on the Delaware reservation in Kansas in 1864. United States bonds of the Creek Orphan Fund were pledged to the Ohio Canal Company. A House investigating committee, looking into the Indian attorney business in 1872, concluded that an Indian claims agent would "buy or sell, corrupt or be corrupted, whichever promises the most money."

It is doubtful whether the injustices suffered by the Indian people could have been as successful as they have been, were it not for the renegades, the traitors, and the Quislings in their midst. Such a man was Elias C. Boudinot, who has become a hero to the white establishment, but no hero to the American Indian tribes, whose property he gave away or sold at meager prices, whose nation he helped to destroy.

Boudinot submitted treaty drafts extremely generous to United States corporations; he favored large grants of land for railroad rights of way; and was so much a friend of an ally of the corporations that he was dubbed "either a designing knave or a contemptible fool." It was the corporations, it was said "that was responsible for such a freak of evolution of a tribal citizen as the character of Elias C. Boudinot."[20]

Examples of violations of the Indian treaties are too numerous to mention. But decisions of the Supreme Court have affirmed the tribes as self-governing entities, and such affirmation is generally based on these canons of law:

1. Ambiguous expressions in treaties must be resolved in favor of the involved Indian parties.[21]
2. Treaties must be interpreted as the Indians themselves would have foreseen and understood them.[22]
3. Treaties must be liberally construed in favor of the Indians.[23]

Indian treaties are not to be read like ordinary legal documents. The courts have ruled that the historical circumstances surrounding treaty negotiations require canons which act in favor of the tribes. Those rules have been applied to statutes, executive orders and agreements made with the tribes.[24]

The leading case on the question of treaty abrogation is the 1964 Supreme Court decision in *Menominee Tribe v. U.S.*[25] This involved a treaty reserving lands to the tribe "as Indian lands are held."[26] The State of Wisconsin argued that the Menominee Termination Act of 1954 made all state statutes applicable on the former reservation. The statute in question was silent on this point. Finding the Act's legislative history ambiguous, the Court looked to later congressional enactments, and noted that *Public Law 280*, passed by the same congress, specifically exempted Indian hunting and fishing rights from state jurisdiction. In view of this, the Court found that congress did not intend to eliminate Menominee hunting and fishing rights. It held that the Termination Act did not abrogate Indian treaty rights. The court also declared that it did not believe congress intended to abrogate Indian treaty rights in a "backhanded way."[27]

The question of "Indian sovereignty" is important because the issue of Indian title to their land and assets is involved in a determination as to just what "sovereignty" or quasi-sovereignty means, and upon what foundation Indian tribal title rests.

Determinations of Indian tribal title have been made by the courts. In all cases, such title has been seen as different from the usual private title held by individuals. Nor is it similar to title held by the federal government in public trust. It has its roots in the treaties and agreements made with the tribes, in the fact that the tribes and nations gave up their continent to foreigners, and that such treaties and agreements may not be unilaterally abrogated, as a matter of "natural law."

A Supreme Court ruling is presumed to settle a particular case, set a precedent for cases that may follow, and thereupon enter into the realm of inherent and practical law unless congress enacts legislation to the contrary. Even at that point, congressional statutes may be struck down by the high court as unconstitutional. This process relies upon the separation of powers which is a tenet of the United States Constitution, residing in the executive, the congressional, and the judicial sectors of the American democracy, and the Constitution.

Supreme Court decisions may differ from time to time on the same general question to be adjudicated. And they do. It's almost a game between attorneys, therefore, in the adversary system of justice prevalent in the United States. Ultimately, the Constitution is the supreme test. Even the Constitution has been variously interpreted, providing an important forum for opinion and judgment. Opinions have been rendered by the Supreme Court that have been judged to be misleading because they may be based on misinterpreted information, information not made available, or even the changing social conditions. In time, as has been found, following decisions mend the wrongs done earlier, and provide yet another round of cases to be considered. Nations founded on democratic principles use the precepts of justice founded in law, both "natural" law and law based on the Constitution.

References are made to Indian tribal title as "aboriginal title," or "title of occupancy." These titles are not passive expressions of an idea, or an exercise in literary phraseology. They are active, and can be adjudicated, explained, and confirmed.

Rulings of the courts, however, have been violated on the grindstone of bureaucratic pragmatism and subservience to the corporate powers. Thus, government agencies have in the historic past violated Supreme Court decisions as well as congressional statutes. The violations are continuing.

Under the guise of the United States as ultimate sovereign, to which the tribes are subject, the treaties have been attacked as "stale," and the rights of the Indian tribes have been opposed. Curiously, those now attacking the treaties and the rights of the tribes as original owners of the land, do not identify where United States sovereignty resides. Congressman Lloyd Meeds, for example, would have us believe it resides in the congress. The congress vows it resides in the people, primarily because each senator and representative must stand for election periodically. The people, however, are vastly misinformed about nearly all issues, and certainly about the character and positions of their congressmen whom they are asked to usher into yet another term in office.

The Supreme Court, however, probably exemplifies the existing sovereignty of the nation, and the ultimate authority can be said to be put into action only through a constitutional amendment, which must be passed by thirty-eight of the fifty states. Even in this respect, true democracy "American style" can be challenged. For it is not the people who have an opportunity to vote on an amendment to the Constitution. It is the state legislatures which make the decisions.

At every step of this process, all of which generally embodies the extraordinary complexity of "United States Sovereignty," violations of the ultimate sovereignty of the people are committed. The people of America are well aware of this. Hence, frustration and general pessimism is shown in the miserably small number of voters who decide elections, and vote on every level of the governmental process in which there are ordinances or propositions to vote upon.

A judicial discussion, known to Indians as "the Great Debate of the 1970s," has been proceeding, and the attorneys on both sides are the protagonists. Attorneys cite court decisions. And a single decision of a single court in a single case, is usually utilized by both sides—defense and adversary. The discussion centers around the concepts and practical meaning of "Tribal Sovereignty," and "Tribal Self-Determination," and "Jurisdiction over Tribal Affairs," such as taxation. Both sides of the cases being prepared for adjudication write articles and profound expositions of their respective positions.

Considering the conditions described above, it would appear to be a fruitless excursion into an imaginary situation, even to take such discussions seriously. Except that the issues are critical to the whole future of the Indian world. To the ordinary hogan-living, hut-occupying, impoverished Indian who is trying to maintain his culture, his language, and his dignity, and primarily to survive, all these questions have little practical meaning. The Indian tribes, and the Indian individuals do not have even the rights owned by everyone else in the conduct of their affairs, and the decisions determining their destiny. They are surrounded and engulfed by regulations of the federal government, of the Department of the Interior, of the Bureau of Indian Affairs (let us not forget the "regs" of every division of the BIA), as well as the laws and regulations of city, county, and state to which he is subjected when working or living off the reservation.

One young Indian, listening to a speaker at a hearing of the American Indian Policy Review Commission, asked: "What's all this about sovereignty? I guess it's a good idea. What I'm worried about, though is my right to vote in my tribe without the BIA saying my vote don't count." He was referring to the Comanche Indian tribal situation in Oklahoma.

26

In positions being advanced by some politicians and their attorneys, it is claimed that congress has the right to unilaterally abrogate Indian treaties. This is challenged by the Indian tribes, on the grounds of injustice, the sacred nature of the contractual agreements such as treaties, and historic as well as legal obligations of the United States. It is a fact that the United States has never abrogated an Indian treaty. By devious means, it is true, it has attempted and succeeded in amending treaties, but in all cases the changes were made by way of another treaty, or a treaty amendment. What further proof is needed of the role of Indian tribes as accepted and acceptable legal entities?

Indian tribal property might better be viewed (if a parallel may be loosely cited) as a cooperative enterprise in which all the members have equal rights, operating under special conditions emanating from the unique position of the American Indian as original owner of the land. Freed from onerous federal regulation, the tribes could well set an example to the country as a whole, of an economy that is far more efficient than the present killing competitive society. In this competitive society, the small homeowner, the struggling farmer, and the "little man" who wants some land for his partial subsistence, is faced with extinction.

Indian tribal property and the right to self-government does not pose a threat to American democracy, as some would have us believe. Indeed, it is true democracy in action.

The mutual interests of Indians and nonIndians, in their struggle against domination of the corporate powers, has a basis for cooperation and should be encouraged.

The fact of corporate ownership of property and the monopolistic practices inherent therein, is accepted by the judiciary as well as the general public and state governments. But Indian tribal ownership is generally questioned if not resisted.

While efforts to completely destroy the Indian tribes and nations, confiscate their land and natural resources, and eradicate the Indians as a race have largely been unsuccessful, new attempts were evident in the 1970s. In part, this offensive has been a "backlash" because of some Indian successes in the courts; in part they have occurred because the federal government is at last providing funds for economic and social changes in the life of the Native American. These latest attempts to destroy the tribes are being made through the congress. The prospect is that this offensive against the Indians will continue. The congress dishonors the country through such proposals to legislate the Indians out of existence.

27

The offensive has its ideologists, and a leading congressional ideologist of the attack is treated in another part of this book. It should be noted, however, that some ideas are being advanced, particularly by the said congressman's legal "alter ego" which may confuse the uninformed. Some of these concepts are considered here.

An article re-printed in the *Congressional Record* (February 4, 1977), contains most of those concepts, seeking to denigrate the historic federal-Indian relationship, and eliminate the Indian tribes as political entities for all time. Quotations will be referred to as the statements appear in the *Record*.

The writer, Frederick Martone, asserts that the Constitution, through the 10th Amendment, "does not provide for Indian tribes," And, the writer concludes, "since no other provision of the Constitution can be read as a source of tribal power, it apparently forecloses the tribes' constitutional right to entity status."

The article reaches such a conclusion in these words: "The conclusion is supported by what little there is in the *Federalist* regarding Indians or Indian tribes. Alexander Hamilton saw the Indians as savages, the natural enemies of the United States, and a justification for a standing army under the Constitution. The Indian nations were a threat to the Union."[28]

Mr. Martone, author of this contorted reasoning, either has not read the *Federalist* with any care, or he assumes that his readers won't bother to examine it. The *Federalist* was published and written by three men who participated in framing the Constitution: Alexander Hamilton, John Jay and James Madison. The purpose of the articles was to sway the thirteen colonies towards adoption of the proposed Constitution (nine of the thirteen were necessary for ratification). Objections confronted by the supporters of the Constitution were of a states' rights nature, and included opposition to such federal controls as a mandatory standing army, a national banking system, the right of the federal government to negotiate and make treaties, and national regulation of trade with the Indians. The *Federalist* authors argued vehemently for a strong, centralized, powerful federal government.

The author of the article opposing Indian tribes "as entities," has decided that Indian treaties are not treaties. But judicial decisions, even to the present day, do recognize Indian treaties. If the opinions of the framers of the Constitution are to be considered at all, then they should be considered in the light of the whole, not of the part deemed convenient by Martone. Thus, *Federalist* articles say, regarding *treaties*:

"A fifth class of provisions in favor of the federal authority consists of the following restrictions on the authority of the several States. '1) No State shall enter into any treaty, alliance, or confederation . . .' The prohibition against treaties, alliances, and confederations makes a part of the existing articles of Union; and for reasons which need no explanation, is copied into the new constitution." (Page 277, by James Madison.)[29]

Madison continues, " . . . as the constitutions of some of the States do not even expressly and fully recognize the existing powers of the Confederacy, an express saving of the supremacy of the former would, in such States, have brought into question every power contained in the proposed Constitution." (Pages 283–284.)

Thus, he states, " . . . as the constitutions of the States differ much from each other, it might happen that a treaty or national law, of great and equal importance to the States, would interfere with some and not with other constitutions and would consequently be valid in some of the States, at the same time that it would have no effect on others."

Madison is arguing that the federal government alone must have the authority to make treaties. And this, in effect, is the foundation of the federal-Indian relationship, since Indian treaties were made with the federal government following adoption of the Constitution. He warns that " . . . the world would soon have seen, for the first time (if states had the right to make treaties) a system of government founded on an inversion of the fundamental principles of all government; it would have seen the authority of the whole society everywhere subordinate to the authority of the parts; it would have seen a monster, in which the head was under the direction of the members."

John Jay, also contending for a strong federal government, opposing state controls as demanded by the thirteen states, and arguing for a national standing army, observed,

"Not a single Indian war has yet been occasioned by aggressions of the present federal government, feeble as it is, but there are several instances of Indian hostilities having been provoked by the improper conduct of individual States, who, either unable or unwilling to restrain or punish offenses, have given occasion to the slaughter of many innocent inhabitants." (Page 16.)

Continuing his argument that the right to negotiate and sign treaties must remain a federal power "with the advice and consent of the Senate . . ." Jay says: " . . . under the national government, treaties and articles of treaties, as well as the laws of nations, will always be expounded in one sense and executed in the same manner—whereas adjudications on the same points and questions, in thirteen States, or in three or four confederacies, will not always accord or be consistent; and that, as well from the variety of independent courts and judges appointed by different and independent governments, as from the local laws and interests which may affect and influence them."

Thus, the philosophy advanced by Jay and others in the making of treaties as well as in developing a court system, was the foundation for the present United States system concerning both. A federal court system emerged in which the lower courts proceed to the higher on state levels, and recourse is had to district appellate courts, and finally to the United States Supreme Court.

Jay continues in the same vein: "The just causes of war, for the most part, arise either from violations of treaties or from direct violence. America has already formed treaties with no less than six foreign nations, and all of them, except Prussia, are maritime, and therefore able to annoy and injure us. . . . It is of high importance to the peace of America that she observe the laws of nations towards all these powers, and to me it appears that this will be more perfectly and punctually done by one national government than it could be either by thirteen separate States or by three or four distinct confederacies." (Page 14.) It is noted that the Indian nations were not mentioned in this statement by Jay. But at no time did any of the framers of the Constitution deny that treaties with Indians were any less important than the treaties with foreign governments.

Indeed, why should the Indians be considered "foreign" governments, since they were the original owners of the land, and might better have been considered (as they were) "Native governments from whom the land must be purchased, stolen, or taken by fraud in order to acquire the continent in the name of the United States."

The words ascribed to Hamilton are these: "The savage tribes on our Western frontier ought to be regarded as our natural enemies, their natural allies, because they have most to fear from us, and most to hope from them." (Page 144–5.) Hamilton was referring to "growing settlements subject to the dominion of Britain, colonies and establishments subject to the dominion of Spain, and the vicinity of the West Indian Islands, belonging to these two powers . . . having a common interest." A strong federal government, with a national standing army, Hamilton believed, would best be able to restrain the British and Spanish outposts than any armed force of the states. The fact that Hamilton was an ethnocentrist and a racist is not a surprise. So too were most of the founding fathers.

Interestingly enough, Hamilton adds these concerns, in his *Federalist* article: "No person can doubt that these (military posts) will continue to be indispensable, if it should only be against the ravages and depredations of the Indians . . ." (Page 146.) Then he asserts, "It may be added that some of those posts will be keys to the trade with the Indian nations." (Page 146.) "*Nations*?" But Hamilton, on another page, has described the Indians as "savages." Savage or not, Hamilton considered the Indians as *nations* with *governments*; he knew the United States must deal with them as nations.

One of the critical questions addressed by the framers of the Constitution was the provision that "the President shall make treaties, with advice and consent of the Senate . . ." Hamilton opposed the sharing of such responsibility by the House of Representatives. This issue became one of recurring conflict between the two houses of congress historically, and continued until the ending of treaty making with the Indians in 1871. It continues today in other areas of treaty responsibility.

Martone and his congressional customers are arguing for states' rights in Indian affairs, an issue that began in 1787 and continues even to this day. But Hamilton, whom this gentleman is so fond of quoting as considering the Indians to be "savages," also said this in connection with the question of states' rights and the supremacy clause of the Constitution:

" . . . the danger which most threatens our political welfare is that the State governments will finally sap the foundations of the Union; and might therefore think it necessary, in so cardinal a point, to leave nothing to construction. Whatever may have been the inducement to it, the wisdom of the precaution is evident from the cry which has been raised against it; as that very cry betrays a disposition to question the great and essential truth which it is manifestly the object of the provision to declare." (Page 192.)

The founders of the Constitution had certain ideas about the form of government considered best suited for their democracy. Alexander Hamilton, in answer to objections to the supremacy clause in the Constitution wrote:

The treaties have as objects "contracts with foreign nations, which have the force of law, but derive it from the obligation of good faith. They are not rules prescribed by the sovereign to the subject, but agreements between sovereign and sovereign. The power in question seems therefore to form a distinct department, and to belong, properly, neither to the legislative nor to the executive. The qualities elsewhere detailed as indispensable in the management of foreign negotiations, point out the Executive as the most fit agent in those transactions; while the vast importance of the trust, and the operation of treaties as laws, plead strongly for the participation of the whole, or a portion of the legislative body in the office of making them." (Page 4,467.) He was therefore in favor of the Senate having the "advice and consent" power in the making of treaties.

In further considering the treaties with Indian nations, Martone states: "What was perhaps natural, truly necessary, in the seventeenth and eighteenth centuries became an embarrassment by the nineteenth century." The principal "embarrassment" suffered by the United States is the stigma of dishonor it bears in its relationships with the American Indians during the last two hundred years. Such a statement is utterly repugnant to a democratic society, which America asserts it is. It is a mockery of decency in law, morality, and relationships with the world.

The Martone concepts also include this apologistic theory of the need to abrogate the Indian treaties. In his view:

"The fact is that Indian tribes were conquered, subjugated, and cast into a position of virtual subordination . . . an Indian tribe is not an internationally recognized sovereign, the status of the tribe under the United States Constitution should be examined. The Constitution does not, in fact, contemplate a role for the tribe in the federal system, i.e., the existence of the tribe as a self-governing legal entity is not constitutionally guaranteed."

A response to this idea, in view of historic fact and present reality, can be stated thus:

Certainly the Indian tribes are not now "foreign nations." In fact, they never were. They were, and are *Native Nations*. They gave up the status of external sovereignty upon signing treaties with the United States, accepting the doctrine of internal sovereignty under the federal government, and reserving to themselves certain lands, the rights to natural resources, and self-government. A trustee relationship was established, in order to guide and oversee these obligations of the federal government.

Another argument proceeds from this, that the Indian tribes and nations do not have internal status as "foreign" powers, now that the United States has relegated them to a position of colonial quasi-sovereignty. It is also admitted that for two hundred and eighty-four years, the natives were treated as Native Nations, negotiating treaties with European foreign nations (not only the colonies). Although the Court decisions and the statutes designate the Indian nations as "foreign" entities, this is a misnomer, as any logical mind will note

It is dishonest to claim that since the Indians have been placed under the dominant sovereignty of the United States, they are to be treated as though they never existed as independent nations. Or, as though their race has disappeared, their tribes extinguished, and their rights completely obliterated. Such an unconscionable, dishonorable statement cannot be excused. The arrogant statement that Indian nations are *permitted* to exist (see Meeds Dissent) is irresponsible and repugnant to American concepts of law, of the nation's innate fairness and honesty, and of the basic tenets of justice.

The burden of the Martone philosophy is that the tribes have no sovereignty, are not entitled to self-government, do not exist as "entities," and should be made subject to the states for purposes of government including taxation, jurisdiction, and use of natural resources.

This gentleman writes like a disembodied theorist. Obviously the man knows nothing about Indian affairs. The only accuracy in this article is recognition of the fact that society changes, and that changes have taken place that place different constructions on relations of the Indians to the dominant society. There his understanding of reality dies, and he descends into the depths of ignominious debasement of the historical process.

Society has changed, and is still changing, but the changes are not understood by Martone and his friends. There is a movement for social change in the world today. The country is moving in a direction opposing colonialism, demanding self-determination, approving the right of the tribes to self-government. There are allies working for Indian tribes today who were never known before, and this country's citizens will not permit the final destruction of the original native peoples of the land. The words of the Indian Self-Determination Act recognize the tribes as "entities"—at least.

The inherent sovereignty of the Indian tribes and nations is a fact. The engineers of the United States government were not fools or dupes, or unaware of the realities of life in 1787. They dealt with the Indians through treaties and agreements because the native peoples were political entities, sovereign in their governments. But the tribes have been duped into dependency through legislation. Their natural democratic processes have been crippled. Laws have been passed and programs instituted "for the betterment of the Indians" according to an alien culture, and without tribal consent as a rule.

What were the intentions of the founding fathers, who framed the

Constitution and treated with the Indian tribes? Here is that part of one treaty that more honestly describes the intent of the federal government:

"The Cherokee Nation having already made great progress in civilization and deeming it important that every proper and laudable inducement should be offered to their people to improve their condition as well as to guard and secure in the most effectual manner the rights guaranteed to them in this treaty, and with a view to illustrate the liberal and enlarged policy of the Government of the United States toward the Indians in their removal beyond the territorial limits of the states, it is stipulated that they shall be entitled to a delegate in the House of Representatives of the United States whenever Congress shall make provision for the same." (Treaty with the Cherokees, 1835.)

The Cherokees moved to the new Territory, created a government based on the model of the United States Senate, House of Representatives, and the Judiciary, formulated a Constitution based on that of the United States, and flourished.

An attempt is made by Martone to denigrate the massive work of Felix Cohen and the *Handbook of Federal Indian Law*. The new ideologists have launched an insolent attack against him, thus:

"A recurring theme in materials relating to federal Indian law is that one man, Felix S. Cohen, single-handedly slowed the process of history . . . The New Deal brought men to Washington who, for the first time, were of the opinion that there might yet be a continuing role for the tribe in the federal system. Felix S. Cohen was such a man: he drafted the Indian Reorganization Act of 1934 and, while an employee of the Department of the Interior in 1942, he published a book which became a cause celebre in the world of federal Indian law." (*Record*, Page S2355, February 4, 1977.)

Cohen worked through the United States government. With its help and approval, he produced the *Handbook*. He worked at a time when it was considered that the best policy would be assimilation of the Indian tribes into the federal system. The Indian Reorganization Act was not a panacea for Indian problems, nor was it approved by most tribes. But it did end the infamous General Allotment Act, and it did recognize Indian governing bodies and the right to self-government. Except that tribal government was to be based on the European model, thereby reducing Indian culture and traditional forms of government. Furthermore, it gave the Secretary of the Interior almost dictatorial power over the tribes.

But Cohen performed a real service to the nation and the Indian people, documenting the legal decisions up to the time of *Handbook* publication, interpreting them from the viewpoint of the international community and the natural law of nations, as well as the Constitution, and insisting that the treaties were valid, ongoing instruments of tribal sovereignty.

The scurrilous attack against him by legal pygmies like Martone will only end in exposing both the ideology and the practices of lawyers who are joining forces with the reactionary elements of the nation, to the end that the Indian tribes may be obliterated.

In 1787, the States fought for independence against federal domination, opposing a national army, the supreme power of the United States federal government to make treaties, and a national court system.

In 1977, the States are demanding power over Indian lands. They call it "jurisdiction" in Indian affairs. They want the right to allocate and adjudicate water rights, lease reservation land, enforce taxation, control the courts, and make tribal governments subservient to state agencies.

The Indian tribes and nations were pawns in the battle between the states and the federal system in 1787. They are political pawns in the struggle today between the states and the federal government for control over the natural resources. That's what it is all about.

Finally, Martone expresses the ideology of all reactionary politicians who have at their service attorneys with a similar view. They are descending to the vilest types of public incitement. Their propaganda is designed to inflame the general public and instigate fear, such as was rampant during the days of "western expansion," and "manifest destiny" of the United States. This is seen clearly in the opening remarks of Martone's article:

"The United States is in the midst of a new civil war. Unlike the last civil war, it is not between the states and the Union; rather it is a challenge by American Indian tribes against the states and the United States. Unlike the last one, this civil war has seen many of the battles occur in state and federal courts. Though the war began when the first white men settled on the North American continent and has continued unabated to the present, the struggle has reached a new stage in which the Indian tribe rather than the settler is on the offensive. This new offensive has been a fertile source of legal issues of which the most basic is the question of tribal sovereignty."

This war is an offensive against the American Indian. But the war is being met with defensive actions in which the Indian tribe is struggling to maintain its independence, its culture, and its people as original owners of this land. The so-called "victories" won by the tribes are only shadows compared to the rights legally and morally belonging to the American Indians.

Reference is made to the "trust relationship" of the United States with the Indian tribes. A trust relationship, in the context of the implementation of federal/Indian relationships through the Interior Department and the Bureau of Indian affairs is more than a fiduciary trust. It is a legal trust, guaranteeing the protection of the assets and persons of the tribe against the assault of other entities (such as the states) and the corporate powers.

Interior negotiates and approves leases, licenses, contracts and especially those concerned with the use of tribal lands for energy-producing purposes. The states should be aware of the fact that if these lands were totally under the jurisdiction of the federal government, without the tribal system of balance and consent, the lands and its resources would certainly not be placed in the states, but in the hands of oil and mining companies under federal contract, which would eliminate taxation.

In the 1835 treaty with the Cherokee Nation, as well as in other treaties, it is stated, ". . . the sum of $75,000 shall be paid to the *Secretary of the Interior* as *trustee* for the Cherokee Nation of Indians.

And again, in the treaty with the same tribe, in 1868, it is stated: "Whereas, for the purpose of enabling the Secretary of the Interior *as trustee* for the Cherokee Nation of Indians, to collect the proceeds of sales of said lands . . ."

It is interesting to note that President Franklin D. Roosevelt appointed former commissioner of Indian affairs, John Collier, to remove Japanese citizens and immigrants from their homes along the west coast to concentration camps, euphemistically called "Relocation camps." Roosévelt stated, in announcing the appointment, that Collier was eminently qualified because of his experience in dealing with persons who lived under similar circumstances, reservation Indians.

In 1950, another president, Dwight D. Eisenhower, appointed a former head of the Japanese-American Relocation Centers, Dillon Myer, to be the commissioner of the Bureau of Indian Affairs. Myer acquitted himself as dictatorially among the Indians as he had among the Japanese concentration camp residents. Surely, in both Roosevelt's and Eisenhower's minds there must have been a comparison between the way both men saw the relocation camps, the concentration camps, and historic Indian reservations.

"Minorities" such as the Hungarian, Italian, Irish, Jewish, Russian, etc. have a homeland to which their culture clings. Their ancient traditions originate in those lands, and their memories return, often nostalgically sometimes hopefully.

But the Native American has no other place, no other culture, no other homeland, than here on this continent. Deprived of his land, he is deprived of his culture. Deprived of his language, his culture is lost. The American Indian has endured, despite genocide, foreign diseases, and the destruction of his economy.

Thus, as one writer has said, "The disappearance of the Indian communities by assimilation has a crucial finality that assimilation can never have for other American minorities who become assimilated can still look toward a homeland from which they came, a viable tradition and culture which dignifies their origin. For the Indian, the tribal community is the only carrier of his tradition; if it disintegrates and disappears, his tradition becomes a matter of history and he loses part of his identity." Alexander Lesser (1961:17) ("Education and the Future of Tribalism in the U.S. The case of the American Indian," *Social Service Review*, Vol. 35, No. 2, June, 1961.)

The new ideologists, in their insolent campaign against the American Indian tribes, are following upon the footsteps of another apologist for American colonialism as practiced against the natives, Frederick Jackson Turner.

Turner's thesis that America moved into the west's "vacant land " gave morality to the pioneers and gold miners, as well as the railroad corporations, as they took land belonging to the Indians in their relentless movement to the west. His philosophy has been discredited. It is an archaic concept renounced by responsible scholars. However, it served its purpose in dispossessing the Indian.

The likes of Martone are now attempting to completely eradicate the Indian, mouthing phrases such as "equal rights," and denigrating the Indian treaties, which are the supreme law of the land. During the last months of 1977, at least six bills were introduced into the House of Representatives, all attempting in various ways to accomplish what Martone could only talk about.

The whole process is dishonorable, illegal, and unworthy of the American people. Such bills, if passed by the congress, would make a mockery of the United States President's posture as defender of human rights.

CHAPTER 1
References

1. J. Smith, *Appeals to the Privy Council from the American Plantations,* 1950, 418-442.
2. Felix Cohen, *Handbook of Federal Indian Law*, p. 33.
3. Ibid at 34.
4. *Turner v. American Baptist Missionary Union*, 24 Fed. Cas. No. 14251 (C.C. Michigan 1852).
5. Quoted in *The Delaware Indians*, C.A. Weslager, p. 508
6. See *Worcester v. Georgia* 6 Pet. (1832).
7. See *The Iroquois in the Founding of the American Nation*, Donald Grinde, Jr., 1977.
8. 48 Stat. 25 U.S.C. 1934
9. Choate v. Trapp, 224 U.S. 665, 1912; Morrow v. United States 243 Fed. 854, 8th Cir. 1917; Solicitor's Opin. on Taxability and alienability, 59 Lands Dec. 348, 352, 1922; Op's Solic. Dept. of Int. M 25737, Mar. 3, 1930; Ops Sol'r Dept of Int. M. 13864, Dec. 24, 1924.
10. Hearings Before Subcomm, Sen. Comm. on Ind. Aff. pursuant to S. Res. 79, 70th Cong. 2d Sess, 1928.
11. 47 Stat. 1568, 1933, 25 U.S.C. # 407a, 407b note, 1946.
12. 48 Stat. 108, 1933, 25 U.S.C. # 331 note, 1946.
13. Mineral Leasing Act of 1938, 52 Stat. 347, 1938, U.S.C. #396 et seq. 1946. And annotations in 25 U.S. C. #390, 592, 593, 601, 613, 622 (Supp. 1951).
14. President's veto message of S. 1407, Oct. 17, 1949, appears at 95 Cong. Rec. 14784, 1949. After the veto the bill was redrafted eliminating state law and order provisions to which the Navajo had objected, and as amended was passed and signed by the President. 64 Stat. 44, 1950, 25 U.S.C. # 631-640 (Supp. 1952).
15. Information supplied by *The Washington Connection*, 1977.
16. The Corporation and the Indian, H. Craig Miner, Univ. of Missouri Press, 1976.
17. Ibid.
18. Ibid.
19. Ibid.
20. Ibid.
21. McClanahan v. State Tax Comm. 411 U.S. 164, 1973. "Judicial Review of Indian Treaty Abrogation," 63 Cal. L. Rev. 1975. C. Wilkinson and J. Volkman.

22. Jones v. Meehan, 175 U.S. 1, 1899.
23. "Judicial Review," supra, 617 n. 78.
24. 391 U.S. 404, 1968
25. Treaty with Menominee Indians, May 12, 1854, 10 Stat. 1064, 1065.
26. 391 U.S. at 412.
27. Article in *Congressional Record*, Feb. 4, 1977. Quotations are from this reprir of the *Harvard Law Review* article
28. *Congressional Record*, p. S253, col. 3, Feb. 4, 1977.
29. *The Federalist* No. XLIV, 1888 edition.

"The history of the United States Government's repeated violations of faith with the Indians thus convicts us, as a nation, not only of having outraged the principles of justice, which are the basis of international law; and of having laid ourselves open to the accusation of both cruelty and perfidy; but of having made ourselves liable to all punishments which follow upon such sins—to arbitrary punishment at the hands of any civilized nation who might see fit to call us to account, and to that more certain natural punishment which, sooner or later, as surely comes from evil-doing as harvests come from sown seed."

A Century of Dishonor
Helen Hunt Jackson
1881

Chapter 2

THE NEW WAR
AGAINST THE INDIANS

So long as the Indian remained locked in the stereotype of a vanishing race, dressed in buckskin and feathers, providing an exotic interest to the American scene, there was relatively little open antagonism, even though there existed a continuing racism. The Indian wars seemed to be a thing of America's romantic past. Even now, it is not clearly understood that these Indian wars were defensive wars against invasions of white settlers and gold miners, invasions of the United States government in violation of solemn treaties with the tribes and nations. The valor and uncommon bravery of those Indians who led the massive and militant defense will yet become part of the saga of American heroism. The dedication of those Indian people who continued to fight under the leadership of their chiefs and medicine men will yet become known as a lasting contribution to American revolutionary action and thought, far more a war for American rights than that of the official American Revolutionary War.

In the late 18th and throughout the 19th century, the Native was herded onto reservations, where he was left to linger in poverty in virtual concentration camp conditions, while federal officials and Indian agents lined their pockets through the many fraudulent practices committed against the tribes. Food and supplies promised in treaties were either not forthcoming, or were sold on the black market by Indian agents who unashamedly stole both supplies and food, leaving decaying meat and the poorest supplies to the Indians.

Government policy swayed to and fro in a crazy rhythm of improvisation, or policies based on greed, as well as those that were the result of pressure brought to bear on the federal government by the states, the settlers, and the gold miners. The most abysmal ignorance was displayed by the federal government, concerning the trust obligations of the United States to the tribes, the cultural differences between Indian and nonIndian, and the basic needs of the Indian people.

Religious groups and white-controlled humanitarian organizations generally embodied the worst of the growing paternalism towards the Natives. Finally, the federal government, jockeying precariously between policies of assimilation and the growing recognition that the tribes simply would not disappear together with their unique cultures, originated what has become known as the "Relocation Program." Indians were induced to go to the cities for training in the arts of the technological world. There they were dumped into housing that in most cases was ghetto-based, into jobs that were dead end, and training that failed to lead to professions and occupations. The litany of that period provides the crassest example of government ignorance of the Indian situation.

The "Indian problem" did not go away. It worsened. The policies of the Eisenhower administration, which espoused the termination of federal-Indian relationships, was shown to be a failure, a gross injustice added to a history of injustice.

The current period of Indian affairs now began. Tribes found that termination brought deeper poverty, hopelessness, despair, thrusting the Indian into the darkest regions between two worlds, that of the Native American and that of the Euroamerican.

Throughout the period of attempted assimilation, the stealing of Indian lands, termination, impoverishment of the people, violation of treaty obligations, plans and programs were proposed. Surveys and investigations took place, the most famous of which was the Brookings Institution-directed Meriam Report of the 1920s and 1930s. It became fashionable to expose the awful results of government neglect and misconduct towards the tribes.

On another front, the stereotype of the vanishing Indian, the buckskin and feathers hero of state fairs and county pie-throwing contests, was attacked. The Chicago Indian Council criticized the school books as they described Indian history and culture. Later the American Indian Historical Society would put the textbook correction struggle into perspective and would open the door to changes and the organization of Indian publishing ventures. A conference of Indian and nonIndian scholars and leaders took place in Chicago in 1928, which drew up resolutions and outlined the sorry conditions of the Indian people. Many scholars, sick with the sight of the Indian condition, sought to bring the conditions to public attention. Surveys by anthropologists, field work by archaeologists, brought more interest to the American Indian even though most of the surveys invaded the privacy of Indian homes.

Suddenly the sleeping giant awoke. Publicity attended the takeover of Alcatraz Island, Wounded Knee, the Bureau of Indian Affairs building in Washington, D.C., and a flurry of other "takeovers." World attention was focused upon the Indian situation through the extraordinary militant actions of groups of Indian people. The occupation of Alcatraz Island drew the eyes of the whole world to Indian affairs. Regardless of criticisms and differences of opinion among the Indian people themselves, this event became symbolic of Indian resistance. The occupation of the village of Wounded Knee in South Dakota followed soon after, and the armed camp set up by the Indians brought world attention to the situation in one of the largest Indian reservations in the United States, Pine Ridge. It became clear that Pine Ridge was only one of many such enclaves of poverty, hopelessness, frustration, brutal power exercised both by Indian renegades and government officials against the Indian people.

The occupation of the Bureau of Indian Affairs building in Washington, D.C., which took place just prior to the Wounded Knee event, was not supported by most Indian people, and few if any Indian tribes. But it threw a harsh light on the growing militancy and aggressiveness of Indian people. It was clear that there were some among the Indians who would rather die than continue living in the sordid economic and culturally-deprived conditions in which they found themselves.

The United States government continued to play football with the "Indian problem." Plans for change were proposed. Schemes of action based on legislation were laid out in neat outline and complex graphs. The Nixon Administration declared, in what was Mr. Nixon's finest hour, that there was an unconscionable conflict of interest within the government as it lumbered through its trusteeship over Indian affairs. It must be ended, Nixon said, in his State of the Union message in 1970. But Nixon, famous for his game plans, had no adequate, operative game plan to end the conflict of interest.

All this stirring of the national conscience, this futile attempt to cause positive change in Indian affairs, lacked a critical ingredient. The Indian people themselves were not consulted. They were not asked what they felt their needs were. They were not brought into the policy-making process. The historic dance of the government continued, bowing and scraping first to one high-powered pressure group, then to another. The result was an indescribable deepening mess that best described the "Indian situation."

The power structure of the United States remained fully in charge of Indian affairs. The trust relationship was officially and regularly violated. The conflict of interest continued. Indeed, when the special water commission was set up in the Department of Interior, charged with the task of protecting and adjudicating Indian water rights, the real intent of the government was finally made clear. Mr. Hans Walker, a Mandan Indian, was placed at the head of this commission. But when the question of conflict of interest was raised by the American Indian Historical Society, acting on request of the Jicarilla Indian Tribe, in an official letter to Walker, he responded demanding "specific examples of conflict of interest," and expressing disbelief in the existence of such a conflict. Walker's files were overflowing with such specific examples. Indeed it is not at all unusual for the federal government to exploit what is euphemistically known as an "Indian leader" to carry on its nefarious activities.

But Indian people were now becoming more sophisticated. Some were graduates of institutions of higher education. Many were experts in fields of technology. And the tribes began to develop muscle. Buttressed by the militant actions of Indian groups, and with the spotlight of national and international attention upon the Indian condition, the tribes began to go to the courts in a new wave of litigation. Litigation is not a novel exercise for Indian tribes. They have gone to the "Great White Father" from historic times onward. The Great White Father finally became known to them as being represented by the courts, and finally by the United States Supreme Court. It can safely be said that there are more backwoods, uneducated Indian lawyers than in any other group of the American population. The people poured over the law books. Felix Cohen's Manual on *Federal Indian Law* could be found in at least one home on every Indian reservation. Briefs, findings of fact, and the processes of litigation became a topic of conversation over the dinner table. There were many occasions when Indian "grass roots lawyers" even challenged the well-educated attorneys holding memberships in the American Bar Association. Successfully. One famous and successful Indian attorney, Tom Sloan, an Omaha, finally rose to the august position of being accepted by the courts. He was uneducated.

The Indians trusted nobody. They watched their attorneys; they watched the Commissioner of Indian Affairs. They gathered information on the workings of the government and particularly that of the Department of the Interior. People who had little or no education, ordinary farm people, ranchers, those who lived on a bare subsistence level of less than $1,000 a year for the entire family, became skilled tacticians and laboriously spelled out the decisions of the courts.

However, they were "taken" again and again. But not without a fight. Thus, as only one case, the California claim, in which the tribes had been victorious in a suit claiming 95 percent of the State of California, they ultimately found themselves captured by their twenty-two attorneys, representing more than 200 tribes of the state. The compromise settlement, amounting to 47 cents an acre for the finest mineral and farming land in the world, was consummated through fraud and misrepresentation, forced down the throats of the Indian people through the illegal manipulations of the Bureau of Indian Affairs. But not without a fight. Groups and tribes resisted the so-called settlement, and the authors were part of this movement. The Indian people who worked to defeat this compromise settlement labored for two years, day and night without end, using their own meager funds. They were defeated, largely through the use of Indian renegades whose names should be engraved in steel in the hearts of all our youth.

To this day, however, there are many Indian individuals who have refused the payment for their homeland, amounting to an average of $600 for each individual, and the authors are only two of this group. The struggle continues, moreover, as the Pit River Indian Tribe demands justice and an exposure of the Bureau of Indian Affairs manipulation of their tribal vote, an illegal action, authenticated as such in court documents.

Within the last five years, Indian tribes engaged in litigation have been winning some victories. The Supreme Court, compelled to be guided by the Constitution and the Indian treaties, as well as the solemn agreements and executive orders committing the federal government to trust responsibilities for Indian economic development, education, and general welfare, has found for the Indians in a number of lawsuits.

This was particularly evident in suits involving Indian water and natural resource rights. A decision of the court in the early 1900s declaring that Indians have "prior and paramount" rights to their waters, now known as the "Winters Doctrine," became the center of a new battleground. Decisions of the courts in cases such as the fishing rights suit in the State of Washington, in which Judge George Boldt declared the Indians have rights to 50 percent of the fish catch, actually abrogated their treaty rights, which gave them unlimited fishing rights. It was a partial victory nevertheless.

Cases at court have been won. Others were lost. But there was a stirring and rumbling among the tribes which could not be silenced.

Indian affairs certanly cannot be separated from the affairs of the nation as a whole. This became evident when there was irresistible proof of water shortage, energy shortage, and continuing demands for land. The history of Indian affairs, in which white people in many cases were permitted to own land on Native reservations, added an even more ominous note to the conflict now erupting between Indian and nonIndian. The conflict is currently showing its form and structure, increasing in strength, and growing because of the illiteracy of the American public in Indian affairs, and the ignorance of many state and federal officials as to the legal status of the Indian, the status of the treaties the Indians have with the United States government, and the pressure of huge corporations and monopolies demanding access to Indian land and resources.

The new war against the American Indian is taking shape.

The organizations and individuals who are marshalling the forces of government and the general public in this Indian war are becoming known and familiar figures. Congressmen who depend upon their constituencies for re-election are bowing to the pressures of the dominant, corporation-controlled groups in their states. It seems clear that the recommendations of the American Indian Policy Review Commission will meet with organized opposition in the Congress, and at the very least, efforts will be made to emasculate most of the recommendations for change.

This war against the Indians is taking certain forms, and some of these are explored here:

THE ORGANIZED OFFENSIVE

With the opening of the 1970s, Indian tribes began to see some practical victories in the courts. Suddenly whites living on or near reservations felt threatened. Instigated by monopolistic corporations, ranchers and large landowners, these white people formed groups, held meetings, and organized a national anti-Indian movement. This was at first considered to be a "backlash" against the Indian gains in the courts. Soon it became an open, strident offensive against the tribes. Unwitting white people were induced to join the movement. The dissemination of misinformation caused a further expansion of the anti-Indian membership. Following are some of the organizations and organized movements that are currently engaged in lobbying for legislation and disseminating misinformation. The objective is to abrogate Indian treaties.

THE INTERSTATE CONGRESS FOR EQUAL RIGHTS AND RESPONSIBILITIES. Heading the Anti-Indian Offensive, this organization is a response to Indian claims for land, demands for protection of their natural resources, protection of their water rights, the right to enact ordinances and impose taxes, and insistence upon the conditions and powers of their tribal sovereignty.

ICERR claims memberships and chapters in approximately 25 states. It was formed in 1975 at a meeting in Utah, and was incorporated August 2, 1976. Its stated goal is "to halt a nationwide drive by professional Indians and attorney groups from taking over vast natural resources."

An ICERR report reveals these persons as incorporators: Jack Freeman, of Faith, South Dakota; Marian Schultz, of Batesland, South Dakota; and Robert Halferty, of Mission, South Dakota.

South Dakota has been a center of oppression and terrorism against Indian people. The takeover of the hamlet of Wounded Knee resulting from this oppression brought worldwide attention to the Pine Ridge Reservation and the conditions of its people. It is significant that all three incorporators are from the State of South Dakota.

Officers of the corporation, which has nonprofit status, according to its report, are: Howard Gray, of Seattle, Washington; Elmer Winter, of Mahnomen, Minnesota; Paul Wood, of Warwick, North Dakota; Marian Schultz; Dan Dennis, of Roosevelt, Utah; and Frank Lawyer, of Idaho Falls, Idaho.

Quite possibly its directors change, because Mayor Hollis Hollinger of Roosevelt, Utah, has been listed as vice president of ICERR in some news releases.

Tom D. Tobin, an attorney of Winner, South Dakota, is listed as the organization's "registered agent" at this time. The town of Winner is noted as the ICERR national headquarters. An office in Washington D.C. serves as the center for its lobbying efforts.

At a meeting held in Missoula, Montana in November, 1976, delegates insisted that the "United States Constitution takes precedence over treaties. Congress should enact laws clarifying jurisdictional conflicts that victimize nonIndians."

Clearly, the developing conflict involves a demand to abrogate Indian treaties. According to the ICERR declaration of purpose:

"We believe that constitutionally guaranteed rights should be protected without regard to race, and that all citizens should bear equally the responsibilities and burdens of citizenship as prescribed under the laws of the states and their political subdivisions."

A further statement makes the point that "all state and local laws shall apply within all reservations and to all tribes and tribal members equally." ICERR has also resolved that "the constitutional rights of citizens should supercede treaty rights of some Americans; Indian reservations should not be enlarged by boundary changes; jurisdiction of tribal governments over nonIndians who have no voice in the tribal government should be prohibited; members of Indian tribes who claim not to be subject to the laws and responsibilities of nontribal governments should not have the right to participate in those governments; and grants of public funds to any group of people based on their race and denial of public funds to other groups because of their race should be prohibited."

Here the group's ignorance is exhibited. Indian rights are not racial rights or privileges. They are political rights, stemming from their treaties, the highest law of the land; as well as from Executive orders, agreements and compacts with the United States that have the same weight and legality as the treaties.

MONTANANS OPPOSED TO DISCRIMINATION is a branch of ICERR. They are represented by attorney Lloyd Ingraham, of Ronan, Montana. They represent nonIndians located on or near the seven Indian reservations in the state. State Senator Carroll Graham (D-Lodge Grass), is a white resident on the Crow Reservation. He is a leading member of MOD, and has introduced legislation in the Montana Senate asking Congress to grant the states full jurisdiction over nonIndians who live on reservations. Graham's resolution was co-sponsored by thirty-four senators.

A related organization, active in Montana, is called the CIVIL RIGHTS ORGANIZATION, and is operating on the Crow Reservation. When the Crow Indians won the Bighorn River bed in federal court last year, a legal victory based on proof that the riverbed had been illegally taken from them, the nonIndian residents on and near the reservation became irate. The tribe subsequently broke unfair leases with major energy companies, won the right to tax their coal, and instituted a law and order code. The Crow Tribe was finally exercising its right as a government.

The hostility that has developed through the national organization ICERR is expressed in their pamphlet, which asks and answers the question:

Could it be that nonIndians have no business on reservations?
Answer:
Why not? If nonIndians have no business on reservations, then Indians have no business off-reservation.

MOD delegates who have represented the organization include: Rick Reid, Tom Reid, Jerry O'Connor and Lloyd Holen of Poplar; and Richard Wagner of Nashua. All represented the Fort Peck Reservation chapter of Montanans Opposed to Discrimination.

At these meetings, the MOD representatives denied repeatedly that they harbor "racist attitudes." But these same delegates demand a "retraction of preferential treatment for minorities."

A local chapter of MOD has also been formed in other areas of the state, including Malta. The chapter leaders in Malta are Al Minugh and Bud Walsh of Dodson; Pete Clausen and Dick Kalal of Zortman, Bill Powell of Chinook, and Xarley Smith of Malta.

In late 1977 the United States Commission on Civil Rights investigated charges of civil rights violations. Complaints involved both MOD and ICERR. Sessions of the Commission, held in Seattle, Washington aired the growing conflict between the Indian reservations, many white residents on the reservations, and the state officials. A statement by the Commission said "The Commission may look into allegations that there are groups with ties to right wing or anti-democratic organizations that are trying to gain power over Indian people, or trying to deny them their civil rights," according to Roger Finzel, Washington, D.C. attorney for the Commission.

At last report, MOD had seven chapters in the State of Montana. The Interstate Congress has held meetings in all the western states, and is spreading its activities all over the country.

Many other smaller groups have set up shop in the states. One of these is the CITIZENS LEAGUE FOR CIVIL RIGHTS IN MINNESOTA. The League was formed as a result of the Lac Courte Oreilles Indian tribal code, which closes reservation waters to unlicensed, nonIndian fishermen. According to its statement, it was founded "by individuals and business people who are concerned over the threat to individual rights and privileges as outlined in the Declaration of Independence and guaranteed to each by the Constitution and the Bill of Rights." Mr. Richard Greiner, owner of Greiner's Highland Resort, is one of the League's active members. His resort is adjacent to but not on the Lac Courte Oreilles Indian (Chippewa) Reservation. Greiner complained that "My business is shot for this year. The few who have called about resort reservations are planning to go elsewhere."

THE MASHPEE ACTION COMMITTEE. Less than a month after the Wampanoag Indians of Mashpee filed their case in court claiming their land was illegally taken from them, approximately five hundred residents of this resort town organized the Mashpee Action

Committee. Acting with indecent haste, without attempting to understand the facts of the case, and certainly not talking to the Indians themselves, the residents stated their goals: "to seek federal relief from the financial chaos that resulted from suddenly clouded land titles, and to keep residents informed on the developments of the legal battle."

Rick Reid, a rancher from Poplar, Montana, speaking at a meeting of the Mashpee group, talked about "the strength of the American system; the mixing of cultures that makes the whole stronger than its parts; the right of individuals to determine their destiny."

In a nostalgic spasm of patriotism, Reid described "The American Dream," and told about his homesteading grandfather, revealing that three generations of his family have lived on the Indian land he now occupies.

Reid's farm is on the Fort Peck Sioux Reservation. His grandfather was one of a mob of foreigners who invaded Indian country with the blessing of the Federal Government, and grabbed Indian land, leaving the Native Americans in poverty, surrounded by generally hostile whites. It was only one more injustice and indignity practiced against the Indian people. Only now are they beginning to lift themselves from their degrading poverty brought on by a swarm of homesteaders.

Opposing the Mashpee Indian claim, there is also the Gay Head Taxpayers Association. The town of Mashpee is a small community located just over the Cape Cod Canal, where many middle and upper income retired people and resort owners live. While Indian claims have been filed by Northeast tribes in other areas of the eastern seaboard, the Mashpee claim is the only one involving an entire town. The Mashpee Action Committee has a close relationship with Interstate Congress, and many Mashpee white residents are members of ICERR.

Another organization, at last report, has been formed in Mashpee, called the Mashpee Coalition for Negotiation. It is considering some sort of negotiated solution with the Wampanoag Indians.

But Samuel P. Sirkis, speaking for the Action Committee, opposes negotiation. He labels the Indian claim "a grave injustice perpetrated against innocent property owners. The federal government must intervene," he concluded.

WYOMING CITIZENS FOR EQUALITY IN GOVERNMENT. This group held a meeting in late 1977. About fifty nonIndian residents of the Wind River Reservation, and representatives from Utah, South Dakota, and Nebraska attended. The group has singled out the tribal government system and the Bureau of Indian

Affairs as the root of most of the troubles between Indians and nonIndians on the reservations. According to their statement, published in the *Riverton (Wyoming) Ranger,* they wish to protect nonIndian rights and property. They also want to "upgrade the quality of life for the Indian on the Reservation and to bring the Indian the same rights as the nonIndians seek."

The Wyoming Citizens group asserts that "the tribal council system is alien to the Indian's traditional ways, as well as being contrary to Democratic principles."

Action urged by the Wyoming group includes the correction of "inequalities and the inverse discrimination on reservations through the courts and the legislatures, both in the states and nationally."

THE LUMMI PROPERTY OWNERS ASSOCIATION, operating in Oregon on the Lummi Reservation. Wally Armstrong, president, has attended meetings of Montanans Opposed to Discrimination, and participates in their activities. In a statement to the press, Armstrong said:

"We seek to protect our own rights." The issues of conflict, he explained, include the Indians' legal jurisdiction within reservation boundaries, (a question that arose at Lummi during a sewer district fight between the tribe and nonIndian residents). This group questions Lummi Tribal Police authority over nonIndians. "We also have certain disputes over water rights," he said. "The Indians claim they own all the ground water. We claim if we buy land we get the water rights." He has indicated the group is in favor of lobbyist pressure on Congress.

The Indians living on the reservations have reacted to all this activity, at first with patience and a willingness to sit down and discuss issues. Then with growing impatience at the lack of understanding shown by the leaders of the anti-Indian groups. The spirit of antagonism to all these challenges to Indian jurisdiction over their own governments was coming to the surface at the end of 1977. The reaction of one tribal governing group is typical.

Norman Hollow, Fort Peck tribal chairman, expressed the reactions of tribal members to the offensive being launched against Indian rights, saying in an interview with the Wolf Point, Montana *Herald-News*: "The Supreme Court has ruled that reservations include all areas within the exterior boundaries of the reservation. If we want to exercise that right we have the prerogative to do so.

"They (MOD) are forgetting that it's tribal land in the first place set aside for members of the tribe to make a living. The MOD people are seeing that the land is slowly going back to the Indian

51

people. That's where it belongs anyway. We're slowly squeezing out some of the white ranchers. That's what MOD doesn't like.''

Clark Madison, executive director of the Fort Peck Planning District explained that ''During the 1900s the tribe lost an average of 7,000 acres of land a year when Indians who were completely impoverished sold it to nonIndian farmers and ranchers.

''The tribe was gradually losing its land base, so we obtained loans in order to buy our land back from individual allottees. When the nonIndian guy could no longer have the option of buying the Indian's land he complained.''

On the issue of water rights, which was forcefully raised by MOD, Madison said, ''This tribe is just as worried about water rights as the nonIndians are. I believe that in the future the Fort Peck Tribes will bring it to litigation. So if MOD makes some definite statements about what their water rights are it's wrong, because it hasn't been litigated yet. But the Indian people have a treaty with the American Government protecting their water rights.''

When Montanans Opposed to Discrimination raised the question of litter and garbage on the reservation, tribal board member Jesse Kirn retorted, ''I don't know what they're talking about. In the last couple of years the tribe's made some real good progress in cleaning up the reservation. They shouldn't forget that it's all tribal land, and that these towns are using our land for dumping grounds.''

Barney Lambert, a member of the tribal executive board, stated in the same interview, ''The Indian is just beginning to stand up for himself. Indians have been in the dark all these years and are finally beginning to realize how they're being ripped off, and this is what MOD doesn't like. It's as simple as that.''

Hollow, concluding the interview in a spirit of cooperation, noted, ''It's never too late to sit down and discuss some of these issues. The MOD members are airing individual gripes and problems, which they should be bringing to the tribe. But these problems are being used in the broadest way, so as to set up a platform and make up a program directed against the Indians.''

The Fort Peck responses are quite typical of the Indian viewpoint on most reservations which are now confronted by the offensive launched through the Interstate Congress .

THE FLATHEAD RESERVATION. This Montana reservation presents even more serious problems than most. There have been disputes about shoreline rights to Flathead Lake, as well as over tax-free sales of cigarettes on the reservation. When Indian individual allottees sell their land back to their tribes, that piece of land is removed from Lake County's tax rolls. The nonIndian groups circulate stories of Indian neighbors who are no more than 1/16th Indian blood, with rights on their reservation.

The Flatheads say that their overwhelming problem is to consolidate tribal lands. Lost property taxes are more than compensated for by federal support of local schools and economic activity generated by the reservation, they explain.

The root trouble here is the shifting policy of the Federal Government generally without either consultation or agreement with the tribes. Assimilation was the government policy some thirty years ago. The Bureau of Indian Affairs could note, in 1957, that the Flatheads were "advanced in the stage of integration with the dominant culture." In the 1960s, when Indians were seen as continuing their culture, as well as still in a condition of abject poverty, the government's policy changed to one of self-determination. Younger, more aggressive, educated Indian leaders appeared.

Today, on the Flathead reservation and others across the nation, young and professionally qualified Indian men and women, some with legal backgrounds, are returning to their birthplaces and finding employment in health, welfare and natural resource programs.

The imposition of local taxes on Indian reservations would be a crippling blow to local Indian economies, and the tribes will oppose such acts to the limit of their endurance.

The whites are unwilling to wait out the interregnum, when Indian practicality and governmental justice together with the cooperation of the local and state communities could well find solutions to problems such as a shrinking tax base, drought, and a tightening economy. Here, as well as elsewhere, the hidden arm of the big landowners, the energy companies, and the corporations, is instigating hatred and antagonisms, just at a time when the Indian tribes appear to be coming out of their poverty and neglect.

SPORTSMEN AS STORM TROOPERS?

One of the first to open an offensive against the Indian tribes was the sportsmen's organizations. The attack was brought on by the struggle of the Indians of Washington to protect their fishing rights. A decision was subsequently rendered by the Court permitting Indian tribes fifty percent of the fish catch. Organizations such as the National Wildlife Federation, Trout Unlimited (as well as its affiliate the American League of Anglers) and nearly every wildlife and "nature loving" sports group has joined a national effort to demean the

American Indian, deprive him of his fishing and treaty rights, and enlist the millions of sportsmen in a lobbying attempt to legislate against Indian rights.

These groups have considerable power, largely through their various magazines and periodicals. One article in *Outdoor Life* (May, 1977) by Richard Starnes, states that Indians "are threatening the nation's whole machinery of game and fish conservation." An inaccurate and degrading article in *Conservation News,* published by the National Wildlife Federation, brought some objections from its members and readers. The response to these objections, from Thomas L. Kimball, executive vice president, was a recommendation that the writers read the booklet *Indian Treaties: American Nightmare,* which is filled with inaccuracies and misrepresentation about Indian fishing practices and treaty rights.

The records provide ample evidence that the streams, lakes and oceans of this nation have been vastly over-exploited both by the commercial fishermen and many sportsmen. Whole populations of deer and other game animals have been wiped out by hunters who have no care for conservation or wildlife management. There are about five hundred Indian individuals who fish for subsistence or for a livelihood, or hunt for food.

There are about ten million nonIndians who fish and hunt for sport. There are thousands of sports stores who depend for a living upon the equipment and clothing purchased by the sportsmen and commercial fishermen. Huge corporate businesses supply these people, and the commercial fishermen. Those are the groups responsible for the offensive against the Indian people by sports and so-called conservation groups. Is it possible that so few Indians could deplete the waters of this land, to the extent that the whole nation might be deprived? It's just not logical. Tribes in the State of Washington have initiated fishing codes that effectively protect the salmon and other fish.

As another example of the wreckage in which wildlife and game has been found is the pollution caused by industries which dump their garbage and chemicals into the lakes and rivers of the country. The single example of Lake Michigan proves the point. This lake is uninhabitable by fish. The same is true of nearly every lake and stream in the country where industries are located.

The sportsmen's organizations do not represent their members. They represent the corporations manufacturing equipment and sports goods, and those who fish commercially. But without considering the opinions nor the interests of their memberships, these groups have formed a lobby to influence the United States Congress in passing legislation removing fishing and hunting rights from tribes. *Conservation News,* as only one example, endorses the activities and legislation proposed by Interstate Congress for Equal Rights and Responsibilities. (January 15,1977.)

Such antagonism has been developed by the sportsmen's organizations that it would take a huge program of information to allay the fears of the general public, and bring the facts to light showing that the Indian tribes do not deplete the waters, do not pollute the streams, and that an "overcatch" and "overfish" of the streams is the great exception and certainly not the rule of the tribes.

What is being induced and actively encouraged by the sportsmen's organizations is an open, armed offensive against the Indian people. Sportsmen as Storm Troopers is not far off, unless the truth is brought to bear on the subject of Indian fishing and hunting rights. Another chapter deals with the unjustified charges of the sportsmen's groups, as expressed in the "American Nightmare" book referred to above.

The National Wildlife Federation includes in its membership both sportsmen and environmentalists. According to its vice-president, Thomas L. Kimball, "the policies of the federation are developed by delegates convening in annual meetings," (personal letter). A resolution adopted by this organization at its 1977 convention states:

"Whereas various Indian tribes are asserting rights to various fish and wildlife resources, as well as rights in and to public and private lands and/or the timber and minerals located thereon; and many of the rights asserted are based upon treaties executed between various Indian tribes and the United States Government many years ago when conditions were vastly different; and many of the assumptions on which these treaties were based, such as the inexhaustibility of certain resources, have proved to be inaccurate; and

"Whereas decisions by various courts interpreting various Indian treaty provisions relating to fish and wildlife resources have made the effective management of various fish and wildlife resources virtually impossible; and

"Whereas the lack of effective management threatens, in some cases, the continued existence of certain publicly-owned fish and wildlife resources . . ."

Given these reasons, the Federation then resolves to recommend to the congress that it take "immediate action to define Indian hunting and fishing rights, as set out in the treaties."

The congress is also urged to "confirm authority of the various states to regulate off-reservation hunting and fishing activities of all

Americans, Indians and nonIndians alike, for conservation purposes."

The Federation also resolved that it reiterate its continuing adherence to the principle that just Indian claims should be compensated for by suitable means other than discriminatory allocations of natural resources."

The war against the Indian is thus joined by professed environmentalists, those purporting to protect "natural resources" who have themselves destroyed those very natural resources, depleted the fish and game and debased the environment.

What is being proposed is either amending the treaties, which would necessitate the approval of each tribe that has been a party to each treaty; or a unilateral amendment to the treaties which would make a farce of the United States as an internationally responsible government; or the complete abrogation of the treaties resulting in the destruction of the tribes.

The Indian tribes are exerting self-government, which includes the right to control the use of the natural resources, and their right to fish and hunt according to treaty conditions and as a result of their ownership of these lands.

THE STATES AND CORPORATE POWER

A historic example can be cited of the position of the states, their control by corporate powers, and their continuing effort to end Federal-Indian trust relationships.

In 1852-1854 Congress mandated an investigation of the tribes in California, and sent out a delegation charged with negotiating the treaties with the more than 200 tribes of that state. Eighteen treaties and one agreement were signed in good faith. Conditions pledging government protection of the Indian people against the genocidal gold miners and settlers were written into these treaties. Reservations were laid out in metes and bounds, and the Indian tribes, while opposing removal from their homelands, finally signed the treaties. They ceded most of the State of California to the Federal Government in the treaties, reserving the land set aside for themselves, together with the resources and rights which they had as nations.

The tribes moved forthwith to these new lands. They fulfilled all conditions of the treaties. But the California state legislature, pressured by powerful ranchers and mining companies, passed a resolution opposing ratification of the treaties, and instructed the congressional delegation to actively oppose ratification.

In 1854, in executive session, the Senate read each treaty three times as provided by law, and systematically refused ratification of every treaty. The tribes were not informed of this action. More than fifty years later, the Indians became aware of the failure to ratify.

The power of the state legislatures over the Senate and the House of Representatives is greater than one imagines. The State of Maine, reacting to the claims of the Passamaquoddy and Penobscot Tribes, instructed their congressional delegation to work for the abrogation of all treaties and for legislation denying the Indians' claim.

The State of Washington, where fishing rights, water rights, and tribal jurisdiction have become prime issues, instructed its congressional delegation to work for legislation voiding legal decisions by the court favoring Indian fishing rights. Congressman Lloyd Meeds obliged, by introducing legislation in the House of Representatives that would effectively void the court's favorable decision, and ultimately abrogate Indian treaties. Another congressman, Jack Cunningham, introduced legislation requiring the brutal abrogation of Indian treaties forthwith.

Governor Slade Gorton of Washington proposed that the federal government, or even the state government "buy off Indian fishing rights." The Indians rejected the proposal out of hand.

In New Mexico, state legislators are confronted by a joint resolution providing for the disqualification of Indian voting rights. The resolution, which would amend the state constitution, proposes that only "Every citizen of the United States, who at his place of domicile is subject to the civil and criminal jurisdiction of the State of New Mexico. . . . shall be qualified to vote at all elections for public officers of this state or its political subdivisions." The Pueblos of New Mexico, the most ancient peoples of North America, having towns older than any town in America, with the most ancient native culture of all Indians in the country, have resisted all efforts to destroy their tribal governments. They have been subjected to every indignity known to man, have been deprived of their rights as human beings; their waters have been illegally taken; their land has been under presure of being exploited and placed beyond their control. New Mexico was the last state to grant citizenship to the Indians. An act of Congress granted citizenship to all Indians. But New Mexico (and also Arizona) refused this right until 1948, and only then by court order.

State officials, in an attempt to justify demands for taking jurisdiction over tribal resources and requiring taxes on tribal enterprises, utilize these concepts as justification:

The tribes are receiving services from the states for which they do not pay, it is said, thus forcing an additional financial burden on the states.

Untrue. Tribal members shop at off-reservation stores and businesses and provide a livelihood subject to taxes for such business.

Tribal members, many of whom live off the reservation, do pay taxes, both income and use.

The states receive federal monies for education based on attendance by tribal members' children.

A state like New Mexico reaps considerable money through the exploitation of Pueblo ceremonies and the interest shown by visitors who swarm into the state every year.

Persons who are not allowed to vote in tribal elections are being subjected to taxes. This is taxation without representation, the states say.

Untrue. The tribe or Pueblo, is a government, and no one is permitted to vote who is not a member of their community. Just as one living in the state of Arizona cannot vote in New Mexico.

The whole question of tribal jurisdiction, its powers to govern itself, is inherent in this claim for "representation" which in itself is another offensive against tribal rights, and the Indians' right to exist as a people, guaranteed to them by treaties, statutes, and executive orders.

The fifty states have a larger bureaucracy than even the Federal Government has, although this is not generally known. Besides the state agencies and legislatures, there are interstate organized groups functioning efficiently. The National Governors Conference, the National Lieutenant Governors Conference, the National Attorneys General Association, and the Council of State Governments are only a few official, well organized groups operating with their own leadership, and their own bureaucracy.

The Council of State Governments has its own headquarters, its own publishing house, and its own staff. Conferences are held on a regional basis throughout the year. Committees are set up to consider judicial, educational, crime and justice, and a host of other

58

issues in which all the states are concerned.

In more recent actions, various interstate organizations have formed Task Forces on Indian Affairs. The last 1977 meeting of the Council of State Governments, Western Region, passed a resolution endorsing the "Dissent" of Congressman Lloyd Meeds, which objected to the recommendations of the American Indian Policy Review Commission, and would unilaterally abrogate Indian treaties.

It can be expected that these state agencies and organized groups will enter full force into the offensive against the American Indians. They are state supported with funds. They receive federal grants. They have funds that are available for their programs and their anticipated publicity campaign against the rights of the tribes to self-determination and self-government.

Behind all these activities is the corporate power of the United States. Coal mines in Montana and Arizona, oil in Oklahoma, minerals in most of the western and midwestern states, water for strip mining coal, and water for irrigating the huge ranches owned by the corporations . . . all these are of importance to the corporate powers of North America.

A historic parallel is provided by the history of Oklahoma, in which railroad and land speculating corporations finally overwhelmed the Cherokee, Choctaw, Osage and Chickasaw Nations, although the tribes had sought to "get into the establishment," by investing money in corporation stock.

The corporations had their way. Indian land was taken. The railroads took as much as twenty miles right of way on each side of the railroad line, and the tribes were finally legislated out of their independent governments. The fact that they still survive and are even now regaining their strength is a tribute to the Native power of dedication and endurance.

A factor encouraging state-tribal hostility is the role of the Federal Government, which has produced regulations in which neither the states nor the tribes can function. The government has neither protected the Indians against the incursions of state agencies and corporate powers; nor have they aided the states through a careful weighing of justice on both sides, encouraging negotiations fair to each. There have been occasions in which the states have been able to compromise with the tribes, or at least negotiate amicably. But with the present condition of the federal bureaucracy, and its failure to clearly support the decisions of the Courts on Indian rights, such negotiations have had little effect.

Acts of the Congress have produced only further confusion, since the agencies of government bureaucracy (notably the Department of the Interior) regularly violate these laws, and issue rules which in themselves void the very laws they are pledged to uphold.

The states, confronted by dwindling tax bases, their costs of government climbing, see the Indian reservations as lucrative sources of income. The use of reservation land, most of which constitutes the last frontier capable of supplying oil, minerals and energy producing resources, is a prime objective of the state legislatures and their agencies. Indian water rights infringe upon the uninhibited population growth of metropolitan cities like Los Angeles with their ghetto-infested peoples. Not all legislators are in favor of abrogating Indian treaties, destroying Indian governments, and wiping out the Indian people. But those who are resisting are in a slim minority.

An appeal to the general public, which votes for the legislators, is the only element that could turn things around. It wouldn't be the first time that the Indian tribes have won the support of the American people to the cause of justice.

There is a persistent prejudice in American thought against the concept of property held in common. Indian tribal property is conceived as a "socialistic" doctrine, antithetical to the American urge to independence through private property. While the philosophical and economic basis of this antagonism is not the purpose of this book, some consideration should be given to the realities of property relations in American society.

These realities include the fact that private property held by individual homeowners and small farmers no longer exists in this society. The homeowner is rarely free from the burden of high-interest mortgages. The small farmer finds it impossible to subsist on the products of his farm and is faced by competition by the big landowners and agribusinesses.

Huge corporations now control or own outright a major portion of the land. Railroads, oil and mineral companies, manufacturing establishments, coal companies, and real estate speculators now own real property in land and structures to an alarming extent. What they do not own outright, they hold ironclad leases on, and quite often the big corporations don't even find it necessary to expend capital investment on land. They can get the use of it through the federal government, which grants permits for grazing cattle, mining, exploration in the name of the public interest but the profits of which redound to the corporate powers.

Huge parcels of land are in the public domain, controlled by the federal government. There is more federal land that has thus been taken off the tax rolls of the states, than there is Indian reservation land. Some of this land is in the possession of the federal government for ostensibly laudable purposes. As examples, one might point to the national park system, the open space projects, and reserves held for use by the United States Armed Forces. However, the national park system does not hesitate to grant licenses to concessionaires, providing a profit to favored recipients. In beautiful Yellowstone Park, the park system has granted rights to deface the land and natural features such as mountains and rock formations, to Hollywood producers who usurp the rights of individual vacationers.

THE MEDIA

Media coverage of Indian issues can generally be characterized in these ways:

There is a lack of understanding of the Indian relationship with the Federal Government. There is a failure to develop background information for newspaper reporters and staff writers concerning Indian history, cultures, and government. Because of the tendency to publish what is most sensational, there is a concentration on "takeovers" and militant actions. Indian successes are almost totally ignored. Indian failures and mistakes are widely publicized.

There is a group of ethnocentric media publishers and reporters whose reputation and circulation brings them broad readership, and makes them dangerous purveyors of misinformation and racism. Their policies and ideologies are followed by the mass media. Among these is Randolph Hearst, owner of the Hearst newspaper empire. In editorials, Hearst has espoused the destruction of Indian tribal government jurisdiction, and promoted the assimilation ideas that have long since proved to be unworkable, and opposed by the tribes. At the same time, some Hearst reporters (Lynn Ludlow, Mark Hatfield, of the *San Francisco Examiner*), have shown great sympathy for the Indian people and have attempted to cover current affairs with integrity.

Kevin Phillips, a Hearst syndicated columnist, has degraded Indian people and displayed an ignorance of Indian affairs scarcely matched by any other writer. Book reviews published in the *San Francisco Chronicle* and *Examiner* have misinterpreted Indian history and cultures, and have often degraded the Indian.

The *New York Times* has some reporters and staffers who attempt sincerely to cover Indian news with integrity. But they lack the background necessary for understanding. An article in the *Times*

61

(September 29, 1977), as only one example, deals with the whales as an endangered species. Boyce Rensberger, in a by-lined article, states that "Eskimo native rights" conflict with the demand by conservationists to protect the whales by limiting or ending the Eskimo right to hunt the whales. The reporter claims that Eskimos have been killing ten to fifteen times more whales than they have heretofore. While the article attempts to be fair, the implications are clear: Eskimos are responsible for the reduction in the whale population.

It is not mentioned that nonIndian whalers, including Japanese and those of the Soviet Union, are largely responsible for the loss in the whale population. Or that the regulations concerning whale hunts by Eskimos have saddled them with a ridiculous type of weapon, which all too often maims the animal and leaves him to die. The Eskimo people have hunted the whale since time immemorial. Their hunts even today result in such a small percentage of the whole that it is ridiculous to make it into an issue. Nothing has been said, furthermore, about the cruelty of the nonIndian sportsmen who hunt without care for protecting the continuing existence of the whales.

The publication titled *American Opinion* touts itself as "the foremost conservative journal" in the country. An article by one Alan Stang, titled "Red Indians," utilizes the misinformation gathered by the Federal Bureau of Investigation through the informer Douglass Durham. The article states the Indians must be made *genuinely* independent "by abolishing the B.I.A. and the Reservation system in which they are wards—slowly, so as not to victimize old people—and then leaving them alone to live on their present land or wherever (and how) they like . . . But the first order of business is to stop the American Indian Movement from terrorizing American Indians into submission . . ."

There is not one iota of accuracy in that statement. The allegation that AIM "terrorizes" Indian people is so ridiculous as to be characterized as a cynical, deliberate, falsehood.

Kevin Phillips, mentioned above, refers to Indians before white contact as "people so primitive they couldn't invent the wheel." Randolph Hearst echoes the Phillips racist position. In one editorial, Hearst declared " . . . the original occupants of the land were the most primitive of people who had never thought of the wheel, had never learned to use metals, and knew nothing of the spinning and weaving of fibers. If the white settlers brought the Indians nothing but those gifts and skills, they were well paid for the land."

The ignorance of this man is appalling. The Indians knew of the wheel, but didn't need it. They made beautiful textiles. They wove from cotton, skins, and bark. They used metals including copper and gold. They developed corn, peanuts, squash, potatoes, and at least fifty other plants domesticated only in North America and transplanted for the use of the whole world. Even had this not been an inaccurate and unfair description of Native civilizations, the "settlers" had no more right to take the land from the Indians than the Dutch in Rhodesia would have in taking white-owned land from Americans.

The *Wall Street Journal*, official organ of financial interests (The Dow Company), prides itself on telling all sides of a story. Their bias in connection with American Indian issues has been shown time and again, however. It's the choice of news that indicates the editorial policy of any publication, not only its content and tone. The *Journal* has given considerable space to the "economic woes" suffered by the white populations of New England because of Indian tribal claims. Several articles relate how land titles are clouded; individuals must wait before they can sell their land; and businesses can't get loans until the suits are settled. There have been no articles describing the Indian condition, the fraud practiced against them in the taking of the land, and what has happened to them since the whites took control of their land.

It would be unfair not to point to the many small newspapers that attempt to tell all sides of the issues, including the Indians'. The *Billings Montana Gazette* has published articles explaining the Indian position. The *Bangor Daily News* has shown sympathy for the cause of the Indians, even though "sympathy" doesn't get rights settled. The *Boston Globe* even exposed textbooks degrading to Indians (June 31, 1977). However, these same newspapers also misinterpret Indian affairs, and the *Globe* cannot be considered a particular "friend" of Indian causes.

The Rev. Lester Kinsolving, a columnist who writes for McNaught Syndicate, has been a consistent antagonist of Indian rights. A recent column (*San Francisco Progress*, November, 1977), severely criticizes the Methodist Church for aiding Indian causes, and gave prominence and praise to Congressman Lloyd Meeds and Jack Cunningham, both of Washington, who have introduced bills intended to unilaterally abrogate Indian treaties and vastly curtail the self-government rights of the tribes.

An example of media bias is shown in articles published by a newspaper that has the respect of the American public because of its work in exposing the Watergate scandal which led to the resignation of a president of the United States. Dealing with the claim of the Maine Indians for land illegally taken from them, the *Washington*

63

Post says (March 8, 1977):

"So ancient agreements have suddenly been reopened, casting doubt on all the property rights and investments built up in good faith over nearly two centuries. It is hard to see where the justice lies in this."

The State of Maine has illegally taken land from the tribes. The Indians have attempted to receive a hearing in court since 1957. The tribal governments have offered to negotiate and mediate their claims. But the state's representatives in congress, and many nonIndian owners of large parcels of land, have been obdurate in refusing to negotiate.

The *Post* shows its bias further, in recommending that the tribes' claims to land be extinguished, and "allow them to seek damages in the Court of Claims . . . It seems to be a reasonable approach to cases in which no perfect justice can be found," the *Post* says.

While bemoaning the situation of the "states and citizens who face enormous losses," the *Post* fails to mention that the Indians have been deprived for nearly two hundred years, and have had no help whatever from the state that took their land. Neither does the *Post* mention that the Indians have declared publicly that their claim is largely against "major landowners," such as the paper producers, Georgia-Pacific Corporation, Diamond International Corporation, and International Paper Company.

Republican Congressman William Cohen of Maine, in a statement before the House of Representatives (*Congressional Record*, March 1, 1977, p. H1533-4) stated that the Maine Indians lost their land "by conquest." If the land was lost by conquest, why then did states negotiate and sign treaties with the tribes in 1794 (Passamaquoddy), with the Penobscot Indians and Massachusetts in 1796 and 1818? In addition there were various subsequent purchases, easements, and state projects, in which the state failed to obtain federal approval and ratification according to the Indian Trade and Intercourse Act of 1790. Maine was a part of Massachusetts until 1820, but these two tribes remained within Maine territory at the time the state was formed out of part of Massachusetts.

The tribes claim they were the victims of fraud, failure to apprise them of the Indian Act of 1790, and that treaties were signed illegally, so that they have retained original possession of the land.

Representative Emery, speaking before the House on the same day, declared that the state had title to the Indians' property as a result of "conquest," because Massachusetts had declared war on the Passamaquoddy and Penobscot Indians in 1755 during the

French and Indian war. If that is so, then the Indians didn't know it. What the congressman fails to mention is that these two tribes supported the Americans in their Revolutionary War of 1776, that the Mashpee lost more lives in that war than did the whites of that town, and that these tribes were allies of the Americans during that war, practically the only Indian tribes that did support the colonies.

In recent years the television media has attempted to describe the Indian situation, primarily in areas yielding to romantic and sympathy-provoking visualizations. Public Broadcasting has drawn upon Indian history, as well as current affairs, to interest their viewers. But, except for a few radio stations in small towns, there is no impact upon the television industry through the entry of Native Americans into the media. Here too there is a lack of background information, and a failure to understand events which makes it impossible to successfully interpret issues.

Indian events, particularly lawsuits, are of special interest to publications like *Nation*. In the July 2, 1977 edition of this periodical, there is palpable evidence of a threat to the Indian tribes in this statement: " . . . when victims of political or social injustice turn to courts for help we frequently do not like judicial solutions and so defy them . . . Unless . . . real give-and-take is negotiated in political forum, the Maine Indians' legal victory stands in danger of being ignored. Their case may well become another example of politics in disregard of the law." This is an example of the cynical attitude to the law, now being expressed by the general public, and most particularly by the lawmakers themselves. It is not only the Indian who is subjected to violations of the law. The Native Americans will find a vast number of supporters who also want to see the laws enforced, in all the affairs of the nation.

Reaching the general public is a paramount requirement for success in obtaining support for Indian programs and policies. During the 1920s and 1930s, John Collier (who became Commissioner of Indian Affairs), was successful in working on certain aspects of Indian issues because he could gain the support of the media. *Sunset Magazine* was his principal medium of publicity for a long time. Through *Sunset* he obtained columns of space in mass media newspapers. This publication made its reputation through its sponsorship of Indian issues. You wouldn't believe it today. It's impossible to get even a book reviewed in *Sunset* dealing with an accurate and knowledgeable description of Indian events and history.

The Indian tribes and the people have, with a practical view to relating the news fairly, founded their own publishing houses and their own newspapers. Most tribes have newspapers. Most Indian centers are publishing newsletters. Indian national organizations publish their own papers and newsletters. There are also some sophisticated learned journals published by Indian people in scholarly organizations and through universities.

A listing of recommended newspapers and journals published by the Indians themselves is found in the appendix. Not all the newspapers are listed. But those that have been active for a number of years and can give a rounded out view of what is happening among the Indian people and in the tribes is supplied.

INDIAN RENEGADES

"Your hereoes are not our heroes," said an Indian speaker at a meeting of the California State Education Commission in 1970, as he criticized textbooks used in the schools.

Indian renegades have helped the states, the white-dominated establishment and the corporations. The fact that they were few was of no avail. Those who wanted the Indians out of the way, who coveted their land and resources, were expert in the art of utilizing the renegades. Treaties were signed by unauthorized Indian persons, particularly those treaties that followed the original compacts between the two governments, the United States and the Indian Nations. These treaties reduced even further the land held by the tribes.

Elias Boudinot, who is lauded as an example of an Indian who was a "true leader," by textbook writers and some historians, has been despised by the Cherokees ever since he sold the nation down the river and conspired with railroad corporations to defraud the Indians of their land, their stock in railroad companies, and then helped to destroy the Cherokee National Government in Oklahoma. Indeed, a congressional committee noted that Boudinot's "personal greed . . . seems to overleap his love of his own people."

History is filled with such information. People such as the renegades and traitors to the Indians, cannot be expected to be more loyal to their corporate friends. Boudinot himself, together with two or three other Oklahoma tribesmen, was closely linked to oil and energy corporations.   (For information on Oklahoma and Indian renegades, see *The Corporation and the Indian*, by H. Craig Miner 1977.)

The textbook writers and the media persist in making heroes of those who were traitors to the Indian people.

Two such renegades have surfaced in the affairs of the American Indian today. They are, mercifully, only two of a small minority.

Billy Bigspring, Blackfeet rancher in Glacier County, Montana, who runs 2,000-3,000 head of cattle, works with Interstate Congress for Equal Rights and Responsibilities. Bigspring believes that "we shouldn't have tribal courts. We can't get justice from tribal courts. NonIndians on the reservation should be involved in making decisions because whatever happens on the reservation can affect them. I think the reservations should be terminated." (ICERR pamphlet, 1977.)

The latter statement explains the reasons for the former. He wants the reservation to be terminated from its trust relationship with the federal government. The tribe has already lost most of its land because legislation such as termination, enacted in the 1950s, won the support of corporations and legislators.

Bigspring opposes the position of the tribes regarding water rights. He says, "If the individual land owner wants to sell his land, the water should go with the land."

Arrogant ignorance is displayed in this statement. By consistent and continuing decisions of the highest court in the land, it has been acknowledged that the waters in, surrounding and traversing reservation land belong to the tribe. Bigspring has no rights to the water; he has the use of it as an individual tribal member. According to Felix Cohen, "In accordance with the doctrine that the United States has exclusive jurisdiction over reservation lands unless it has specified that state statutes shall be controlling, it has been held that an allottee cannot under the state laws relating to appropriation of water acquire any right whatsoever in waters reserved to the tribe." (Cohen, *Handbook*, p. 220.)

Bigspring wants to sell his land. The tribe wants the land to remain in tribal control. They have the right to protect their water. The issue is one with which the tribes are familiar. Preservation of the tribe, the culture, the people, depends upon the land. Selling land to nonIndians brings a further reduction in the tribal land base. Without a land base there is no tribe, no culture, no identifiable people.

Glenn F. Godden is another rancher and realtor. He is said to be one-quarter Cherokee, born in Redfield, South Dakota. He declared in a newspaper interview: "What we want is an end to reservations. We are all native born Americans. Our particular ethnic heritage is an accident. We should all live together equal under the law."

The reservation land is all that is left to the tribes, out of the entire continent they once owned. Would Godden accept the taking of their inheritance from his children and grandchildren? Do the heirs of Rockefeller, Ford, Morgan, and Hearst accept that they must be "equal" in poverty with the rest of the nation? Indians today are not merely "descendants." They are the heirs of those who owned the continent, and have now only the pitiful remnants of a huge estate.

Bert Wolfe is president of the Citizens League for Civil Rights. He says he is three-quarters Indian and grew up on a reservation. He stated, at a meeting in Mashpee in late 1977, "I am from Stone Lake, Wisconsin. I don't think that if Sitting Bull, Crazy Horse, Geronimo and Chief Joseph were here they'd roll over in their graves. I think they'd pat me on the back.

"The reservation is the worst thing that ever happened to Indians," Wolfe declared. "They have produced qualities and minds steeped under socialistic conditions. After six generations of control, this 'government product' hasn't got the gumption or the motivation to face the real world."

This "real world" is one of savagery, exploitation, fraud, and deceit. Wolfe will find it difficult, when the exploiters are finished with him, to live within it peacefully and well. The references to Indian leaders got a round of applause from the white audience, but such theatrical manifestations only serve to distort the truth.

There are others, but few indeed, and the Indian people must deal with them, as they deal with others who have no understanding of the Indian situation, its historic relationship to current affairs, and the kind of life the Indians could have had if tribal self-determination had been exercised in good faith. Government controls and bureaucratic mismanagement have been and still are responsible for the failures seen so far in the Indian condition.

It is claimed by those who would wipe out the Indian tribes and the Indians as a people, that "treaties are a dead letter; they are old; they are stale; they no longer apply." This is sheer nonsense. The Bill of Rights could be construed as "stale," if such judgments be accepted. The treaty made with Panama, and with foreign nations may be construed as "stale" if those now warring against the Indian tribes and nations are to be given credence.

It is a sad commentary on American education that the unique relationship with the Indian tribes has not been taught, nor has it been understood as a basic tenet of our democracy. The United States Government has dealt with the Indians historically and until this day, as one deals with nations, as political entities having governments, with special relationships that have been developed throughout the history of this nation. These relationships have been confirmed again and again with the greatest dignity, by the highest courts of the land, and are justified by international law.

A vicious attack has been launched against the American Indians. This attack is led by the Interstate Congress for Equal Rights and Responsibilities. The falsity of their very title proclaims their intention to deceive the American public. The title might better be "The Interstate Congress for Equal Rights and Responsibilities for White People Against Indians." The irresponsible leaders of this group have unleashed the Four Horsemen of the Apocalypse: Racism, Greed, Fear and Ignorance. The intended victim is the American Indian.

Given the facts, the American people would reject out of hand the brutal, unreasonable, and illegal position of this group.

The offensive against the American Indians wears many coats, and supports many self-serving interests. What has not been understood is the fact that Indian people, despite their many differences, are united against this offensive as never before. Organizations, well educated and well trained Indian people, experts in management, teachers, dedicated people who are determined that the Indian nations shall endure, are alive and well in this country. There is a broad segment of this nation that can be expected to join the Indians in a counter-offensive to protect their rights and their very survival.

"In 1871, Congress, either ashamed of making treaties only to break them, or grudging the time, money, and paper it wasted, passed an act . . that no Indian tribe should hereafter be considered a foreign nation with whom the United States might contract by treaty.

" . . . they added to the act a proviso that it should not be construed as invalidating any treaties already made. But this sense of obligation must have been as short-lived as shadowy, and could have had no element of shame in it, since they forthwith proceeded, unabashed, to negotiate still more treaties with Indians, and break them;

" for instance, the so-called 'Brunot Treaty' with the Ute Indians in Colorado, and one with the Crow Indians in Montana–both made in the summer of 1873.

"They were called at the time 'conventions,' or 'agreements;' but the difference is only in name. "

A Century of Dishonor
Helen Hunt Jackson
1881

FRIEND INTO FOE:
THE MEEDS DISSENT

When the United States Congress established the American Indian Policy Review Commission in 1975, it was fully intended and anticipated that the voice of the Native American would be heard. Federal relations with the Indian people, their tribes and nations, was to be thoroughly examined. Data was to be provided authenticating charges of neglect, violations of Indian treaties, mishandling of Indian affairs, and conflicts of interest existing between the United States and the interests of the Indian tribes.

To a great extent the voice of the Indian was heard (although there are some who charge this was insufficient). Tribes provided documented evidence of violations of the trust responsibility and obligations of the federal government. Data was provided in quantity fully sufficient to support the final recommendations made by the Commission in its Report. Recommendations were made to change the situation under which Indian tribes were subjected to the illegal taking of their land and natural resources, and Indian people were deprived of such rights as education, economic development and self-government.

The Commission voted on each recommendation as well as upon acceptance of the Report. Painstaking discussion was held on every aspect of the documented evidence, on every recommendation, and on the general ideological basis for the Report itself. Of the eleven members of the Commission, only one dissented from the Report and Recommendations. That one was Representative Lloyd Meeds, vice chairman of the Commission.

Congressman Meeds dissented from the basic line and the legal documentation presented in the Report. He disagreed with the Recommendations, and drafted an official Dissent to the Report and Recommendations. The Commission obliged Meeds with a payment of $25,000 for hiring the services of one Frederick Martone, an Arizona attorney, for research and help in drafting the Dissent.

Meeds has been active in Congress in connection with Indian affairs. He was hard at work for passage of the Alaska Native Claims Act (which will prove to be one of the greatest disasters experienced by the Native people), the Menominee Restoration Act (which, although it did restore federal recognition to this Indian nation, also burdened it with a requirement that it come under the Indian Reorganization Act, opposed by many Menominees), and the Indian Education Act of 1972 (still being subjected to various changes in order to make it possible of significant progress in Indian education).

He is considered by many Indian people to have been a friend. There are many who believe he has shown his true ideology throughout the process of legislation in the House of Representatives, with one hand obtaining certain successes, and fixing an iron grip on Indian initiative with the other.

The basic text of the Meeds/Martone Dissent is provided in this chapter. This document, as no other in American history, displays a complete lack of understanding of Indian relationships with the Federal government, historically and in current times. It initiates, as no other document does, an ideology by which the opponents of Indian rights are now being guided in their offensive against the American Indian. It is a manifesto of the dominant society's establishment, directly aimed at abrogating Indian treaties unilaterally, as the final goal of the establishment.

The Meeds/Martone dissent is now being utilized by those who are orchestrating and structuring this war against the Indians. Following his declaration of policy through the dissent, Meeds introduced the first of what may be construed as a series of legislative proposals. This legislation would emasculate tribal sovereignty and Indian rights; it would in all practical ways destroy the treaty obligations of the United States.

Meeds is a skilled politician, trained in the House of Representatives over many years. He has some oldtime friends among the Indian people, who are aghast by his present position. This congressman just barely inched through his last election, winning by a little more than 500 votes. It is certain that these few votes, putting him back in the Congress, were provided by the Indian people, who had a right to expect that he would work for their interests. It is claimed, however, that the pressures of his constituency have caused this "change" in the congressman. Justifying his introduction of legislation that would oppose the interests of the Indian people in his state, Meeds explained it in the most cynical way, saying that since he was not "pushing" the bill, it should not be taken seriously. However, even the most unsophisticated political flunkey would know that the bill need not be "pushed" at all. Judging by the great corporate bodies and defenders of states' rights over Indian rights, the support to his dissent and to his legislation as well, comes almost automatically from such groups.

A resolution passed by the Western Conference of the Council of State Governments in September, 1977 illustrates this support. The resolution is found in the Appendix.

An explanation is due as to the handling of the Meeds/Martone text of the Dissent. The authors have separated the text into more manageable paragraphs. Some liberty has been taken in the paragraph introductions, such as placing introductory phrases in bold-face type. Unless absolutely necessary to an understanding of the text, citations are not used since they are given in the responses that are made a part of this chapter. In many cases, such as the last pages of the text, the complete wording of the dissent is given unchanged. Those desiring to examine the entire document may obtain it through the Government Printing Office. It is titled *American Indian Policy Review Commission Final Report,* and was submitted to Congress May 17, 1977 (Volume One of Two Volumes). The Dissent is found on pages 571 through 612.

THE SEPARATE DISSENTING VIEWS OF CONGRESSMAN LLOYD MEEDS, D-WASH. VICE CHAIRMAN OF THE AMERICAN INDIAN POLICY REVIEW COMMISSION

By Lloyd Meeds

A Partial Condensation

"Unfortunately, the majority report of this Commission is the product of one-sided advocacy in favor of American Indian tribes. The interests of the United States, the States, and nonIndian citizens, were largely ignored.

'' The reports of the task forces and the final report of the Commission were often based on what the members wished the law to be. Recommendations ignored contemporary reality. As an example, the report of Task Force No. 1 would require the return to Indian possession and jurisdiction of large parts of California, Oregon, Nebraska, North Dakota, South Dakota and Oklahoma. Despite contemporary litigation, most Americans are justified in believing that 400 years have been sufficient to quiet title to the continent.

'' The Commission saw its role as an opportunity to represent to the Congress the position of some American Indian tribes and their nonIndian advocates.

'' This Commission failed to consider the fundamental and controversial issues in contemporary Indian law. Instead, it assumed as first principles, the resolution of all contemporary legal and policy issues in favor of Indian tribes. The report is advocacy and cannot be relied upon as a statement of existing law nor as a statement of what future policy should be.''

RESPONSE: In its DECLARATION OF PURPOSE, the Congress declared that not only was it necessary to "conduct a comprehensive review of the historical and legal developments underlying the Indians' unique relationship with the Federal government," but also to determine "necessary revisions in the formulation of policies and programs for the benefit of Indians." That is what the Commission accomplished, among other things.

The Commission was *mandated,* by the very nature of the legislation, to represent to the Congress the opinions and needs of the Indian people and the tribes. Certainly it is an advocacy position. The "interests of the United States, the States, and nonIndian citizens" have indeed been most adequately represented in the past and always have even taken priority over the interests of the American Indians.

The statement that the findings of Task Force No. 1, and its recommendations would require the return to Indian possession of "large parts" of six states is a scare tactic. Undoubtedly the congressman knows better. In fact, in all the cases at court the position of the tribes has been, as noted in official statements and in many briefs, to eliminate from consideration of return of land or compensation of the same, small businesses, homeowners, and small farmers.

However, as has been noted in a response to the dissent (see footnote), the dissent has delineated the principal areas of conflict in the Indian and nonIndian communities. It has squarely presented the question of whether the predominant, nonIndian community views itself as a conquering, suppressive force intent upon destroying the American Indian nations and tribes. The large percentage of nonIndians do not, in fact, subscribe to the vindictive conqueror concept as outlined in the Meeds document.

The average nonIndian subscribes to the concept that this nation owes to

---

*See William Veeder, Memorandum to Sen. James Abourezk, Chairman, Select Committee on Indian Affairs Relative to "The Majority Report" Vis-a-Vis "The Dissent," May, 1977.

the American Indians a trust responsibility, which should and must be performed within the concepts of the Constitution and the principles of democracy derived from the American India:1 which founded this nation.

THE DISSENT BY MEEDS

"The fundamental error of this report is that it perceives the American Indian tribe as a body politic in the nature of a sovereign as that word is used to describe the United States and the States, rather than as a body politic which the United States, through its sovereign power, permits to govern itself and order its *internal* affairs, but not the affairs of others.

'The report seeks to convert a political notion into a legal doctrine. In order to demythologize the notion of American Indian tribal sovereignty, it is essential to briefly describe American federalism. (Note: A description of federalism follows, insisting generally that there are only two sovereign entities, the United States and the States.)

"The blunt fact of the matter is that American Indian tribes are not a third set of governments in the American federal system. They are not sovereigns. The Congress of the United States has permitted them to be self-governing entities but not entities which would govern others.

"The erroneous view adopted by the Commission's report is that American Indian tribal self-government is territorial in nature. On the contrary, American Indian tribal self-government is purposive. The Congress has permitted Indian tribes to govern themselves for the purpose of maintaining tribal integrity and identity. But this does not mean that the Congress has permitted them to exercise general governmental powers over the lands they occupy.

"The Commission has failed to make the distinction between the power of American Indian tribes to govern themselves on the lands they occupy, and their proprietary interest in those lands. Mere ownership of lands in these United States does not give rise to governmental powers. As landowners, American Indian tribes have the same power over their lands as do other private landowners"

RESPONSE: Indian tribes have vastly different proprietary interest in their land than "other private landowners." Their interest is based on the fact that this whole continent was once the possession of the Indian nations, having a complex and acknowledged civilization, with governments and laws, and a democracy understood by those who lived within its borders. Further, how does one exercise self-government if jurisdiction and control over their property such as land and natural resources is denied them?

THE DISSENT BY MEEDS

" Indian reservations exist within the boundaries of the States and within the United States. Reservation Indians are citizens of the States in which they live and of the United States. They are subject to the laws of the United States, but for the exercise of congressional power, reservation Indians are subject to the governmental power of the States in which they live. A tribe's power is limited to governing the internal affairs of its members."

RESPONSE: In support of the conclusion reached in the last paragraph above, there are cited three sources[1]. As to the first authority cited, which is the report of the Arbitration Tribunal, this did not and could not constitute binding authority on anyone except those immediately involved.

As to *McIntosh* and *Cherokee Nation,* Supreme Court decisions, there are repeated references made to them, and the same will be made in the responses. Their inapplicability will be explained.

The dissent makes a sweeping assertion that the Indian nations "lost" their tribal sovereignty and "are permitted to exist" as political units "by virtue of the laws of the United States and not any inherent right to government, either of themselves or of others." There are no further authorities for this assertion. _____

THE DISSENT BY MEEDS

" The doctrine of inherent tribal sovereignty, adopted by the majority report, ignores the historical reality that American Indian tribes lost their sovereignty through discovery, conquest, cession, treaties, statutes, and history."

RESPONSE: LOSS OF SOVEREIGNTY THROUGH DISCOVERY. What is meant by "discovery?" Discovery, according to European history, occurred in 1497, when Cabot sailed south down the Atlantic Coast of North America to the present State of Virginia, claiming the area for King Henry VII of England. International agreements of that era, it is true, had made a compact that the nation "discovering" any part of the New World would hold prior rights to that area.

It is also a historic fact that North America had been discovered by the Native peoples some thousands of years before the first European set foot on their land. They had built civilizations upon that land, establishing their governments and laws by which they lived within their nations. The literature is filled with authentication of this historic fact, even though fraudulent historians of the dominant society have sought to prove otherwise.

The dissent cites *Johnson v. McIntosh* in support of this position,[2] but that case does not state anywhere that the Indians lost their tribal sovereignty. It says that among the potentates of Europe, the Nation having discovered a tract of land on the North American Continent — due to its magnitude, there was enough for everyone — there would be no violation of one potentate's "discovery" as against another potentate's "discovery."

Moreover, the potentates, among themselves, did not consult the Indians, but decided that Indian nations and tribes could not sell their lands to any potentate but the one who had made the alleged discovery.

How could the rulers of empires of Europe destroy the sovereignty of the Indian tribes without the knowledge of the tribes?

There was no destruction of the inherent power of the tribes to govern themselves. The dissent fails to comprehend the difference between the power of self-government and the European title to land, and flounders badly throughout the document in its attempt to denigrate tribal sovereignty.

What does sovereignty mean? It means the power to govern. It does not have the meaning historically ascribed to that word in which only kings, queens and potentates are sovereign. It also means the right to own property. But sovereignty does not emanate from the ownership of land, nor is there any authority which would support the concept that, in some manner, sovereignty emerges from the land occupied by the tribes.

The dissent, using *McIntosh* in denying tribal sovereignty, is mistaken in the reference. Rather than denying tribal sovereignty, this decision repeatedly makes reference to the continued existence of the tribal governments and that this existence was recognized by the great powers of Europe.

Tribal sovereignty has been and is recognized by the United States of America.

Reliance is placed by Meeds upon *Cherokee Nation*[3] to support the concept that "discovery" destroyed tribal sovereignty. A reading of this decision does not support the contention. There was involved, in this decision, the question of whether the Cherokee Nation came within the purview of the provisions of the Constitution, which confers original jurisdiction upon the Supreme Court, involving " . . . controversies between a state . . . and foreign states."[4] The Supreme Court said "No." It stated the Cherokee Nation did not come within the category of "foreign states," as contemplated in the Constitution. Also, as to another citation used in the Dissent, *(Worcester v. Georgia),* this decision was made the year following the *Cherokee Nation* decision. In *Worcester,* the full extent, nature and character of Indian tribal sovereignty are reviewed in detail.[5] *Worcester* was rendered eight years subsequent to *McIntosh* and there was no attempt to reverse *McIntosh* by *Worcester.* The *Worcester* decision defines and declares the vitality and existence of Indian inherent tribal sovereignty in such terms as are today viable and applied by decisions rendered recently by the highest court.[6]

In *Worcester v. Georgia,* the Supreme Court decided that: "the very term 'Nation,' so generally applied to them (Indian Nations), means 'a people distinct from others.' The Constitution by declaring treaties already made, as well as those to be made, to be the Supreme Law of the Land has adopted and sanctioned the prior treaties with Indian Nations, and consequently admits their rank among those powers who are capable of making treaties."[7] There is no legal precedent whatever to support the statement contained in the Dissent that "discovery" caused the Indian nations and tribes to lose their sovereignty.

RESPONSE — SOVEREIGNTY LOST THROUGH CONQUEST:
The Meeds document shows that its authors have not carefully examined their own sources. Indeed, we are instructed by *McIntosh* that France

Spain, Great Britain and later the United States, at the time of *McIntosh* and before that time, refrained from asserting " . . . claims to their lands, to dominion over their persons. . . "[8]

Clearly, at the time of *Worcester,* (1832), conquest had not destroyed tribal sovereignty.

Neither can the decision in *Cherokee Nation* be relied upon to support the concept that the tribes had lost their sovereignty through conquest. Justice Story, in his *Commentaries on the Constitution,* describing *Cherokee Nation* correctly and realistically and not chauvinistically, said:

"Upon solemn argument, it has been held, that such a tribe is to be deemed politically a State; that is, a distinct, political society, capable of self-government; but is not to be deemed a foreign State, in the sense of the Constitution . . . "[9]

RESPONSE: LOSS OF SOVEREIGNTY BY CESSION. During and subsequent to the Revolutionary War and until the time that the United States ceased, in 1871, to enter into treaties, substituting agreements and other arrangements tantamount to treaties, there were cessions of property made by the Indian nations and tribes to the United States.

Those treaties involved without exception an exercise of Indian tribal authority. The United States, as a party to the treaties, recognized tribal sovereignty of necessity. Not only that, but recognizing the requirement that only a tribe holding sovereignty could sign the treaties, the United States took the trouble in many cases to commit fraud, by arbitrarily naming certain Indian renegades as "chiefs," or even "kings," and obtaining fraudulent signatures to those treaties, by which it was placed before the President and the Senate for confirmation, in an attempt (successful of course) to prove that the tribes had agreed, as they were required to agree as sovereign nations, to the treaty in question.

Cession means the assignment of a right or claim, a transfer usually evidenced by a treaty of sovereignty over territory of one sovereign state to another, apparently willing to accept it.[10] Cessions of property have been made to this nation, and it has also ceded property. But those cessions, all involving sovereignty, did not in any sense impair the sovereignty of this nation or those with whom it covenanted.

Neither did cession impair the sovereignty of the Indian nations which were the cessioners of land to which they had a valid claim. From the first treaty entered into with an Indian nation, the Delawares, in 1778, it is recognized that the nation dealt with the Indian nations as equal sovereigns. The Indian tribes and nations are recognized as having sovereignty to this day. Subsequent treaties established and recognized that Indians had the sovereign rights to enter into the treaties.

When Congress declared unilaterally, that "No Indian nation or tribe within the territory of the United States shall be acknowledged or recognized as an independent nation, tribe or power with whom the United States may contract by treaty . . ."[11] this important proviso was added: "But no obligation of any treaty lawfully made and ratified with any such Indian nation or tribe prior to March 3, 1871 shall be hereby invalidated or impaired."

There were about 400 treaties in existence in 1871, when the Congressional Act became law. Their sovereignty continues to this day. The sovereignty of those Indian nations cannot be destroyed by the cessions which were usually contained in those covenants.

RESPONSE — SOVEREIGNTY LOST BY STATUTES: Treaties are, by constitutional edict, the supreme and sacred law of the land. There are no statutes that repeal this principle declaring that treaties in existence in 1871 are invalid. Indeed tribal sovereignty is confirmed by the conduct of the Executive and Judicial branches of the United States.

The plenary power of the Congress relates only to legislative functions. One authority states: "In the main . . . that instrument (the Constitution) . . . has blocked out with singular precision and in bold lines, in its three primary Articles, the allotment of power to the Executive, the Legislative and the Judicial Departments of the Government. It remains also true, as a general rule, that the powers that have been conferred by the Constitution to one of these Departments cannot be exercised by another."[12]

Justice Story stated, regarding the separation of powers of the government: "The object of the Constitution was to establish three great departments of government . . . The first to pass the laws, the second to approve and execute them, and the third to expound and enforce them."[13]

It is irresponsible to declare tribes have no power independent of the plenary power of Congress. By confirming treaties and otherwise, Congress has explicitly recognized the tribes have power of the highest dignity. At no time has Congress destroyed sovereignty. Rather than enacting statutes to destroy Indian sovereignty, Congress has wisely and on numerous occasions taken advantage of Indian sovereignty and relied upon it as a method to accomplish its policies. In the 1975 Self-Determination Act, the Congress declared: "The Congress . . . finds that: (2) The Indian people will never surrender their desire to control their relationships both among themselves and with nonIndian governments, organizations and persons."[14]

By the same Act, the Congress also declared: " . . . its commitment to the maintenance of the Federal Government's unique and continuing relationship with and responsibility to the Indian people through the establishment of a meaningful Indian self-determination policy which will permit an orderly transition from Federal domination of programs for and services to Indians to effective and meaningful participation by the Indian people in the planning, conduct and administration of those programs and services."[15]

It should also be stated that bureaucratic suppression of Indian nations' and tribes' sovereignty does not obliterate that sovereignty.

RESPONSE — LOSS OF SOVEREIGNTY BY HISTORY: The Meeds/Martone document makes a fallacious argument, in a contortion of the law and of history itself unequalled in modern times. These two men, with no knowledge of and certainly no scholarly accomplishments to point to in the discipline of history, have put together a jangle of words to sustain an erroneous position.

There is no evidence in history that tribes and nations of America have lost their sovereign powers through history. True, they have consistently struggled to maintain and protect their sovereignty. That is what Congressman Meeds should have pointed to with pride, as a member of Congress, elected by the people, including Indian people, to that high position . .

In reaching for authentication in "history" to prove that Indian tribes have lost, surrendered, abandoned, or had destroyed their sovereignty, Meeds/Martel have overreached themselves. History, on the contrary, gives clear evidence of the undying intention of Indian people to protect their sovereignty. Congress and the Courts of this land have recognized this fact throughout the history of this nation, despite the many crimes that have been committed against the Natives.

THE DISSENT BY MEEDS

" The supreme law is, of course, in the United States Constitution. It is obvious that there are but two sovereigns, the United States and the States. And to the extent that American Indian tribes may claim a position in the interstices of the Constitution on which to ground a constitutional guarantee of separate tribal existence, the 10th Amendment rather plainly destroys that argument. Since the draftsmen separately delineated foreign nations from Indian tribes in Article I Sec. 9(3), Indian tribes were, even at that early date, not considered foreign nations.

" The consent, or lack thereof, of the ancestors of contemporary American Indians to the Government of the United States is quite irrelevant to the applicability of the sovereignty of the United States to American Indians and their tribes. Nor may anyone exempt himself from the sovereignty of all the people. Our predecessors fought a war among themselves over this and the question is settled. It is too late in the day to seek to recreate 400 years of history."

RESPONSE: The sovereignty of the United States has been acknowledged time and again by the Indian people, the tribes and nations. It is a sovereignty born of democratic thought, in which the Indian people participated as inspiration, and the history is very clear on that score.[16] The service of American Indians in two world wars and two unauthorized wars is testimony of that. But, as the Meeds/Martone document states, law follows reality. The reality of law these days is that it must serve the people. It exists by virtue of the support of the people. It was "law" in Hitler Germany to massacre Jews. It is "law" in Rhodesia to deny the majority Blacks the right to govern, participate in governing themselves, and vote. It is held that the Congress has the right to unilaterally abrogate Indian treaties. While not arguing that point, even though there is ample evidence it would be unconstitutional, it is worthy of note that such a unilateral abrogation would bring down upon the Congress the wrath and hatred of the entire world.

It is unnecessary to "recreate" the 400 years of history. That history is part of the history of this nation, and the Indian nations are bone and sinew of that history. To attempt any step that would destroy the unique relationship of the Indian tribes and nations with this federal government would vindicate those who point to the hypocrisy of the demand for "human rights" all over the world by the current President of this nation.

80

THE DISSENT BY MEEDS

" Tribal government, no doubt had one purpose when Indians were neither citizens of the United States nor of the State in which they lived. Under the 14th Amendment, citizens of the United States are citizens of the State wherein they reside. American Indians, therefore, are citizens of the State and the United States. They cannot now claim that their tribal entity gives to them a source of governmental power in an extra-constitutional sense.

" Law follows reality and experience. Accordingly, the Supreme Court's treatment of the role of the tribe in the Federal system has reflected the realities of the tribe at the time the Court has dealt with the problem. But from the very beginning, the Court made it clear that Indian tribes were not sovereigns. The Court described Indian tribes as 'domestic dependent nations.' This was no doubt true in 1831. As the Court made clear, tribal Indians were 'aliens, not owing allegiance to the United States.'

" The Commission, in essence, is making political recommendations under the guise of legal doctrine. This Commission uses the word "sovereignty" as it is politically used by Indian tribes "without regard to the fact that as applied to Indian tribes 'sovereign' means no more than 'within the will of Congress.'

" The Commission report neglects to mention that there is not a single case of the United States Supreme Court which has ever held that tribes possess inherent tribal sovereignty such that in the absence of congressional delegation they could assert governmental power over nonmembers of the tribe, and exclude State jurisdiction."

RESPONSE. THE FOREGOING CITATIONS PROVE OTHERWISE. It is eminently clear that the Meeds/Martone dissent is using inaccurate citations, and misrepresenting the facts, in order to prove a political viewpoint, which is that there is in the nation, on the part of powerful forces, a demand for total extinction of the Indian tribes.

The word "sovereigns" is used in the dissent in an incorrect connotation. No Indian, truly a member of that proud race, and no Indian tribe has ever claimed to be a sovereign, regardless of the popular misconception fed by Hollywood and the media, defining certain suspect individuals as "princesses," or "kings," or "princes."

Indian tribal powers of a sovereign nature, as nations with valid and ongoing treaties, agreements and compacts with the federal government, are still in existence. This includes control of tribal assets and property, and the right to make and enforce its laws.

THE DISSENT BY MEEDS

" The Commission has converted the doctrine of tribal self-government into a doctrine of general tribal government by taking a quantum leap forward without any adequate legal foundation. The Commission has not even explained why, for policy reasons, it would be a good thing for Indian tribes to exercise general governmental powers over the lands they occupy.

'' The Commission makes much of the fact that reservation Indians want to be left alone and be free of State interference (even though they are citizens of the State, vote in State elections, and help create State laws which are inapplicable to them), yet fails to understand that by arguing for the exercise by Indian tribes of general governmental powers, Indian tribes cannot be left alone.

''The Commission's recommendations would leave us with the following results: Reservation Indians would be citizens of the State but be wholly free of State law and State taxing schemes. Reservation Indians would have all the benefits of citizenship and none of its burdens. On the other hand, nonIndian citizens of the State would have no say in the creation of Indian law and policy on the reservation, even if they were residents of the reservation, and yet be subject to tribal jurisdiction. NonIndians would have all the burdens of citizenship but none of the benefits.''

RESPONSE: Meeds acts as though he did not know that Indians living and working in the cities, off the reservation, do pay taxes. Indeed they do, and quite often most heavily. Even new and untried Indian businesses, such as The Indian Historian Press, are overburdened with taxes so that fully one-third of the so-called proceeds are paid out in taxes.

He also should be glad of the fact that Indians vote in State elections. He would have not been reelected in the State of Washington otherwise.

White people resident on Indian reservations have certain liberties and enjoyments not held by others. If the title to some of these lands were ever subjected to comprehensive investigation, the chances are very good that many of them would have no title at all, except by the questionable device of adverse possession. It is amply proven that many of these deeds to Indian lands, while allowed under the Dawes Allotment Act, were stolen from the Indians through the device of Bureau of Indian Affairs agents simply making over some deed to these white people. Many Indians didn't even know their land had been sold, until many years after the fact.

The devices of land ownership loss to the Indian nations are dealt with ir another chapter, but if American citizens who are citizens of the state o Florida (as one example), go to another state, they must observe the laws o that state, while for a time not being able to vote in the host state. A citizen of Florida who votes in one county, may not vote in another.

White people, or nonIndians generally, having chosen to occupy land on Indian reservations, must subject themselves to tribal jurisdiction and authority. It may be better for them to have this kind of authority than what exists in most cities and states today. The belief that there is something reprehensible in the tribal authority is compounded of racism and misrepresentation.

THE DISSENT BY MEEDS

" By adopting the doctrine of inherent Indian tribal sovereignty the Commission looks at the original powers of the tribe and concludes that the tribes have retained all those powers except where expressly limited by the Congress. The Commission's point of departure is faulty. The focus is not on the nature of the prior rights of tribal government. The question is by what mandate do tribal governments govern today?

" Under our Federal Constitution, there are but two sources of power: the States and the United States. Territorial governments derive their power from the United States. The Commission would assert that Indian tribes exercise powers of self-government in some extra-constitutional sense.

" It is one thing for the Congress to permit tribal Indians to govern themselves and not be subject to Federal constitutional limitations and general Federal supervision. It is quite another thing for Congress to permit Indian tribes to function as general governmental entities not subject to Federal constitutional limitations or general Federal supervision. The position adopted by the Commission would have Indian tribes exercising powers which the United States itself cannot exercise because of constitutional limitations."

RESPONSE: The Meeds dissent speaks of Federal supervision as being necessary in case the tribes exercise self-government. That is what has been the case since the Federal Government began. It is the reason for the existence of the Commission in great part. The Federal supervision has been filled with conflict of interest, with mismanagement, misappropriation of Indian funds, misuse of authority, and a host of the most pernicious practices seen by "civilized" man.

THE DISSENT BY MEEDS

" There is no adequate theoretical basis for the assertion of inherent tribal sovereignty. The assertion of inherent tribal sovereignty proves too much. It would mean that whenever there is a group of American Indians living together on land which was allocated to them by the Federal Government, they would have the power to exercise general governmental powers. The source of those powers would then be some magical combination of their Indianness and their ownership of land.

" It is clear that Indian tribes do not govern themselves under State power. It is equally clear, however, that they govern themselves under the Federal power, and like all Federal power, their powers are specifically limited and the limitation with respect to tribes is one of self-government rather than the government of others.

" It is one thing for the Congress to permit tribal Indians to make their own laws and be ruled by them without State interference. It is quite another for the Congress to permit tribes to exercise general governmental powers without general Federal supervision. War, conquest, treaties, statutes, cases, and history have extinguished the tribe as a general governmental entity. All that remains is a policy.

" That policy is that American Indian tribes may govern their own internal relations by the grace of Congress. General governmental powers exist in this country only in the United States and the States.

" A particularly pernicious consequence of the existing scheme is that in those political subdivisions of a State in which reservation Indians are a majority, they can control that level of government and, for example, set property tax rates which are applicable only to nonIndians. This has in fact occurred and is no mere potentiality. The Commission appears to be content to accept representation without taxation and taxation without representation. Our forefathers were not.

" In support of its argument that Indian tribes by treaty have retained to themselves inherent powers of self-government, the Commission relies upon *U.S. v. Winans*. It is true that there is dictum in that case to the effect that the treaty in that case ''was not a grant of rights to the Indians, but a grant of rights from them — a reservation of those not granted.''

" This dictum raises the question of whether, in instances where the United States required Indians to relocate themselves and put them on reservations, the United States reserved the land for Indians, or whether the Indians reserved the land for themselves.''

RESPONSE: In precisely the same manner as the existence of Indian tribal sovereignty has been challenged in the dissent, there is further attack upon the rights and interests which the Indian nations and tribes have reserved for themselves.

The statement in the dissent that the Commission report relies on the *Winans* case, is in error. The Commission report relies upon an abundance of authority, in addition to the *Winans* case, authorities rendered by the Supreme Court and other courts antecedent and subsequent to *Winans*.

The dissent attempts to put the question upside down when it asserts that the treaty in the *Winans* case did not, in effect, apply to tribes relocated on other than aboriginal land. The dissent also states that its authors ''reject the broad assertion that tribal Indians have reserved to themselves inherent rights of self-government and property.''

However, the *Winans* decision proves and is authority for the proposition that the sovereign power of tribes over their properties, held and occupied by them from time immemorial, were reserved to the extent that they were not specifically granted by their treaties.

Winans proves that the Indian nations and tribes, when they exercised their sovereign powers to enter into treaties, were proceeding at the highest dignity of sovereignty when they executed the treaties, and when they retained all that they did not grant by their treaties.

In the most explicit terms, the Supreme Court held that, in that instance, the Yakima Indian Nation reserved properties which it did not convey. It retained title to those properties. The Congress of the United States recognized full title in regard to those reserved properties which were not granted by the tribe.[17]

The most crucial feature of the *Winans* decision is the posture of the United States in negotiating and consummating that treaty. Thus was recognized, by the treaty itself, that not only did the Yakima Indian Nation have the power to enter into that arrangement of such high dignity, but it also was the owner of the land and the appurtenances to the land retained by the Yakima Indian Nation. The Yakima treaty was entered into on June 9, 1855. There, it was declared that certain tribes "are to be considered as one nation, under the name of 'Yakima,' with Kamaiakun as its head chief . . . "[18]

There is then set forth in that treaty a description of a vast area of land in the central portion of the present State of Washington. The United States, as a sovereign, accepted a conveyance from the "Yakima" Nation as a sovereign. The sovereignty of that Indian nation is repeated. Then, proceeding on the basis of one sovereign consummating a treaty with another, the treaty continued, in Article 2, that, "There is, however, reserved, from the lands above ceded from the use and occupation of the aforesaid confederated tribes and bands of Indians, the tract of land included within the following boundaries, to wit . . . " A description of approximately one and a half million acres of land *retained* by the Yakima Nation follows.

This proviso in the treaty is set forth in the *Winans* case: "The exclusive right of taking fish in all the streams where running through or bordering said reservation, is further secured to said confederated tribes and bands of Indians, as also the right of taking fish at all usual and accustomed places . . . "

THE DISSENT BY MEEDS

" But this question must yield to a conceptual distinction. It is one thing to say, as the Court said in *Winans*, that Indian treaty rights belonging to Indians whose aboriginal possession was not disturbed by the treaty but rather confirmed, are rights reserved by the tribe. It is quite another thing to say that any tribe anywhere has reserved to itself the land on its reservation and various rights to self-government. The leap is unwarranted. The treaties vary. The reservations vary. Many Indians now exist on reservations which have no relationship to ancestral or aboriginal homes. Hence it is clear that in these instances. The United States reserved the land for Indians.

" It is wholly erroneous to adopt, as this Commission has, the position that tribal Indians have reserved to themselves all rights not specifically extinguished by treaty.

" It may be, as in *Winans*, that the relationship between the United States and a particular Indian tribe was one of arm's-length bargaining such that it could be said that a tribe actually reserved rights to itself. On the other hand, the relationship between the United States and other tribes was characterized by war and destruction. When these relationships culminated in peace treaties, it is simplistic, to say the least, to assert that the Indians reserved anything to themselves. It is clear that in most instances, the United States as the victorious party, dictated the terms of the treaty and reserved for the Indians various parcels of land.

" As I have rejected the broad assertion of inherent tribal sovereignty, I also reject the broad assertion that tribal Indians have reserved to themselves inherent rights to self-government and property rights. Generalizations such as these have no place in law, and must yield to a judicious consideration of relevant treaties, statutes, State enabling legislation, history, and contemporary fact. The nature and scope of tribal self-government is too important to be left to case by case adjudication.''

MEEDS RECOMMENDS

" *I recommend that Congress enact comprehensive legislation which clearly defines the nature and scope of tribal self-government and makes it clear that the governmental powers granted tribes by the Congress are limited to the government of members and their internal affairs, and are not general governmental powers.*

" Whether Indian tribes are to exercise governmental authority over nonmembers goes to the very roots of Indian law and policy. The question ultimately goes to what the purposes are for allowing Indian tribes some of the powers of government, or whether indeed those powers are not tied to any specific ends at all. The question is whether Indian governmental power is an instrument of Federal policy defined by its ends or whether it is an absolute prerogative without a limiting purpose.

Indian peoples do not have and have not been accorded any right of government good against the sovereignty of all the people. They are not given the power of government for its own sake. Rather, it is the policy of the United States to allow some Indian peoples to exercise some governmental powers over themselves for a purpose. The purpose is to allow peoples of distinct cultures, most of whose ancestors were present in this land before the nonIndians came to it, to decree with their own norms of conduct and to control their affairs so as to preserve their own cultures and values.''

RESPONSE: The question of whether the United States reserved or granted to the tribes their land in exchange for cessions of land, or whether the tribes granted to the United States has been raised in the dissent. Taking only one example: In 1855 the Treaty was signed by the United States with the Blackfoot Indians in Montana.[19] Following that treaty, a covenant was entered into on May 1, 1888. The Court of Appeals for the Ninth Circuit traced the unbroken chain of title of the Blackfoot Nation down to 1888. The Court's opinion was subsequently affirmed by the Supreme Court, and became distinguished in jurisprudence as the Winters Doctrine. This important assertion was made by the Supreme Court in that case:

"By the terms and provisions of this treaty, the Ft. Belknap Indians (part of the group of Indians who signed the 1855 treaty), reserved to themselves the 'uninterrupted privileges of hunting, fishing, and gathering fruit, grazing animals, curing meat, and dressing robes.' ''[20] The area set aside for the tribes, (*not granted by them*), embraced the Milk River, which had its source in Montana but entered Canada and returned back into the United States. Down through the years the Federal Government recognized that 1855 treaty, although at times the Government acted to limit the area embraced within the treaty.

Another assertion by the Court of Appeals for the Ninth Circuit, later affirmed by the Supreme Court, bears recalling:

"When the Indians made the treaty granting rights to the United States, they reserved the rights to use the waters of the Milk River at least to the extent reasonably necessary to irrigate their lands. The right so reserved continues to exist against the United States and its grantees, as well as against the state (Montana) and its grantees." The Supreme Court recounted the beneficial uses for which the Indians had retained, did not grant, their rights. Those Indian rights could be applied to "beneficial use, whether the lands were kept for hunting, 'and grazing roving herds of stock,' or turned to agriculture and the arts of civilization."[21]

The issue was whether the May 1, 1888 agreement with the Indians and the United States was vitiated when Montana was admitted into the Union in 1889. The Supreme Court rejected that concept, saying: ". . . it would be extreme to believe . . ." after the 1888 agreement was executed that ". . . Congress destroyed the reservation and took from the Indians the consideration of their grant, leaving them a barren waste—took from them the means of continuing their old habits, yet did not leave them the power to change to new ones."[22]

In still another case, it is reaffirmed that when the Indians executed their treaties, reserving lands and appurtenances to themselves, it was in the full exercise of their inherent sovereign powers.[23]

This is the *Ahtanum* case, in which the Court of Appeals for the Ninth Circuit said (citing *Winters* and quoting from *Winans*:

"That the (Yakima) treaty of 1855 reserved rights in and to the waters of this stream for the Indians, is plain from the decision in Winters v. United States, 207 U.S. 564."[24] Further, the Court insisted that: "When the Indians agreed to change their nomadic habits and to become a pastoral and civilized people, using the smaller reservation area, it must be borne in mind, as the Supreme Court said of this very (Yakima) treaty, that 'the treaty was not a grant of rights to the Indians, but a grant of rights from them—a reservation of those not granted.' " (United States v. Winans, 198 U.S. 371, 381.)[25]

Still further, the Court clearly identifies the error in concepts proclaimed in the dissent by Meeds, relative to the status of Indian nations and tribes when they signed treaties:

"Before the treaty the Indians had the right to the use not only of Ahtanum Creek but of all other streams in a vast area. The Indians did not surrender any part of their right to the use of Ahtanum Creek regardless of whether the Creek became the boundary or whether it flowed entirely within the reservation."[26]

The Supreme Court, in another case, recently made this comment: "It must always be remembered that the various Indian tribes were once independent and sovereign nations, and that their claim to sovereignty long antedates that of our Government."[27]

THE DISSENT BY MEEDS

" It is also sometimes urged that tribal governmental power, including power over nonIndians, derives from tribal ownership of the beneficial interest in trust lands. But whatever authority Indian tribes may have over trust property (which is far less extensive than the prerogatives of property ownership which is not subject to Federal fee interests), those rights are ultimately rights to control property itself, not rights to control activity or property of others. Indian tribes, like other landowners, may expel trespassers or sue them for damages. But there is no doctrine whereby when entering the land of another, one consents to any general lawmaking and enforcing authority of the landowner merely by virtue of being on his land."

RESPONSE: As recently as 1975, the United States Congress, in enacting the Indian Self-Determination Act, recognized tribal sovereignty and authority in these words:

"The Congress finds that . . . (2) The Indian people will never surrender their relationships both among themselves and with nonIndian governments, organizations and persons." The Congress "declares its commitment to the maintenance of the Federal Government's unique and continuing relationship and reponsibility to the Indian people through the establishment of a meaningful Indian self-determination policy which will permit an orderly transition from Federal dominance of programs for and services to Indians to effective and meaningful participation by the Indian people in the planning, conduct and administration of those programs and services.''

A question may be asked, in the interests of sheer logic: ''How does any entity exercise self-government, without jurisdiction over their property, and upon those located on, visit, or do business on their property?

The statement that Indian governments have ''not been accorded any right of government good against the sovereignty of all the people,'' is evidence of the dissent's clear intent to develop an offensive against the tribes. How does Meeds determine that Indian self-government would be used against the ''sovereignty of all the people?''

The congressman treats ''the preservation'' of Indian cultures and values as though this were capable of accomplishment in a vacuum, without a viable government, and without the controls inherent in the very concept of self-government.

THE DISSENT BY MEEDS

'' There are few values more central to our society than the belief that governments derive ''their just powers from the consent of the governed.'' Government by Indian tribes over nonIndians, if allowed to take place, would be a clear exception to that principle. A heavy burden of justification should fall on those who would subject some of our citizens to the coercive powers of others without any opportunity or right to join in the deliberations and decisions which determine how that power is to be exercised. Those who assert that Indian tribes should be allowed to rule nonIndians offer little justification other than an appeal to the abstraction of ''sovereignty.'' But our society sees no distinction between the rulers and the ruled; all citizens enjoy both statuses. There is little reason shown why academic deductions from the metaphor of ''sovereignty'' should take precedence over the Declaration of Independence and the first principles of democracy.''

RESPONSE: Corporations and individuals have heretofore experienced a bonanza through an opportunity to increase their wealth and to be free from responsibility for the expense of government. Reservations have been a refuge against taxation. Using Indian land and resources without participating in the costs of government cannot help the tribes develop economic self-sufficiency. The tribes are now attempting to develop and strengthen their governments, to protect their resources, and are enacting ordinances requiring payment of taxes. This is necessary if the tribes are to become independent of federal funding.

Meeds terms this process ''coercive.'' He relates it to the Declaration of Independence, whose very precepts are founded upon Indian concepts of democracy. There is no conflict between the principles of democracy and the right of tribes to self-government.

As governments, the tribes have the right to govern, to do all that a government does. Felix Cohen, in *Handbook of Federal Indian Law* (pages 122-59), expresses this inherent right as follows:

Indian self-government . . . "includes the power of an Indian tribe to adopt and operate under a form of government of the Indians' choosing, to define conditions of tribal membership, to regulate domestic relations of members, to prescribe rules of inheritance, to levy taxes, to regulate property within the jurisdiction of the tribe, to control the conduct of members by municipal legislation, and to administer justice."

Cohen, in this government-approved manual of Federal Indian law, cites many court decisions. It would be redundant to repeat them here.

Meeds, in his dissent, raises the question of taxation "without representation." There are numerous cases in law to support the tribal authority to tax, both their own members, members of other tribes, and nonIndians having business or performing functions, or residing on their lands.

(Meeds, by the way, might better spend his time and talents in a consideration of the illegal and inequitable taxing system in this country, in which there is a tax on tax, if he is so intent upon upholding the principles of democracy.)

Discussing "The Taxing Power of an Indian Tribe," Cohen states that, "One of the powers essential to the maintenance of any government, is the power to levy taxes. That this power is an inherent attribute of tribal sovereignty which continues unless withdrawn or limited by treaty or by act of Congress is a proposition which has never been successfully disputed." (Page 142, *Handbook.*)

Referring to the case of *Buster v. Wright* (135 Fed. 947, CCAS 1905, app. dsm. 203 U.S. 599), Cohen describes the case of the Creek Nation, which had imposed a tax or license fee upon all persons, not citizens of the Creek Nation, who traded within the borders of that nation. Plaintiffs in the case were traders doing business on town sites within the boundaries of the Creek Nation, who sought to enjoin officers of the Nation and of the Interior Department from closing down their business and ousting them for nonpayment of taxes. On demurrer, the plaintiffs' bill was dismissed by the trial court, and was later affirmed by the Court of Appeals for the Eighth Circuit, and finally by the United States Supreme Court. The opinion of Judge Sanborn in the Circuit Court of Appeals "illuminates the entire subject," Cohen asserts, and quotes Judge Sanborn:

"The authority of the Creek Nation to prescribe the terms upon which noncitizens may transact business within its borders did not have its origin in an act of Congress, treaty, or agreement of the United States. It was one of the inherent and essential attributes of its original sovereignty. It was a natural right of that people, indispensable to its autonomy as a distinct tribe or nation, and it must remain an attribute of its government until by the agreement of the nation itself or by the superior power of the republic it is taken from it."

Referring to the landmark case *Cherokee Nation v. State of Georgia,* Judge Sanborn continues, "Originally an independent tribe, the superior power of the republic early reduced the Indian people to a 'domestic dependent nation,' yet left it a distinct political entity, clothed with ample authority to govern its inhabitants and to manage its domestic affairs through officers of its own selection, who under a Constitution modeled after that of the United States, exercised legislative, executive, and judicial functions within its territorial jurisdiction for more than half a century.

"The governmental jurisdiction of this nation was neither conditioned nor limited by the original title by occupancy to the lands within its territory."

Quoting yet another case, Cohen states, "An opinion of the Attorney General dated September 17, 1900, quoted with approval in *Morris v. Hitchcock,* declares:

" 'Under the treaties with the Five Civilized Tribes of Indians, no person not a citizen or member of a tribe, or belonging to the exempted classes, can be lawfully within the limits of the country occupied by these tribes without their permission, and they have the right to impose the terms upon which such permission will be granted.' "

The records are filled with decisions by the courts upholding the right of the tribe to tax, to restrict entry upon their lands, to make conditions for occupying reservation land either by taking up residence or engaging in any work.

Even more recently, in 1976, a Supreme Court decision ruled that the Indians on reservations have a right to self-rule without outside interference, affirming Indian sovereignty, and the right of the tribes to tax.

The case involved the Leech Lake Reservation in Minnesota. The county attempted to exact a personal property tax on the mobile home of Russell and Helen Bryan, located on the reservation. The state of Minnesota argued, in the ensuing lawsuit, that a 1953 federal law gave states the civil jurisdiction over reservations, as well as the right to tax. In 1975, the Minnesota Supreme Court upheld the state. In 1976, the United States Supreme Court reversed the State Supreme Court and disallowed the property tax.

In a unanimous decision written by Justice William J. Brennan Jr., the Supreme Court said that the 1953 federal law was meant only to provide Indian reservations with law enforcement services, if they had none of their own, as well as the white man's court system through which Indians could resolve civil matters. The 1953 act, the Court said, was not meant to "result in the undermining or destruction of such tribal governments as did exist . . . (making them) little more than private, voluntary organizations, a possible result if tribal governments and reservation Indians were subordinated to the full panoply of civil regulatory powers, including taxation, of state and local governments."

In still another case, a federal judge in South Bend, Indiana upheld an ordinance passed by the Continental Congress in 1787, ruling that the great-grandson of an Indian war chief does not have to pay taxes on his land.

Judge Allen Sharp said that the chief Swimming Turtle (Oliver Godfroy), is not obliged to pay taxes on his 79 acres of land in Miami County, and is entitled to recover about $1,000 in taxes he paid since 1959.

In the August, 1977 ruling, the judge consulted the Northwest Ordinance, originally passed by the Continental Congress in 1787 and approved for a second time in 1789 by the first United States Congress under the Constitution. Judge Sharp said that Godfroy was correct in insisting that his land should be tax-exempt according to Article 3 of the ordinance.

The judge ruled that the descendants of Godfroy's great-grandfather, a war chief called Francis Godfroy, had owned the land since the Federal Government released the title in 1849 in accordance with the Treaty of 1838.

THE DISSENT BY MEEDS

"TRIBAL COURTS: The courts of tribal governments can have no broader reach than the purposes for which Indian tribes are granted governmental power in the first instance. That purpose is to regulate the Indians' affairs among themselves. There is no lack of enforcing authority which would show a practical necessity for subjecting nonIndians to criminal prosecution by the arm of a quasi-governmental entity from which they are excluded from political participation because of accidents of birth.

"The Commission argues strenuously that civil judgments of tribal courts should be given full faith and credit by other courts of the States and of the United States. To the extent that tribal judgments are entirely between members, do not implicate any interests of nonmembers, and are arrived at according to substantive legal rules and modes of procedure satisfactory to the Indian peoples of the tribe whose court has entered the judgment, I see no substantial reason why such judgments should not be afforded full faith and credit. However, judgments against unwilling nonIndian defendants should not be afforded full faith and credit.

" It would be disastrous to Indian interests for tribes to have power over nonmembers. If we assume that the governmental powers accorded to Indian tribes include the exercise of jurisdiction over nonIndians, then the nonIndian majority would have a vital stake in the precise content of all laws enacted by every Indian tribe and in all procedures utilized by them to enforce their laws. Congress would have no choice but to closely supervise Indian governmental decisions in a way which would totally frustrate the very purpose of giving Indian governmental powers in the first place."

MEEDS RECOMMENDS

" I RECOMMEND THAT CONGRESS ENACT LEGISLA-TION DIRECTLY PROHIBITING INDIAN COURTS FROM EXERCISING CRIMINAL JURISDICTION over any person, whether Indian or nonIndian, who is not a member of the Indian tribe which operates the court in question.

"I FURTHER RECOMMEND THAT CONGRESS ENACT LEGISLATION prohibiting Indian courts from exercising civil jurisdiction over any person, whether Indian or nonIndian, who is not a member of the tribe which operates the court in question, unless the nonIndian defendant expressly and voluntarily submits to the jurisdiction of the tribal court after the claim arises upon which suit is brought.

" JURISDICTION BETWEEN STATES AND TRIBES: Several major principles concerning the allocation of powers between States and tribes can be stated summarily. States do not have governmental power over reservation Indians for their activities on the reservation unless expressly granted by the Federal Government. States do have power over the off-reservation activities of reservation Indians. However, Indian reservations are part of the States within whose boundaries they are situated, and the States' powers over their territory are limited only to the extent that Federal law mandates restrictions on those powers."

(Meeds discusses the case of Williams v. Lee (1959) 258 U.S. 218, in which the court ruled that ". . . absent governing acts of Congress, the question has always been whether state action infringed on the right of reservation Indians to make their own laws and be ruled by them." This is the "infringement rule" discussed by Meeds, in which he asserts that the rule "has proved to be a very poor discriminator between permissible and impermissible State jurisdiction because the rule does not identify what the 'legitimate governmental interests' of tribes are over transactions involving both Indians and nonIndians." He then suggests that no infringement of tribal self-government should be found unless the nonIndian activities over which State jurisdiction is sought are part of a complex of activities which are substantially Indian in character.)

" There are also areas in which unitary regulation is necessary and therefore Indian reservations should be subjected to State jurisdiction. One example is the control of air pollution, which respects no political boundaries. Congress has charged States with the achievement of Federal air pollution standards within their boundaries, yet it is argued that the Clean Air Act does not authorize States to apply and enforce their air pollution laws on Indian reservations."

RESPONSE: In taking this position, concerning the rights of the States over Indian reservations in any specific area, Meeds shows his ultimate goal: To place the reservations under State control and jurisdiction. This would be final, irrevocable termination of Federal trust responsibility.

The argument that such matters as environmental protection, clean air standards, zoning regulations, and land use planning should only come within the purview of the States because of the "possibility of self-interested exploitation," has no merit. It is specious at best, and self-serving to the political interests of Congressman Meeds and the power structure he represents.

The tribes can be encouraged to cooperate with state planners, to make agreements with states on many issues (such as they are doing even now), and undertaking the planning and protection of resources and the environment, together with the State agencies. In the fishing rights issue, the tribes have shown great initiative in protecting the fish population. In fact, it is the States that have shown irresponsibility in land use planning, as well as in the enforcement of land use and environmental protection principles and laws.

THE DISSENT BY MEEDS

"LAND USE REGULATION. It is usually felt that only the Federal Government can ultimately control the uses of Federal lands, although the practice of the government is to cooperate closely with local authorities. On the other hand, the existence of jurisdictional islands within urban areas holds out the possibility of self-interested exploitation which would frustrate the very purpose of regional land use planning.

" In the absence of ultimate authority over Indian land use planning lying with Federal officials, the fairest system would be to place final authority in State planning authorities in which Indians would participate equally with other affected citizens."

RESPONSE: Why would the placing of land use planning within the States' jurisdiction be the "fairest system?"

The tribes, as self-governing political entities (not merely landowners), have the right to determine the uses of their lands to their own best interests. The States have the interests of the big corporations at heart, regardless of the protestations of representing "all the people." Continuing raids on Indian lands and resources would be the result of such a proposal as Meeds puts forward.

THE DISSENT BY MEEDS

" TAXATION. THE UNITED STATES SHOULD TAX ALL PERSONS ON INDIAN RESERVATIONS the same as it does persons elsewhere. States should tax nonIndians and their property. Tribes should be able to tax members on their property.

" Neither Indians nor nonIndians on reservations should enjoy exemption from Federal taxation. As citizens of the United States with equal participation in and enjoyment of the benefits of the Federal Government, there is no reason why Indians, any more than anyone else, should receive favored tax treatment from the Federal Government.

"Since nonmember Indians have no right to participate in the government of a tribe to which they do not belong, it would be contrary to the purposes of Federal Indian policy and invidiously discriminatory against nonIndians to allow non-member Indians immunity from State law and taxation merely because they are Indian.

"It may be seriously doubted whether Indian tribes enjoy the right to tax. A few old, lower court cases, none less than 70 years old, recognize that power. I have no quarrel with tribal powers to tax, as long as the power is limited to taxation of members and their property.

"The majority asserts the tribe should be free to tax nonIndians and their property situated on reservations. They deduce this power from the assumption that Indian tribes are general governmental units with authority over all things and persons within their boundaries. Taxation of nonIndians and their property would be especially pernicious because of their exclusion from participation in the political processes which control the supposed power. Tribes have no power to tax non-Indians or their property because tribes have no power at all over non-Indians or their property. Again, tribes have a limited privilege to govern themselves; they have no general power of government within the boundaries of their reservations."

RESPONSE: The question of the right of tribes to tax goes to the heart of the Meeds dissent. With taxation, the tribes can become independent entities, politically and economically, which is what was the purpose and is today the purpose of the Federal Government. With the right to tax the tribes, and all those doing business or resident on the reservations, the states would have an additional and considerable source of income.

The statement that the power to tax is an *assumption* ignores the body of law supporting the right to tax. This is no mere assumption.

The Commission asserts the right of the tribes to tax. It does not propose some new type of ruling, law or regulation. The tribes already have the right to tax, but the Meeds position wishes to remove that right and place the tribes at the mercy of the states, the corporations, and the state agencies.

The statement in the Meeds dissent that "tribes have a limited privilege to govern themselves; they have no general power of government within the boundaries of their reservation," has no merit. Mr. Meeds is attempting to make discriminative law. Either ignorance of the formidable array of court decisions that are diametrically opposed to this position, or ignorance of the law, is responsible for this statement.

Mr. Meeds cannot be excused on the basis that he is ignorant of the law. Quite the contrary. This man is knowledgeable, aware of the sources involved, the court decisions rendered, the "rules of the game."

We have every right to accuse Mr. Meeds of an attempt to denigrate the law, to launch a brutal offensive against the Indian tribes, and all his protestations of "friendship" with Indian people will not absolve him of this attempt to wipe them out. _____

THE DISSENT BY MEEDS

"DUE PROCESS OF LAW. While Congress may insulate Indians from State law and may subsidize their efforts at self government and social welfare, I seriously doubt that Congress could levy a tax on persons or property situated on Indian reservations and then remit those tax funds to the Indian tribes. The same result is achieved by allowing Indian tribes to tax nonmembers on their lands. It is a denial of due process of law for Congress to tolerate a scheme in which the financial burden of supporting Indians and Indian government falls disproportionately on non-Indians or on non-Indian property on Indian reservations."

MEEDS RECOMMENDS

RECOMMENDATIONS. "I RECOMMEND THAT CONGRESS ENACT LEGISLATION CONFIRMING THAT STATES HAVE THE SAME POWER TO LEVY TAXES, the legal incidence of which falls upon non-Indian activities or property. The only exceptions to this blanket recognition of State taxing power over non-Indians should be in the rare situations where comprehensive Federal regulation of specific subject matters would independently preempt State regulation, including taxation, of non-Indian activities on Indian reservations.
"I ALSO RECOMMEND that Congress expressly proscribe taxation of nonmembers or property of nonmembers by Indian tribes"

RESPONSE: The Meeds recommendations merely confirm and expose the attempt to attack the Indian people in their role as tribes and nations having governments. _____

THE DISSENT BY MEEDS

PUBLIC LAW 280, in which States have been granted or have assumed general civil and criminal jurisdiction over Indian reservations.

"The effects of Public Law 280 cannot be conveniently summarized. It allows State enforcement of criminal law and provides a State civil forum for litigation against reservation Indians with certainty that the civil law of the State generally applicable to private persons will be the rules of decision in such cases.

"It is not clear to what extent the granting of criminal enforcement powers to States obligates the States to spend their funds to provide police and law enforcement services on Indian reservations.

"Comprehensive congressional review of Public Law 280, which was intended to reduce jurisdictional problems in Indian reservations, has now produced its own set of wide-ranging uncertainties about the permissible jurisdiction of States within Indian reservations. It is appropriate if for no other reason than to reduce the confusion that now exists about the meaning of the statute.

"The Commission report recommends that Indian tribes subject to State jurisdiction under Public Law 280 be granted the unilateral right to withdraw from such State jurisdiction. This recommendation is overbroad.

"RETROCESSION OF JURISDICTION should be predicated only on particular findings that State jurisdiction under Public Law 280 has resulted in actual harm to Indian culture and values. Immunity from the obligations and restrictions placed on all for public benefit will always be thought desirable by the few who would enjoy the immunity. If withdrawal from State jurisdiction is to be done on grounds of Federal policy, the policy choices should be made by Congress, which can weigh fairly the costs of Balkanizing State jurisdictions as well as the advantages to Indians."

RESPONSE: To make the availability of retrocession of state jurisdiction as being "predicated only on particular findings . . . " further tightens the stranglehold that Meeds would place on the Indian tribes. It is the prerogative of the tribes whether they wish to remain under state jurisdiction in law enforcement proceedings. Public Law 280 was another effort to terminate the Federal-Indian trust relationship. It failed, and many tribes have now taken advantage of the opportunity to turn back that law, which put the tribes under the thumb of state agencies without delivering the services promised under P.L. 280. The states themselves have either abused the privilege, or have failed to perform efficiently and equitably when they performed at all.

The hearings held by the Policy Review Commission give urgent and succinct testimony to this position.

MEEDS RECOMMENDS

" CIVIL JURISDICTION. In many instances, there are no judicial forums in which certain claims can be heard. Existence of these jurisdictional gaps also raises serious constitutional problems. Because of the interplay of federal law and the absence of tribal forums, it will often happen that parties to various transactions will have or not have remedies and enforcement forums depending on their race. Assuming the unconstitutionality of this bizarre system of relief based on race, it is not clear what the consequences should be. Perhaps nonIndian defendants of Indian plaintiffs in State courts should be allowed to raise nonmutuality as a substantive defense to the claims of Indian plaintiffs. Perhaps a nonIndian plaintiff against a reservation Indian could have a claim under the Indian Civil Rights Act to compel the Indian tribe to provide a judicial forum for him such as an Indian plaintiff would have against him in State courts.

" In any event, it is surely unwise and probably unconstitutional to permit the Federal purpose of allowing Indians to make their own laws and be governed by them to reduce down to a system whereby different laws apply to Indians and to nonIndians involved in identical or the same transaction."

"CONGRESS SHOULD ENACT LEGISLATION ALLOWING CIVIL JURISDICTION in state courts against Indian defendants in all cases where there would be jurisdiction in the State courts, were it not for the Indian status of the defendant and where the tribal government of the Indian defendant does not provide a judicial forum to hear the claims against the Indian defendant. Tribal interests in regulating their own members could be protected by providing that tribal rules of decision must be given appropriate weight in the State court proceedings. In the alternative, Congress should bar actions by Indians against nonIndians for claims arising on reservations where tribes have not provided forums for similar actions by nonIndians against Indians."

RESPONSE: To argue that the tribes, in the exercise of self-government and jurisdiction over their own affairs, can have no right in the judiciary arm of their government, is to fly in the face of numerous court decisions to the contrary.

The Commission has stated, in its Report, as Meeds says in his dissent, that "civil judgments of tribal courts should be given full faith and credit by other courts of the States and of the United States "

The Commission was only echoing what the law affirms. But Meeds is attempting to make it appear that the Commission's report is recommending an expansion of tribal powers. Not so.

The powers of an Indian tribe "in the administration of justice derive from the substantive powers of self-government which are legally recognized to fall within the domain of tribal sovereignty." (Cohen, *Handbook,* page 145.)

In all the fields of local government, the judicial powers of the tribe are coextensive with its legislative or executive powers, (59 Fed. 836, CCAS 1894, app. dism. 17 Sup. Ct. 999, 1896). The Court said in the case of *Standley v. Roberts,* " . . . the judgments of the courts of these nations, in cases within their jurisdiction, stand on the same footing and are entitled to the same faith and credit." (P. 845, ibid.)

Said Cohen, "The laws and customs of the tribe, in matters of contract and property generally (as well as on questions of membership, domestic relations, inheritance, taxation, and residence), may be lawfully administered in the tribunals of the tribe, and such laws and customs will be recognized by courts of state or nation in cases coming before these courts."[28]

THE DISSENT BY MEEDS

"THE INDIAN CIVIL RIGHTS ACT OF 1968. In general, the Indian Civil Rights Act is a tremendously important bulwark against the abuse of power, which Indians are no less capable of than other persons. I must dissent from various of the Commission's recommendations to restrict the Indian Civil Rights Act. The Commission report takes exception with some of the provisions of the Act, which for the first time, expressly subjected Indian tribes to constitutional limitations in the exercise of power.

" The Commission suggests that requirements of exhausting tribal remedies before having access to Federal courts to redress tribal deprivations of constitutional rights should be strictly adhered to.

" I favor the more flexible approach to exhaustion which the Federal courts have taken.

" No mechanical rule can be prescribed in advance, and the courts should be free to protect constitutional rights whenever in the circumstances of particular cases it appears that it would not be beneficial to pursue tribal remedies.

" The Commission suggests that Federal court review of unconstitutional tribal action should be restricted to a review on records made in tribal court. There is no justification for this restriction on the ability of Federal courts to protect constitutional rights.

" The Commission objects that the jury trial requirements of the Indian Civil Rights Act are unduly burdensome on Indian governments. While it may well be true that many Indian courts are not well equipped to provide jury trials, this argument weighs against allowing such Indian communities to exercise governmental powers; it does not argue in favor of abridging the traditional procedural rights of our citizens.

" If the minimal constitutional protections which all our people cherish are too burdensome for Indian tribes to provide, then they should leave criminal law enforcement to those agencies which will provide them.

" I likewise dissent from the Commission's recommendation that Indian tribes be allowed to fine criminal defendants up to $1,000 and imprison them for up to a year, rather than the $500 and 6-month limitations which now exist.

" The Commission's recommendation that tribal sovereign immunity from Indian Civil Rights Act suits be expanded is at best shortsighted. If Indian governments are to exercise governmental powers as licensees of the United States, it is imperative that they be fully answerable for the improper exercise of those powers. Tribal sovereign immunity should be drastically reduced, if not eliminated. It should not be allowed to interfere with Federal court enforcement of federally protected civil rights."

RESPONSE: This attempt to emasculate tribal courts is made despite the many court decisions asserting the rights of tribal courts, and the judicial powers of the tribes. The problem is to strengthen the tribal courts, instead of weakening them to the point where they are mere shadows of judiciary systems.

The cynical statement made by Meeds that "If the minimal constitutional protections which all our people cherish are too burdensome for Indian tribes to provide, then they should leave criminal law enforcement to those agencies which will provide them," is entirely unworthy of this lawmaker. Indeed the whole system of justice and law enforcement in this nation is under severe criticism, and a thorough review of the judicial system is needed. Who is Meeds to criticize the tribal courts? Regardless of current weaknesses in the tribal courts, the justice meted out by them far outshines that which one receives in the states' civil and criminal courts.

The value of human life and individual rights involved in the criminal justice system is at stake here, and the states have generally failed to set an example.

Again, court decisions affirm tribal jurisdiction over its own law enforcement activities, and also affirm the rights and legal status of the tribal courts.

In his attempt to abrogate the treaties, destroy the Federal-Indian trust relationship, and emasculate the tribal governments, Meeds has recommended such actions by the Congress as would enforce his position.

The dissent terms the position of the Indian tribes as "licensees of the United States." The tribes are not "licensees." They are sovereign entities, political bodies in a relationship with this nation and its federal government held because of *original* rights, not particularly aboriginal rights, which is usually misunderstood by most people (including congressmen) to mean "primitive" rights.

THE DISSENT BY MEEDS

"FINANCING PUBLIC SERVICES. A major problem in the present allocation of State/tribal jursidction is the fairness of the allocation of costs of government and public services.

" To the extent that chosen national Indian policy entails financial burdens on persons other than Indians, it is neither fair nor rational for those burdens to be cast disproportionately on the taxpayers of the States in which Indian reservations are situated.

" Congress has the power to repeal a treaty by unilateral action (Head Money Cases, 112 US, 580, 599, 1884), (a treaty is subject to such acts as Congress may pass for its enforcement, modification, or repeal.)

" To the same effect are the Cherokee Tobacco, 78 US (11 Wall.) 616, 621, 1870, and *Stevens v. Cherokee Nation* (174 US 445, 483, 1889). Many examples of essential abrogations of treaty rights come to mind, but one that was actually adjudicated, is an example.

" By the Act of June 2, 1924, Ch. 233, 43 Stat. 253 8 USC #1401 (a)(2), the Congress declared that all noncitizen Indians born within the territorial limits of the United States would be citizens of the United States. In *Ex Parte Green*, 123 F. 2nd 862 (2nd Cir. 1941, cert. denied, 316 U.S. 668 (1942), an Indian was inducted into the United States Army. He claimed he was not a citizen within the meaning of the Selective Service Law and that the attempt by Congress to make him a citizen under the 1924 Act violated treaty rights. He argued that his tribe had never been conquered by the United States. The court denied his claim and held that even if his treaty argument were valid, where there is a conflict between a treaty and a subsequent statute, the statute prevails.

" Beyond the practical problems associated with recommendation B is the unenforceability of any such legislation. Suppose, for example, the Congress adopted recommendation B but then proceeded to ignore it. Since subsequent statutes repeal prior ones, and since the self-imposed limitation is not found in the Constitution of the United States, recommendation B would be unenforceable. Recommendation B seeks changes in our constitutional system without the trouble of constitutional amendment."

RESPONSE: The recommendation of the Indian Policy Review Commission is recognition that the intent of the United States regarding its relations with the American Indians must be founded in justice. The unilateral abrogation of a treaty dishonors the nation. It is true that treaties with the Indian tribes have been abrogated and more often than not illegally, by the simple expedient of taking the land. The Commission's Recommendation B simply asserts that unilateral abrogation of any Indian treaty must not be done, and recommends that the Congress recognize this restriction upon its powers.

THE DISSENT BY MEEDS

"TRIBAL INDIAN CLAIMS, STATUTES OF LIMITATIONS, AND PASSAMAQUODDY TRIBE V. MORTON, 528 F. 2nd 370 (1st Cir. 1975). The status of tribal claims to land is best understood by referring to the authority under which the claim is made. In general, a claim would be made under aboriginal possession, executive order, or treaty or statute.

" Because discovery gave exclusive title to those who made it, fee title to the lands occupied by Indians when the colonists arrived became vested in the sovereign. (Johnson v. M'Intosh, 21 US, S. Wheat, 543, 573, 1923) . . . other cases are mentioned . . .

" It was recognized, however, that the Indians had a right to occupy the lands until their possessory right was extinguished by the United States. That right, based upon aboriginal possession, is frequently called Indian title and is good against all but the sovereign. But Indian title is mere possession and not ownership and cannot be terminated by the United States without compensation under the 5th amendment. The power of Congress to extinguish Indian title based on aboriginal possession is supreme. The manner, method and time of such extinguishment raise political not justiciable issues.

" Similarly, an Indian reservation created by Executive order of the President conveys no right of use or occupancy to the beneficiaries beyond the pleasure of Congress or the President.

" Such rights may be terminated by the unilateral action of the United States without legal liability for compensation in any form even though Congress has permitted suit on the claim. This is so because Article IV, Sec. 3 of the Constitution confers upon Congress alone the power to dispose of property belonging to the United States.

" Where, however, lands have been reserved for the use of Indians by the terms of a treaty or statute, and the Congress has declared that thereafter Indians were to hold the lands permanently, the tribe must be compensated under the 5th Amendment if the lands are subsequently taken by the United States.

"The status of tribal land now begins to take form. The United States owned all the land in fee that Indian tribes claimed or now claim based upon aboriginal possession or Indian title, subject only to tribal possessory rights. These lands, therefore, were public lands under Article IV, Sec. 3 of the Constitution. It is only when Congress gives this land back to the tribe by treaty or statute that compensation is due under the 5th Amendment upon a subsequent taking.

"Recall that Indians were incapable of conveying land based on aboriginal possession (Indian title), because they did not own them. Ownership was in the United States. Congress prohibited the alienation of lands occupied by Indians except pursuant to the authority of the United States. (Act of July 22, 1790, ch. 33, 1 Stat. 137). Subsequent Nonintercourse Acts, culminating in the Intercourse Act of 1834, continued this prohibition against alienation but each of the Acts has variations and, therefore, resort to 25 USC Sec. 177 is not enough. Resort must be had to the specific Nonintercourse Act in effect at the time aboriginal possession was extinguished.

" Contemporary Indian claims based on aboriginal possession have, no doubt, been a great surpise and shock to the American people. Such claims cannot be asserted against the United States for a variety of reasons.

"Indian title is not good against the sovereign United States.

The Nonintercourse Acts culminating in 25 USC #177 are not applicable to the United States or its licensees.

"All pre-1946 claims not brought before the Indian Claims Commission under the Act of August 13, 1946, ch. 959, 60 Stat. 1949, amended and codified in 25 USC #70 et seq., prior to 1951 have been forever barred by section 12 of the Indian Claims Commission Act. Section 12 provides that 'no claim existing before such date (August 13, 1946) but not presented within such period (5 years) may thereafter be submitted to any court or administrative agency for consideration, nor will such claim thereafter be entertained by Congress.'

"But entities other than the United States have no such protection against ancient and stale Indian claims based on aboriginal possession. Thus it was that the Passamaquoddy Tribe in the State of Maine sought the aid of the United States in suing the State of Maine for Maine's alleged interference with the tribe's aboriginal possessory rights, Maine allegedly not having complied with the Nonintercourse Act as far back as 1794.

103

" Ordinarily, in this country, the assertion of ancient claims is barred either by applicable statutes of limitations, or by the doctrine of laches. But these impediments are not ordinarily applicable to Indian tribes or the United Staes.

" Now 28 USC #2415, which contains various periods of limitation for actions brought by the United States on behalf of various Indian tribes, is uncertain in its effect. In the first instance, it is applicable against the United States. It may or may not be applicable to Indian tribes. In the second instance, it refers to recognized tribes. Third, it is expressly not applicable to actions which seek to establish title to or the right to possession of real or personal property. Accordingly, existing statutes of limitations are inadequate as a bar to the constant and perpetual assertion of stale claims by Indian tribes.

"The assertion of stale claims which upset certainty in the area of real property law and centuries of expectations, and shock the conscience, cannot be countenanced by our legal system.

" Just as the Indian Claims Commission Act ended with finality the assertion of stale claims by tribes against the United States, similar legislation is needed to bar the assertion by tribes of all stale claims against all parties. I, therefore, propose a two-pronged approach to solve the problem of stale Indian claims.

" The first step is for the Congress to adopt legislation which extinguishes for all time all tribal or Indian claims to interests in real property, possessory or otherwise, grounded on aboriginal possession alone.

" Indian lands held under treaty, statute, Executive order or deed would not be affected. As pointed out above at length, no compensation is due under the 5th Amendment for such extinguishment. This would prevent the assertion of such claims on and after the date of the enactment of such legislation. I see this as essential to the orderly administration of justice in this country.

" To ensure that such legislation would extinguish claims such as the Passamaquoddy's now asserted but not yet reduced to judgment, I would resolve all doubt by recommending to the Congress the enactment of a statute of limitations that all such claims not yet reduced to judgment shall be forever barred.

"This would bar the Passamaquoddy or similar claims and deny to the Passamaquoddy and other similar litigants any right to damages from any parties for trespass on possessory rights. Neither the Passamaquoddys whose possessory rights may have been interfered with, nor the people of the State of Maine or Massachusetts who may have dealt with them in the absence of Federal treaty, are now alive. There is nothing unfair about denying the descendants of the Passamaquoddys a windfall and preventing the imposition of a bizarre and unjust burden on the descendants of the people of the State of Maine and Massachusetts.

"It seems to me that this is the correct solution because history clearly shows that the tribes for almost 200 years acquiesced in their land transactions with Maine and that the Congress had ratified Maine's and Massachusett's actions. We must not be unmindful that ' the architect of contemporary law is always contemporary fact.' (L. Friedman, A History of American Law, 1973.)."

RESPONSE: The Meeds dissent now raises a question that has brought the eyes of the entire nation to the Indian relationship with the United States. The issue is the claim of the Passamaquoddy and Penobscot Tribes for land taken illegally in Maine. Other claims are those of the Mashpee in Massachusetts, and indeed most of the Northeastern part of the United States is involved.

The claims of these tribes are based not only on original possession, but upon the failure to extinguish title to the lands that belong to these tribes. There is no statute of limitations in this case, although Meeds attempts to produce such a statute of limitations through the use of the Indian Claims Commission Act. This Act placed, in effect, a statute of limitations as to instituting certain claims against the government. The subsequent Acts passed by Congress extended the period when tribes could litigate under the Act. But the claims of the Northeastern tribes bear a different character from other claims of the Indian nations and tribes. It is interesting to note that most of the Iroquois Nations fought on the side of the British during the American Revolutionary War. Their reasons for this included the fact that Americans were taking Indian land illegally. It was believed that England would be the lesser of the two evils.

However, both the Passamaquoddy and Penobscot Tribes, as well as the Mashpee, were allies of the struggling new nation. There were more Mashpee Indians who died in the American Revolution than there were whites of the region.

The Passamaquoddy claim excludes homeowners and small businessmen, by statement of their tribal council. But there are huge corporations holding land belonging to the tribes. It is this land that the Indians assert rightfully belongs to them, never having been extinguished because of the Indian Intercourse Acts, in which it was only the Federal Government that had the authority to treat with the Indian tribes.

The dissent errs when it characterizes the Passamaquoddy claim as "stale." The Indian people of the northeastern United States have retained their culture; their languages are still alive; they have been subjected to every racist device known to man since the Europeans arrived on their shores. They now ask for justice, and proper negotiations ought to be conducted to this end. The Department of Justice has recognized this claim; it has not considered it "stale," and has undertaken the case of the tribes. The

President of the United States has not considered these claims as "stale," and has assigned a negotiator for settling the tribes' claims.

It is Congressman Lloyd Meeds who has raised the question of essentially abrogating Indian treaties, continuing the pernicious system of refusing to recognize Indian rights. From his lofty (but precarious) perch as a member of Congress, Meeds has taken the position of the racist, the ethnocentric individual who historically has brought the Indian to his present deplorable situation.

THE DISSENT BY MEEDS

" Definitions: Tribe and Indian: Need for Finality. Because the Constitution grants to the Congress to regulate commerce with Indian tribes (Article I, #8), the recognition of Indians as a tribe, i.e., a separate policy, is a political question for the Congress to determine, and its determinations are not subject to judicial review unless the Congress were to heedlessly extend the label of Indian in an arbitrary way.

"But since the Congress cannot bring a community or a body of people within the range of its power over Indian affairs by arbitrarily calling them an Indian tribe, neither can a tribe. The questions 'who is an Indian' and 'what is a tribe' have no meaning in the abstract. The questions have meaning in law only in the context of the congressional exercise of its powers under Article I #8. Whatever its nonarbitrary exercise of that power is, is the answer to the questions.

" Hence, in any given context, resort must be had to the relevant treaties or statutes by which the Congress has made its declaration.

" The Commission fails to appreciate this fundamental principle of constitutional law. By Chapter 3, the Commission asserts that an Indian is a person recognized as an Indian by his or her tribe or community unless Congress has expressly provided to the contrary.

" Now it may well be that an Indian tribe may refer to this or that person as a member. But such definitions or declarations have no consequence unless the Congress specifically recognizes such declarations under its constitutional power.

"It is for the Congress to say who is an Indian and what is a tribe for purposes of Federal Indian law and policy.

"Assuming the promulgation of adequate standards, the Congress may well have the power to delegate this power to the various Indian tribes. But in the context of the Commission report, this would not be a wise policy.

"American Indians would be entitled to a variety of Federal benefits because they are Indians. That being the case, Congress has a special interest in not delegating its definitional power to Indian tribes. If the people of the United States are to distribute their largess, then the United States must be responsible for its distribution. I would also recommend a limitations period, such that after a reasonable date certain, no person or entity would be permitted to assert that it is an Indian or a tribe for Federal purposes. Failing to do this, the Commission's recommendations could result in an open ended raid on the Federal treasury."

RESPONSE: The Meeds dissent is filled with error, misapplication of decisions of the Courts, and the introduction of an ideology of vindictive extinction of the Indian tribes. No position taken in the Meeds dissent shows this more clearly than the question of determining who is an Indian and what is a tribe.

According to Meeds, "It is for the Congress to say who is an Indian and what is a tribe for purposes of Federal Indian law and policy."

But the Courts have consistently held that an Indian tribe has complete authority to determine all questions of membership in that tribe.

Exceptions have been adjudicated in connection with the preparation of tribal rolls for the purpose of distributing a judgment fund, or in any other way distributing tribal assets. The Secretary of the Interior is at present the final authority in such cases, and it is under his direction that such tribal rolls are established at this time. But the Secretary has more often extended his authority to determining whether an individual may be enrolled as a tribal member or not. This has been done in order to "redistribute" tribal properties and assets, usually to corporations, settlers and railroads. The vote of tribal members was thus rigged, by the expedient of eliminating those members who were expected to vote against such redistributions.

"Who is an Indian" has been determined in a variety of ways by government agencies, by the Bureau of Indian Affairs, by state agencies, and by the tribes themselves. The tribe's power to determine its own membership has been recognized by the Courts, and this power is derived from the tribe's status as a political entity.[29] Historically, the Federal Government has often acted arbitrarily in determining Indian identity, and such determinations have been made in connection with voting on some measure important to the taking of Indian land, or the continuing effort to cause disintegration of the tribe's identity and extinction of the Indian people.

More recent Congressional action has, however, resulted in the recognition of the tribe as sole authority for determining an individual's Indian identity. Thus, in recent acts, Congress has defined "Indian" as one who is a member of an Indian tribe.[30]

Perhaps the crassest example of federal juggling of tribal membership for ulterior purposes is that of the California tribes. During the process of determining the Indians' claim in that state for lands taken from them, the Bureau of Indian Affairs area director, Mr. Leonard Hill, was asked "How do you determine who is an Indian?" Hill replied, "An Indian may be anyone who has any evidence of blood quantum descended from an Indian who was present in this state in 1854." Asked what degree of blood would be accepted for such a determination, Hill said with utmost cynicism, "As low as 1/364th degree Indian blood."

It was the intent of the Bureau of Indian Affairs at that time (the 1960s) to eliminate the tribes as sovereign entities, thus "solving" the Indian problem.

The Bureau of Indian Affairs has no authority for determining an individual Indian's identity, but it has been done, and it is being done today. There are cases decided by some Courts, permitting the Federal Government to make such determinations for economic and political reasons, but the illegality and injustice of this must be clear to anyone. Meeds would put this injustice into law.

The whole question of the very existence of the Indian people revolves around this issue, and the tribes have indicated they will use every method at their disposal to exercise this right, the right to decide who is a member of their tribe, and thus who is an Indian.

THE DISSENT BY MEEDS

" Management of Property Rights to which Indians are entitled by treaty but which exist off the reservation. It is axiomatic that the extent of a tribe's power to govern its own members is limited to the territorial boundaries of its own reservation. Absent express Federal law to the contrary, Indians going beyond reservation boundaries have generally been held subject to nondiscriminatory State law otherwise applicable to all citizens of the State.

" But note that the Congress has the power to immunize reservation Indians from the application of State law off the reservation. But the fact that the Congress has the power to immunize them when they go beyond reservation boundaries, does not mean that the tribe has the power to apply its law to its members off the reservation.

" One would ordinarily associate Federal preemption with Federal jurisdiction. But the United States Court of Appeals for the Ninth Circuit in the case of United States v. Washington, (1976), has leaped from Federal preemption of State regulation of Indian fishing at treaty fishing grounds off the reservation, to tribal regulation of its members off the reservation in the area of Federal preemption. (Though footnote 4, 520 F 2nd at 686-87 is unclear, the opinion of the District Court in United States v. Washington, 384 F. Supp. 312, 410 W.D. Wash. 1974) made it clear that a self-regulating tribe had no authority over nonmembers.)

" It is one thing to say that a Federal treaty grants to an Indian tribe property rights off the reservation. It is quite another thing to say, where the treaty says nothing of the kind, that a tribe may exercise governmental powers off the reservation to enforce its off reservation property rights. The result is wholly unsupported in the law.

"It is as though a court were to hold that property belonging to the State of Washington, but located in the State of Oregon, could be regulated by the State of Washington. So too, a tribe's self-regulatory power does not extend beyond its boundaries. The protection of a tribe's off reservation property rights is to be accomplished under the law of the State in which the property is located.

"If the tribe has federally protected property rights off the reservation, then it is the duty of the State to enforce those rights. If the State does not enforce those rights, then it is within the power of a Federal or State court to enforce those rights. But it is not within the power of a Federal or State court to grant to an Indian tribe regulatory powers beyond the boundaries of its reservation.

"The scheme established by the United States Court of Appeals for the Ninth Circuit is unworkable. I recommend to the Congress appropriate legislation which makes it clear that Indian tribes exercising powers of self-government not only have no authority over nonIndians, but also have no governmental or regulatory authority outside of their reservation boundaries over their own members.

"Such legislation does not affect treaty rights or tribal property rights located off the reservation. But it would preserve intact the concept that a governmental unit's regulatory powers are no broader than its territorial boundaries."

RESPONSE: The Meeds dissent refers repeatedly to the "plenary power" of the Congress. Examining the whole fabric and context of the dissent, one comes to the conclusion that the power claimed for the Congress by Meeds is nothing less than dictatorial.

There are some facts to be considered, however, regarding Federal-Indian relations and Federal policies towards the Indian tribes. In a comprehensive examination of the dissent, Mr. William Veeder, renowned attorney who has been employed by the Bureau of Reclamation as well as the Bureau of Indian Affairs, and now has various Indian tribes as his independent clients, has placed this question in perspective:

"Webster tells us that 'plenary' means 'complete, absolute, perfect and unqualified,' " Veeder notes, (page 58 of the memorandum to Senator James Abourezk regarding the Meeds dissent).

"That full power, however, is limited to legislative action. It is the breakdown in the Executive Branch of the Government that has contributed to much of the failure in Indian affairs. Had there been proper Executive conduct, the history of Indian affairs would not have been so bleak.

"The institutionalized conflicts of interest within the Office of the Secretary of the Interior and the Attorney General of the United States underlie much of the disastrous consequences that exemplify the conduct of Indian affairs.

"Legislation, passed by Congress, may be requisite to totally correct the conflicts of interest in the Interior and Justice Departments. Two glaring examples of the methods used to defeat the power of Congress will suffice to demonstrate the obdurate actions of an intransigent bureaucracy within both the Interior and Justice Departments."

Examples are then given, and the Veeder memorandum states, that, "Irrespective of those basic and all important concepts enunciated by the Supreme Court in *Winters* and *Winans,* the bureaucracy has steadfastly acted to denigrate the concepts of those two keystone opinions."

One such example is a 1977 publication in the Federal Register of proposed secretarial rules regarding the use of water on Indian reservations. The effect of these regulations would deprive the tribes of their water rights.

Another example of Executive action violating the will of the Congress and the interests of the Indian nations is the way the recently enacted Self-Determination Act is being applied. This act has the goal of freeing the Indians from the autocratic control of the existing bureaucracy. However, through administrative rules and regulations by the Interior Department, the bureaucracy has reduced much of this Act to impotency.

THE DISSENT BY MEEDS

" An unduly broad and unwarranted extension of the trust responsibility leads to special obligations in health, welfare, education, and tribal government. The same broad interpretation would result in the extension of heretofore nonexistent legal obligations to off-reservation Indians, terminated tribes and nonfederally recognized Indians.

" As a legislator I must say that many of the recommendations have absolutely no chance of being enacted into law.

" That is because they are oblivious to political reality. The combined effect of a number of recommendations and findings constitutes a degree of separatism which this country is totally unprepared to assume. Some of the recommendations and findings are inimical to concepts we hold sacred as American citizens.

" So in the headlong flight to preserve the uniqueness of the American Indian, the Commission recommendations go too far and in my view threaten the existence of the very thing we seek to preserve. The quickest and most certain way to destroy that uniqueness is to immediately implement all the recommendations of this Commission.

" The backlash of the dominant culture would be swift and sure.

" Even in the absence of backlash, subjecting the nonIndian majority to Indian jurisdiction will effectively destroy the uniqueness of

Indians. The majority would then have a stake in the exercise of power which would be irresistible. Congress would have no choice but to closely supervise Indian governmental decisions in a way that would totally frustrate the very purpose of giving Indians governmental powers in the first instance.

"That would be unfortunate. While it may have been necessary at one time to pursue the melting pot theory in this Nation, we are now big enough, strong enough, mature enough and hopefully wise enough, to countenance and even encourage diversity in our culture.

"The American Indian has a very rich and unique culture. He should be given every opportunity to practice that culture. But the American Indian is also an American citizen. He lives among American citizens. Ways can be found to prevent the collision of his uniqueness as an Indian and the rights of other Americans, including Indians, under the Constitution.

"Legislation, such as the Indian Self-Determination Act, which promotes separateness, should receive priority by the Congress if that is what Indians want. Substantial decision-making by Indians over events which control their lives should be allowed. Legislative action should come from a sincere and realistic desire to continue the special relationship between Indians and the Federal Government. But we must not legislate out of a sense of guilt to excessive zeal to cure all the sins and inequities of the past. Distorting the present and future to atone for the past cannot be the basis of a stable and enduring policy.

"The United States is prepared to accommodate Indian interests, and to provide a substantial degree of self-determination. But there is a point beyond which it cannot go. Our federal framework will not be compromised, nor will the rights of nonIndians be ignored.

"Where tribal aspirations collide with constitutional values, the tribe's interests must yield.

"Nor can the rights of the nonIndian majority be compromised to support tribal aspirations. Doing justice by Indians does not require doing injustices to nonIndians.

"Conclusions. The Commission recommendations for restructuring the Bureau of Indian Affairs are thoughtful and constructive. The many recommendations which call for greater participation by Indians in decisions affecting their lives deserve the support of the American people and the attention of the Congress.

"Much of the report is neither legally nor historically accurate. Most of the inaccuracy springs from the initial erroneous conclusions regarding sovereignty, jurisdiction, and trust responsibility. These very basic and fundamental errors permeate and taint almost every part of the report.

" Indian tribes, because of the misapplication of total sovereignty, become super-governments possessing all authority and powers not expressly forbidden them by Congress.

" Tribal governments, because of the mistaken scope of the Commission's recommendations regarding jurisdiction, hold sway over the lives and fortunes of many who have no representation in the governing body which makes decisions affecting their lives."

RECAPITULATION

Analyzing the basic ideology expressed in the dissent of Congressman Lloyd Meeds, who was vice chairman of the American Indian Policy Review Commission, it can be generally stated that:

1: The ideology expressed by the Meeds dissent (representing a minority of one), amounts to abrogating the Indian treaties, by a slower process than would be accomplished through an outright Congressional law of abrogation, but an end to the treaties unilaterally, nevertheless.

2: The tribes would be reduced to mere clubs, without authority or control over their land and resources.

3: An attack upon tribal sovereignty and self-determination, with its accompanying rights to self-government and jurisdiction over its own affairs, is the ultimate goal proposed by Meeds.

4: Decisions of the Courts affirming tribal sovereignty have been misinterpreted and misapplied by the Meeds dissent, all to the end that the Indian tribes and nations be extinguished, the patronizing phraseology of some portions of the Meeds document to the contrary notwithstanding.

5: The historic position of the Indian tribes and nations, which exists to the present time, is held to be "stale," and Meeds recommends that redress of grievances, claims derived from injustices perpetrated against the tribes, be wiped out through the statute of limitations as indicated in the Indian Claims Commission Act.

6: The language, tone, recommendations, and assertions of legal precedent all point to the innate racist nature of the Meeds ideology.

7: In an effort to pander to the power elements of his constituency, Meeds has placed himself in the position of ideologist of the offensive against the Indian people, vintage 1977 and continuing until stopped by public disgust and rejection of his position and proposed legislation.

As outlined in the Veeder memorandum (page 3), the American Indian Policy Review Commission has made recommendations for remedial action in the Federal-Indian relationships, that can be described in general terms as follows:

1: Corrective action relative to Indian affairs is an imperative necessity which can and must be taken without further legislation. This is the task and responsibility of the Executive branch of government, which has the obligation to oversee the Interior and Justice Departments preventing them from instituting regulations and rules that in effect void Congressional acts.

2: That corrective action demands that the governing bodies of American Indian nations and tribes be fully implemented and utilized to eliminate the wasteful practices, both as to human rights and funds.

3: Equally clear is the fact that the institutionalized conflicts of interest have been, and are now resulting in violations of the rights of the American Indian, individually, and confiscating their property rights, both collectively and individually.

4: Congress should proceed forthwith to develop appropriate legislation for the removal of Indian affairs from the Department of the Interior and to establish an independent agency for Indian affairs.

CHAPTER 3
References

1: Cayuga Indian Claims (Great Britain v. United States), 20 AM. J. Int'l L. 574, 577 (1926) (American and British Claims Arbitration Tribunal) and the cases of Johnson v. McIntosh, 21 U.S. 543, 574 (1823); Cherokee Nation v. Georgia, 30 U.S. 1, 17 (1831).

2: 21 U.S. C. 543, 574 (1823).

3: Cherokee Nation v. Georgia, 31 U.S. 1 (1831).

4: Constitution of the United States, 1787, Article III, Sec. 2.

5: See Worcester v. Georgia, 31 U.S. 515, 558, 560-561 (1832).

6: See McClanahan v. Arizona, 411 U.S. 164, particularly on pgs 168 et seq.

7: Worcester v. Georgia, 31 U.S. 515, 558, 560-561 (1832).

8: Worcester v. Georgia, 31 U.S. 350, 571 (1832).

9: 2 Story, *On the Constitution,* Fifth Edition, Sec. 1101, pg. 44.

10: Webster's Third International Unabridged Dictionary.

11: 25 U.S.C. 71.

12: Kilbourn v. Thomeson, 103 U.S. 168, 191 (1880).

13: Martin v. Hunter, 14 U.S. 304,328 (1816).

14: 25 U.S.C. 450(2), Pub. L. 96-638, Sec. 2, January 4, 1975, 88 Stat. 2203.

15: 25 U.S.C. 450(a), Pub. L. 96-638, Sec. 3, January 4, 1975, 88 Stat. 2203.

16: See Donald Grinde, *The Iroquois in the Founding of the American Nation,* 1977, Indian Historian Press.

17: See Tee-Hit-Ton Indians v. United States 348 U.S. 272, 279, 280 (1955).

18: *Indian Treaties 1778-1883,* Kappler's Third Print (1975). U.S. Government Printing Office, Reprinted by AMS Press, New York, 1975.

19: Treaty with the Blackfoot Indians, October 17, 1855, 11 Stat. 657 et seq. (Effective April 25, 1856).

20: Winters v. United States, 143 Fed. 740, 741 (C.A. 9, 1906).

21: 207 U.S. 564,577 (1908).

22: 207 U.S. 564,577 (1908).

23: United States v. Ahtanum Irrigation District, et al., 236 F. 2nd. 321, (C.A. 9, 1956), cert. den. 256 U.S. 998 (1956); 330 F. 2nd. 897 (1965); 338 F. 2nd. 307 (1965); cert. den. 381 U.S. 924 (1965).

24: 236 F. 2nd. 321, 325.

25: 236 F. 2nd. 321 U.S. 325-326 (C.A. 9, 1956).

26: 236 F.2nd. 321,326.

27: McClanahan v. Arizona State Tax Commission, 411 U.S. 164, 172 (1973).

28: *Handbook of Federal Indian Law,* Felix Cohen, page 145.

29: *Patterson v. Council of Seneca Nation,* 245 N.Y. 433, 157 N.E. 734 (1927); *Delaware Indians v. Cherokee Nation,* 193 U.S. 127 (1904); *Cherokee Intermarriage Cases,* 203 U.S. 76 (1906).

30: American Indian Policy Review Commission Report, See page 108, which cites 25 U.S.C. Sec. 450b(a) (Indian Self-Determination and Education Assistance Act of 1975); 25 U.S.C. Sec. 479 (Indian Reorganization Act); 25 U.S.C. Sec. 1452(b) (Indian Financing Act of 1974).

According to government statistics in the year 1880, there were approximately three hundred Indian tribes living in the continental United States. Of these tribes and nations, Helen Hunt Jackson says:

"There is not among these three hundred bands of Indians one who has not suffered cruelly at the hands either of the Government or of white settlers. The poorer, the more insignificant, the more helpless the band, the more certain the cruelty and outrage to which they have been subjected.

"This is especially true of the bands on the Pacific slope. These Indians found themselves of a sudden surrounded by and caught up in the great influx of gold-seeking settlers, as helpless creatures on a shore are caught up in a tidal wave . . . "

A Century of Dishonor
Helen Hunt Jackson
1881

Chapter 4

THE BIG LIE: A NIGHTMARE
IN THE NORTHWEST

It took the United States three hundred years to defraud the Indians of the eastern seaboard of their land, destroy their economy, and decimate their populations. When the westward expansion began in the mid-1800s, the United States had a military force, and was more experienced in the art of "subduing" the natives. It took them only thirty years to bring the Northwest Indians under United States domination. The struggle was a terrible one. The Indians, who had perceived the United States Army as their friends and protectors, soon grew to distrust them. The settlers and gold miners moved in like a swarm of locusts, confiscating tribal land, killing and destroying wherever they went.

The Indians reacted, when it became clear that their land and their lives were at stake, and the thirty years of American expansionism became thirty years of intense warfare between the Indian nations and the United States. The Indians of the Northwest live in the most beautiful and fruitful part of the North American continent. Their tribes were governed by traditional leaders. They knew a democracy that was foreign to the invaders, in which all the people had a part in deliberations, policy making, and leadership.

Only one report of many, may serve to describe the situation of the Northwest Indians during those years. In 1852, Brevet Brigadier General Hitchcock, commanding the Pacific division, wrote:

"The whites go in upon Indian lands, provoke the Indians, bring on collisions, and then call for protection, and complain if it is not furnished, while the practical effect of the presence of the troops can be little else than to countenance and give security to them in their

117

aggressions; the Indians, meanwhile, looking upon the military as their friends, and imploring their protection."

Corporate power was brought to bear upon the Indian tribes. The railroads wanted land for transportation. The United States Government in 1850 offered "settlers" three hundred and twenty acres of land, with an equal amount for his wife if married, as an inducement to move to the Northwest Territory. (Settlers from 1850 to 1853 were allowed to pre-empt half that amount of land.) There were no restrictions as to what lands could be taken, so the settlers took the best they could find. When gold was discovered, farms were built around the diggings. Thus the better part of the land was soon overrun by the immigrants. No matter where they settled, however, they were on Indian land. The Northwest was no "vacant land," as some historians claim. It was well populated. The tribes utilized the land, and had a complex civilization. Their arts and sciences have been studied, and the results published, proving that this area had some of the most remarkable development on the continent.

By the time the settlers had arrived to take up their three hundred and twenty acres and go to farming, the Indians had established farms of their own. They cultivated the potato, and each family had its own patch of productive land, which they tended with care. The settlers, however, had no consideration for Indian rights. They proceeded to enclose the Indian farms as part of their own. In 1853, Lieutenant Jones, commanding Steilacooom barracks, wrote, concerning this situation: "The practice which exists throughout the territory, of settlers taking from them their small potato patches, is clearly wrong and should be stopped."

Injustice was added to injustice when the miners came. The road from California to Oregon lay across Indian lands. In the state of Washington, the motive was greed for land, settlement of a vast territory rich in timber, open space, and the establishment of a base for future development. But the tribes were now aware that these invaders were not friendly people as they had at first imagined. They fought to protect their people and their land. The Yakima Nation was particularly successful in routing the invaders. By May, 1855, Governor Stevens wrote to the Secretary of War: "When Colonel Wright commenced his march into the Yakima country, early this month, they practically held the whole country for which they had been fighting. Not a white man now is to be found from the Dalles to the Walla-Walla; not a house stands; and Colonel Wright, at the last despatches, was in the Nahchess, in presence of twelve or fifteen hundred warriors, determined to fight . . ." (See Reference note at end of chapter.)

Ending this era of the illegal taking of Indian land (there were no treaties nor agreements with the Indians for cessions of their land until land had already been taken), the United States made treaties with the Indian nations. The land ceded by the Indians was nearly equal to all of New England and the state of Indiana.

The Willamet Valley tribes ceded 7,500,000 acres, for $198,000. The Walla-Wallas, Cayuses, and Umatillas ceded 4,012,800 acres for $150,000; the Yakimas, Pelouses, Klickitats and others, ceded 10,828,000 acres for $200,000; the Nez Perces, 15,480,000 acres for $200,000; the Des Chutes, 8,110,000 acres for $435,000; the Flatheads, Kootenais, and Upper Pend D'Oreilles, 14,720,000 acres for $485,000. It has been calculated that the amount of money paid to the Indians, and doled out in sums, approximately $2,500 to each tribe annually, amounted to about $2.75 a year for each Indian.

The treaty with the Rogue Rivers, (September 10, 1853) ceded 2,180,000 acres of their land for $60,000, or about three cents an acre. An estimate of this tribe's population at the time of the treaty was nearly two thousand; four years later they had no more than nine hundred and nine.

The cessions of land made by the Northwest Indian Nations contained treaty provisions in which the Indians reserved for themselves, certain quantities of land and the right to fish and hunt "till time immemorial."

The result of all this destruction of Indian rights, taking of their property, reduction of their populations, and ruin of their economy was impoverishment of the people. Not until the mid-1900s were the nations able to renew their lives and bring their forces together in order to protect their rights. In the years following the entry of the white settlers upon land of the Northwest tribes, the whites were not satisfied with merely taking the land. They pre-empted water, claiming water rights "because the water goes with the land." Underground water was drained from tribal land; timber was cut without Indian permission and often without their knowledge. The war, although taking on a different character, continued, and the whites by this time had settled and developed towns and cities throughout the Northwest.

The Indian Nations went to court, and there they found some relief, and some justice. The most recent decision favoring Indian rights, was the ruling by Judge George Boldt that Indians had the right to take fish "in all their accustomed places," as provided in their treaties. However, in order to satisfy the sports fishermen and the commercial fishing interests, Boldt ruled that the Indians could take only 50 percent of the fish catch. One of the least known and most powerful structures in the United States is the commercial fishery business. United with them, in a new war against the Indians, are the sports fishermen, who have been led to believe that Indian rights to fish means that there will be a failure in management and preservation of the important resource.

Indians became more militant in the 1970s, and united with whites and blacks to protect themselves. Thus the "fishins," and the encounters with the state's fish and game agencies, became a common occurrence, filling the media with sensational stories of Indian militancy, but without explaining the background or the issues involved.

The State of Washington is the center of the struggle for Indian rights today. That is not to say that the struggle, in the late 1970s, is not equally critical in all other states where there are considerable numbers of Indians and where Indian tribes exist as governing bodies. But the State of Washington has become unique, for here is where the ideologists and propagandists of the new war against the American Indian have their center of activities. Here is where the storm troopers of the 20th century Indian war have marshalled their forces to eradicate the Indian nations from the earth. Here is where corporate power is working behind the scenes to protect their timber interests, to confiscate more Indian land, and to break the power of the Indian governments, without which the tribes could not exist. The propaganda mill on behalf of corporate power grinds out its misinformation. Clearly, there are many who are misguided by this attack upon the Indians. But it is the corporate power which is behind the new war. And Congressman Lloyd Meeds is their prophet.

In May, 1977, two spokesmen for the new Indian war published a book about "the Indian problem." What emerged was one of the most inaccurate, inflammatory documents to reach the printed page in the last fifty years. Titled, *Indian Treaties: American Nightmare*, the authors emerged from the struggle over Indian fishing rights with pretensions to a universal knowledge of Indian history, cultures, and issues. C. Herb Williams, one of the authors, is described as a "full-time writer with a background including nine years as a daily newspaper reporter, another eight in the public relations department of a large natural resource oriented corporation... He published a cover story in *Fishing Tackle Trade News* on the subject "Indian Treaties—Sportsmen's Nightmare."

Walt Neubrech, the co-author, is described as "a former chief of the Enforcement Division of the Washington Game Department for a quarter of a century and was in the center of the Indian Rights controversy. He made some of the decisions that resulted in court cases that hit the U.S. Supreme Court.''

The foreword is written by Thomas L. Kimball, executive vice president of the National Wildlife Federation.

Because of the influence and the millions of members of the sports organizations and the large circulation of their publications, this book had sold 15,000 copies during the first two months of its release.

Despite the patronizing references to the American Indians, whom "We remember as benefactors of the European colonists . . ." (Foreword, page xii) and the authors' recognition that "There is no question that many Indians have been treated as second-class citizens or worse for decades. History records countless injustices done to the ancestors of today's Indians," (Introduction, page 1), the book is the crassest example of *The Big Lie*. This strategy has been practiced by corporations throughout the history of the United States. It is practiced by legislators, scholars, and state governments in their role as representatives of corporate interests. It is practiced even by congressmen who have their eyes on future elections, and know it will be difficult to get support without corporate help.

Just as we have taken the "Dissent" of Congressman Lloyd Meeds to account, in discussing his opposition to the American Indian Policy Review Report and Recommendations, so is it necessary to take to account this ideological Big Lie and expose it. In effect, the Williams/Neubrech opus echoes the proposals of Meeds, together with its effort to ultimately abrogate the Indian treaties and demolish Indian tribal governments. This book is not only an inflammatory invitation to racist groups and individuals to join the new war against the Indians. It is an uninformed and illiterate collection of concepts of racial convenience. Anything goes, including the Big Lie, when corporate interests are at stake.

Here are excerpts from Williams/Neubrech, and responses:

"Claims, lawsuits and court decisions across the nation are granting ever-increasing control of America's fish, game and other resources to a handful of citizens." (Page 1.)

This statement implies the courts are granting the Indian people special consideration. Courts have "given" the Indians nothing. They have upheld the treaty rights of the Indian nations and tribes. Rights to hunting and fishing were reserved by them, as were the reservation lands.

"In many states, Indians claim they are sovereign and independent nations, largely beyond the control of federal and state laws, while they continue to accept and enjoy all the rights and benefits of

U.S. citizenship.'' (Page 1.)

American law has always recognized the sovereignty of Indian tribes. The treaty relationship with the United States is not applicable to, nor is it shared, by any other people in these United States. The status of the tribes remains separate, as legal sovereign communities living on separate lands within the boundaries of the United States. The Indians have citizenship in the states, in the nation, and in their own tribes. This is their right, as original owners of the continent who ceded land to the federal government.

"A small number of America's Indians are fighting the states and the federal government for more and more rights to natural resources." (Page 2.)

The tribes have always had to protect themselves against land-grabbing corporations and the white settlers. Encroachment on their land has been the rule. Nevertheless, much of their water, land, minerals, timber, fish and game has been depleted, with the connivance of the Federal Government. Currently, many tribes are consolidating their efforts to prevent further inroads on their natural resources and their treaty rights.

The Supreme Court decided, in a 1908 ruling, that Indians do indeed have the right to their waters, and has spelled out this right. The authors attack the courts of this land because of their rulings today. They forget that court decisions have from the first establishment of the United States, sought to protect Indian rights, and even this has been inadequate and ineffective against the federal bureaucracy, most particularly the Department of the Interior, which regularly has violated congressional acts and Supreme Court decisions in favor of the corporate powers.

The Indians are not fighting for "more and more rights to natural resources." They are fighting to retain their rights, which have already been violated to an enormous extent. The evidence clearly points to the exploitation, over-use, over-appropriation of waters, and the contamination of this nation's waters through the states, the federal government, the Department of the Interior; all of these entities have been responsive to the demands of corporations whose main goal is the exploitation of the land and its resources.

"Most of this destructive catch (in the Skagit River) was made by Indians with modern boats, powerful motors and nylon nets. They were protected by a federal court decision and encouraged by misleading federal fish biologists."

Indians are blamed for decreasing the fish population, and are charged with exterminating valuable fish resources. It is not considered that commercial fishermen had for years, and still today, take undetermined huge quantities of fish. In many areas surrounding the rivers, lumber interests pollute the streams, destroy the spawning areas, in some areas causing floods that wipe out the spawning areas. In other places in the country, the fish have been depleted because water has been taken from the streams by manufacturing, lumbering, and mineral-producing corporations.

Indians have the right to take fish, and regulate fishing. When a state claims jurisdiction, it is illegal and unjust, considering the solemn treaties made with the Indians. In that case, trouble is inevitable. The tribes have declared they will cooperate with the states in executing equitable fishing regulations. So far, the states have been adamant in favor of total jurisdiction.

Of greater concern is the commercial fishing, both foreign and domestic, the pollution of our waters by all kinds of industry, the rape of forest and mining interests polluting the streams and rivers and demolishing the spawning areas, the damming of rivers with the diversion of water drying the rivers and destroying the fisheries such as has occurred at Pyramid Lake in Nevada and the Jicarilla Apache on the Navajo River. This is not the work of the Indians, no more than it is the Indian's responsibility for depletion of fish populations in the Northwest.

"Usually, a decision in a case of this kind (the Boldt decision) is something of a compromise between the two parties. In the Boldt decision, Indians were granted almost everything they asked." (Page 7.)

These are factitious reasonings. Anyone engaging in court action does so with intention of winning and gaining everything he has a right to. In this case, the Indian Nations had many statutes and Supreme Court decisions upholding their rights.

It was considerate of the commercial and sports fishing interests, for Judge Boldt to limit the taking of fish by Indians to 50 percent, when they are entitled to 100 percent. Nowhere in the treaties is the taking of fish by the Indian Nations restricted to 50 percent.

."The central controversy in the case was the wording in several treaties that Indians could fish at their 'usual and accustomed places in common with other citizens of the territory.

"The state maintained the part of the phrase that said 'in common with other citizens of the territory' meant that both had equal rights, and if it was necessary to regulate fishing in the interests of

123

conservation, the state had that right." (Page 8.)

The rights of Indian Nations have been so misconstrued that the public has a perverted view of the true facts. Referring to the contention that nonIndians, "other citizens of the territory," have rights, it was conceded that they did have *territorial* rights. However, when the Oregon Territory was extinguished and converted into the states of Washington and Oregon, these territorial rights became non-existent. State laws were then instituted for the "other citizens."

But the Indian Nations retained their inviolable treaty rights. It should be emphasized that "The treaty was not a grant of rights to the Indians, but a grant of rights from them, a reservation of those not granted." These reserved rights are private rights and were clearly upheld by the Supreme Court.

The authors complain that state fish and game managers, when confronted with Indian claims say "It can't happen here." Then they assert, "Yet it is happening in state after state, as the courts grant special rights to Indians to take fish and game without regard for state conservation laws. The special rights also are being granted for water, timber, land, and mineral claims." (Page 12.)

Such statements are irresponsible. The courts did not, nor do they, grant "special rights." They are upholding rights reserved by the Indians to themselves. For many years, these rights have been violated. The authors would have the violations become rights taken unto themselves. The above statement is only one of many statements deliberately made to inflame those who are ignorant of Indian affairs, laws, and court decisions.

"Today, the poor conditions on many reservations and among many Indians are used as justification for granting special rights and privileges. (Page 12.)

These so-called "special rights" are not special at all. The Indian people are demanding the fulfillment of obligations stipulated in the treaties, and solemnly enunciated in agreements and court decisions. Most treaties called for the establishment of schools, "with suitable instructors, to provide a smithy and carpenters shop and furnish them with the necessary tools, employ a farmer, a blacksmith and a carpenter," it is stated in one treaty. The government promised to send the Indians a physician. Other treaties were to provide clothing, cloth, needles, farming implements, horses, cattle and provisions. Most of these provisions and cattle were sold by

124

Indian agents to white settlers; very little reached the tribes. Education for a long time was non-existent. The Indian has been on the endangered species list since the coming of the white man. Many tribes vanished as the result of genocide by the white people. The treaties did not fade away and die. They are the supreme law of the land.

All that is wanted by the tribes is that they be given an opportunity to become economically independent, free from federal funds. This cannot be accomplished if the states and the corporations insist on attempting to change the course of history, abrogate the treaties, and condemn the Indian people to perpetual dependence upon the federal government.

"The Klamaths had been officially terminated and no longer were legally Indians as far as the Bureau of Indian Affairs was concerned, yet the Supreme Court ruled they still kept their rights to fish and hunt as they wished within the boundaries of the original reservation." (Page 12.)

The rights to hunt and fish, contained in the treaties, are not terminated, and the United States Government acknowledged this.

"Nor must a tribe have a treaty or a reservation to be granted these rights. Non-treaty tribes of bands which never had a reservation are given rights to wildlife in territory never covered by a treaty.

"New reservations are even being created by executive order even though Congress passed a law in 1871 that no more treaties should be negotiated with the Indian tribes." (Page 12.)

The ending of treaty making through the Indian Appropriations Act of 1871, did not end the taking of Indian land by nonIndians; nor did it end the creation of reservations where, until the mid-1900s, Indians were herded in an attempt to separate them "for their own good" from the rest of the people.

The establishment of executive order reservations goes back to at least 1855. The United States dealt with the Native peoples as independent governments from the beginning, and not only through treaties. Executive orders, statutes, treaties, all have the same force of law, the highest law in the land.

The question of the validity of executive order reservations has arisen from time to time. The doctrine that such reservations have the same status as any other type of reservation was clearly expressed by Attorney General Stone's opinion when Secretary of the Interior Fall attempted to sell minerals from these reservations under laws governing minerals on the public domain. The attorney general held that the proposal was illegal, and declared that "The President had authority at the date of the orders to withdraw public lands and set them apart for the benefit of the Indians, or for other public purposes." The issue is now settled. (340 B.A.G. 181, 1924.)

In view of the fact that many nonIndians living on Indian reservations are dissatisfied and are claiming "discrimination" against them by the tribes, are intimidating the people and governing bodies of the tribes, and are in fact claiming the same rights reserved by the Indians in their treaties, there is a solution that is proposed by some.

There exists a statute that can be implemented by the tribes to solve the distressing situation. The Act of June 23, 1926, (44 Stat. 763) authorizes the purchase by voluntary sale or by condemnation of private lands for the use of Indians, and allocates funds in the United States Treasury not otherwise appropriated to be used for the purpose. This has been done by several tribes, and may be a positive way to avoid antagonisms.

"Not all Indians hunt or fish commercially, so the rights being granted benefit only a part of what is a small number of people." (Page 13.)

It is untrue that there are special privileges being granted to a few Indians. There are no restrictions denying Indians the right to become commercial fishermen, except if a particular tribe chooses to enact such a restriction. Indians have always respected the equality of the law, and observed its precepts. Indeed no special group deserves special privileges, such as the non-citizen aliens now receive. Thousands and thousands of such alien people are in this country, eligible to receive welfare and many other priviliges only 90 days after their arrival.

The Indian is indeed a citizen of the United States. He was a citizen of Spain; he was a citizen of France; he was a citizen of Mexico. When these countries ceded their claims by treaty to the United States, the Indian as a citizen of those countries, was accepted as such with all the rights and privileges accorded him by the former nation.

."Probably no group in America has more diverse viewpoints than American Indians. This has been noted repeatedly by Indian leaders as a problem in getting Indians to work together." (Page 14.)

Conditions affecting various tribes and reservations vary on the basis of geographic location, culture of the people, economics, and religious beliefs. This is true of any people, and the differences among Indian people are small indeed, when one considers their unity on basic, important issues confronting all the people. This is historic fact, and evidence is provided today, by the universal unity of all Indian Nations and tribes in mounting a counter-offensive to the new war against the Indian people.

"The state felt that in the interests of conservation, it should regulate fishing on the Puyallup, regardless of who was involved." (Page 14.)

The Puyallup reservation was originally comprised of a huge acreage. It has been reduced to its present size of approximately five acres. It is insinuated that this small amount of land would preclude treaty rights. But treaty rights are still extant. This area in the state of Washington was claimed by Great Britain. On August 5, 1848, a treaty between the two countries was made. Both countries, on July 1, 1863 entered into a treaty for the settlement of the claims of the Hudson Bay Company and the Puget Sound Agricultural Company. Under this treaty, both countries appointed commissioners to hear their claims. On September 10, 1869 a final award was made to each company, and the two companies then executed deeds to the United States.

On August 14, 1848 Congress created the Territory of Oregon. In Section One of the Act it was provided that nothing therein contained "shall be construed to impair the rights of persons or property now pertaining to the Indians in said territory, so long as such rights remain unextinguished by treaty between the United States and such Indians."

By the Act of March 2, 1853 Congress organized the Territory of Washington out of the northern half of the Oregon territory, and Section Two of that Act provides that all laws of Congress relating to Oregon Territory, not inconsistent with the 1853 Act, were continued in force in the newly created Washington Territory.

"In the interests of conservation" occurs again and again in *Nightmare*. It is stated, in effect, that the only conservationists are the dominant society individuals and corporations. History and current afffairs prove otherwise. No country has so polluted its streams and waters, its land and natural resources, as the United States has. Left to conduct their governments and enact their laws, the Indians might well save this country by enacting viable and practical laws of conservation, about which the sportsmen and commercial fishermen know very little, except what will redound to their own self-serving interests.

In the town of Tyringham, Massachusetts, with a population of

250, it was found necessary to post no-hunting signs at four thousand sites in and surrounding the town during the winter deer season of 1977.

Residents complain that hunters kill livestock, endanger people, destroy fences and blast holes in farm buildings. The worst problems are caused by gunners. Indians do not hunt in this area. These are the depredations caused by whites who shoot anything in sight, leaving dead deer lying along the road and in the woods. It was not explained how many of the thousands of hunters who come in every year are members of the National Wildlife Federation.

" . . . we didn't feel that there was still a reservation, so they would be required to abide by the laws as other citizens did." (Reference is again to the Puyallup Indians, see Page 16.)

These words are taken from Mr. Neubrech's notes. He was a state employee with 25 years of service. There was ignorance of the status of the Indian right to fish, according to Neubrech. More than likely, such rights were knowingly violated, or at best ignored. Some knowledge and understanding of the Indian treaty rights might have averted the ensuing confrontations. The process of peaceful negotiation was defeated, because of the failure of a state official to know the law, if Neubrech's assertions are accepted.

In Chapter 7, ("The Neck of the Funnel") the two authors decry the depletion of natural resources, the destruction of game and fish. Indeed the public is becoming more and more aware of this deplorable situation. But they are not aware of the major factors that have destroyed our once abundant assets.

We decry the extinction of the carrier pigeon by game hunters who did so to supply the tables of renowned expensive hotels, restaurants and epicures, and the slaughter of hundreds of thousands of buffalo by sportsmen and professional hunters for their tongues and hides. This was not done by Indians, despite the Big Lie disseminated by some historians, and propagandists such as the authors under discussion. We have seen sportsmen totally decimate deer herds in many areas, with the sanction of that "special breed of men," the fish and game management departments of the states. In the Kaibab area of Arizona, the head hunters practically destroyed the deer herds. In California the High Sierra area was opened to permit the taking of bucks and does because the game management "experts" determined the deer herds were "too large." Chaos resulted. Anyone big enough to fire a gun bought a license to hunt. It was a slaughter. A person driving through these areas saw spotted fawns, yearlings, does, and cattle strewing the roads. The areas have never recovered. The same happened in southern Oregon, including the Klamath Indian Reservation and the areas of Beatty and Bly.

We have personally witnessed the pollution of our waters, streams and rivers by factories, lumber companies, mining interests, oil corporations and the agribusinesses. We see the construction of dams, the diversion of waters from our rivers, and channelization by the Corps of Engineers as being the greatest threat to fishermen. Many of these projects have been extremely detrimental to the Indian people. The building of dams has forced Indians from their homes. The diversion of waters has killed the fisheries on the Truckee River in Nevada and the Navajo River in New Mexico. This has damaged the age-old food supply of the Paiute and the Jicarilla Apaches.

These are not isolated cases.

"An 1855 treaty extinguished these rights (fishing, Michigan), saying 'the Ottawa and Chippewa Indians hereby release and discharge the United States from all liability on account of former treaty stipulations.' "

Here again the Big Lie is at work. The truth can be ascertained from the treaty with the Ottawa and the Chippewa, executed July 31, 1855:

"The Ottawa and Chippewa Indians hereby release and discharge the United States from all liability on account of former treaty stipulations, it being distinctly understood and agreed that the grants and payments hereinbefore provided for are in lieu and satisfaction of all claims, legal and equitable on the part of said Indians jointly and severally against the United States, for land, money or other thing guaranteed to said tribes or either of them by the stipulations of any former treaty or treaties; *excepting however, the right of fishing and encampment secured to the Chippewas of Sault Ste. Marie by the treaty of June 16, 1820.*" (Emphasis supplied.) (Kappler, Treaties, Page 729).

The Big Lie, set up as a smokescreen by Williams/Neubrech to cover up the nonIndian violators of fish conservation, including commercial fishing interests and sportsmen, was blasted by the *Milwaukee Journal* (May 15, 1977) regarding the illegal fishing in Michigan. District attorney Thomas S. Reynolds, the Department of Natural Resources, and the attorney general's office are reported to be seeking "to break the trout poaching racket" that has flourished quietly for years, but has grown into what officials say is a multi-million dollar nationwide business, according to the *Journal*. The biggest fish dealer in Door County, Wesley Brandy of Sturgeon Bay is quoted as saying "Sure it's going on. I've been here 32 years and it's been going on for that 32 years, except now it's big. Everybody is doing it. But you have got to remember that the guys who call themselves sport fishermen cheat too."

Most of the illegally taken fish is distributed throughout the nation, the center of distribution being Chicago. "Aside from the illegal taking of fish, it was found that the fish are "highly contaminated by polychlorinated biphenyls (PCBs). These chemicals are said to be highly cancer producing substances. The United States Department of Agriculture reported that the trout have high levels of PCB, unsafe for human consumption.

"Many Michigan citizens found it hard to comprehend how one small segment of society could claim rights not shared by all." (Page 34.)

It is to be noted that ignorance of the law is no excuse for violations. This sudden emotional disturbance about "one small segment" of society claiming "rights not shared by all" is not only a Big Lie, but an invention of the authors' self-serving imagination. Just who is claiming they don't have equal rights? The poor sharecropper in the south who works for the big landowners? The unemployed factory worker who depends upon the big companies for his job, all the while watching these companies earning immense profits from the fruit of his labors? Or, the big corporations who are monopolizing the natural resources of this land, manipulating the prices of oil and gas in order to acquire more profits? Suddenly, these two are spokesmen for the general public, who really know better. They know that the "one small segment of society" that is claiming and getting special rights is not the Indian. It is the big corporate power. Rights of the Indian include rights to the whole continent, and we have long since been forced to cede those rights, in payment for which we received small parcels of land and the "right" to continue the fight for these rights from generation to generation ad infinitum. When will it end?

"The name 'Siletz Tribe' is a misnomer, for in the early days, many of the Indian tribes in western Oregon were put together on the reservation of 1,382,000 acres." (Page 36.)

This is falsification, or ignorance, probably both. The Siletz are a Salishan tribe and were the southernmost Salishan tribe on the coast of Oregon. Later, when a reservation was established in Oregon for several tribes, the name was extended to designate all the tribes of the Siletz Reservation.

"The fact that treaties were not formally approved by Congress opens the door for litigation similar to that in Maine." (Page 37.)

The cases are dissimilar. The door had been opened and precedents established long before these cases developed. Congress by the Act of May 18, 1928 (45 Stat. 602) stipulated that the Indians of California might bring suit against the United States for . . . "All claims of whatsoever nature the Indians of California . . . may have against the United States by reason of lands taken from them in the State of California by the United States without compensation, or for the failure or refusal of the United States to compensate them for their interest in lands in said state which the United States appropriated to its own purposes without the consent of said Indians . . ."

In the Act of August 4, 1955 (69 Stat. 460) Congress again identifies the Indians of California as "successors in interest to claims against the United States . . ." as provided by the Act of 1928. In two suits against the United States the California Indians received a meager payment for all land in the present state of California with the exception of Mission lands held by the Catholic Church.

There is no doubt in the mind of any intelligent person, that the Penobscots, Passamaquoddy and other Indian nations have rights in land appropriated by the States without just compensation. This applies to all state governments which have acquired Indian lands under the same circumstances. The Trade and Intercourse Act, which became effective March 4, 1789, and was adopted by Congress in 1790, must be referred to as the law of the land.

This statute (which is still on the books as R.S. 2116, 25 U.S.C. 177) forbade "any sale or conveyance of Indian lands without the consent of the Federal Government."

Succeeding Trade and Intercourse Acts upheld the conditions of that first one. The Supreme Court has, throughout the years, upheld the special relationship of the Indian nations with the federal government as proclaimed by the Trade and Intercourse Acts. The scope of the Acts is demonstrated. In *Federal Power Commission v. Tuscarora Indian Nation* (362 U.S. 99, 119, 1960), the Court said, "The obvious purpose of that statute is to prevent unfair, improvident or improper disposition by Indians of lands owned or possessed by them to other parties except the United States, without consent of Congress and enable the Government acting as parens patriae for the Indians, to vacate any disposition of their land made without its consent."

"Courts today are rewriting many of the Indian treaties of the past. In reality it means judges can make decisions which reflect their own personal, social or political beliefs . . ." (Page 39.)

This attack on the judicial system of the United States, particularly in the higher courts, appears repeatedly in the *Nightmare*, and is itself a nightmare, for it lends comfort and joy to the Nazis, the Ku Klux Klan, and the most reactionary elements in the states and national government, to attack the cornerstone of American law. Indians have been subjected to adverse court decisions, and it is to be hoped that succeeding courts will rule more equitably than those who have ruled against just Indian claims. But the attack on the courts cannot go unchallenged. The courts are certainly not rewriting Indian treaties. They are interpreting them, and in some decisions, more Indian rights were fragmented away, than confirmed.

Decisions of the judges, it is certainly true, depend upon their knowledge, their study of Indian and related affairs, the evidence brought before them, and the justice in the case both historically and in the present day. Some judges may be motivated personally. One cannot subtract the human responses from the law. But the instances when judges have ruled solely because of their personal, "social or political beliefs," exist usually when the courts decide adversely against the Indians. The problem is not so much with the courts, nor with the laws and statutes. The problem is with the federal bureaucracy, which regularly violates the laws and statutes, and historically has violated decisions of the courts.

"It's against this background that courts have been attempting to make up for past wrongs with present decisions which discriminate in favor of Indians." (Page 39.)

One might welcome such a posture on the part of the courts, or on the part of any governmental agency, state or federal. There is no evidence that anyone is "attempting to make up for past wrongs." It's all they can do to give the Indians what has been promised and is lawfully theirs through many treaties and agreements. Illegalities such as the practice of genocide in California and other states; the taking of land by gold miners, land that did not belong to them; the racist attitudes displayed by many frontiersmen and settlers against Indians . . . who shall pay for these unlawful deeds? Reparations have been paid to foreign countries defeated in war by the United States. The Oglala Sioux have yet to be paid for murder and injury sustained by them in the massacre of their people at Wounded Knee. What Indians are receiving today constitutes a debt long overdue, and without interest.

An attempt is being made by Williams/Neubrech, together with others aiding the corporate interests, to inflame and incite the

American public (including those sportsmen who have integrity), against the Indian tribes. This is due to the innate racism and ethnocentrism of these people.

What is racism? It is the assumption that psycho-cultural traits and capacities are determined by biological race and that races differ decisively from one another, usually coupled with a belief in the inherent superiority of a particular race and its right to domination over others; a doctrine or political program based on the assumption of racism and designed to execute its principles; a political or social principle based on racism.

Make no mistake about it. The *Nightmare* has not been brought on by the Indian people, their tribes and nations, who made it possible for the early Europeans to survive on this continent. It is brought on by the inherent, disguised racism of the Williams/Neubrech characters of the Northwest.

What is ethnocentrism? A habitual disposition to judge foreign peoples or groups by the standards and practices of one's own culture; a tendency to view alien cultures with disfavor and a resulting sense of superiority. Ethnocentric: Centering upon race as a chief interest or end; inclined to regard one's own race or social group as the center of culture; exhibiting an incapacity for viewing foreign cultures dispassionately.

Make no mistake about it. The *Nightmare* exhibits every element of ethnocentrism, regardless of patronizing protestations of sympathy for the Indians who "have suffered many indignities."

In addition to the racism and ethnocentrism shown by *Nightmare,* by Congressman Meeds, and their cohorts, the issue is a political one. The relationship between the federal government and the Indian Tribes is a political one based on the supreme law of the land, the treaties, which in fact recognized and still recognizes the Indian nations as independent, sovereign political entities with the right to self-determination, the right to self-government.

"The Equal Protection Clause of the Fourteenth Amendment to the U.S. Constitution takes precedence over an Indian treaty. This viewpoint is held by many attorneys and jurists in America today; but has been ignored as courts make decisions based on the philosophy that we can right past wrongs with decisions that discriminate on the basis of race and religion." (Page 44.)

There have been no decisions pertaining to Indian nations that have been adjudicated on the basis of race. All have been determined on the basis of established law.

Note Article VI, Sec. 2 of the Constitution, in which it is stated:

"This Constitution and the Laws of the United States which shall be made in Pursuance thereof; and all Treaties made, or which shall be made, under the Authority of the United States, shall be the supreme Law of the Land; **and the Judges in every State shall be bound thereby, anything in the Constitution or Laws of any State to the Contrary notwithstanding.**" (Emphasis supplied.)

In 1975, G.M. Dahl, chief of the Enforcement Division of the Michigan Department of Natural Resources made this statement, which the authors of *Nightmare* have exuberantly quoted in their mass of misinformation, thus: "The following summary makes heavy reading. It is not a bumper sticker approach of glib phrases to the problem. Because it represents such a thorough job of research it is reproduced here in its entirety." One would not consider it "heavy reading." Perhaps cumbersome, futile and erroneous, but not "heavy." For instance, this "thorough researcher" errs when he states, "In 1887 Congress provided for the allotment of tracts and reservation land to individual Indians, a policy which was continued and expanded by the Treaty Reorganization Act of 1934 . . ."

The superlative "researcher" errs in at least one important respect. It was not the Treaty Reorganization Act of 1934. It was the Indian Reorganization Act which was passed in 1934, which ended the process of allotments that began with the Dawes General Allotment Act of 1887. Indian allottees have the same rights as any other citizen. They also have the protection of treaty rights and the protection of the United States against encroachment of state laws. There are hundreds of allotments held by Indian people that would, after twenty-five years of governmental protection, be terminated. However, the allotment trust periods have been extended until otherwise directed by Congress. The Indian Reorganization Act of 1934 states, in Section 461, that "No land of any reservation, created or set apart by treaty or agreement with the Indians . . . shall be allotted in severalty, to any Indian." Thus, the I.R.A. ended, and did not "continue" and expand the allotment system.

The Indian people are not being granted "special privileges in violation of the Equal Protection Clause" through racial classification. Most Indian tribes would not ask a state to create such special laws, knowing that the state has no jurisdiction on their reservations, and that they are protected under federal law.

Finally, the two *Nightmare* propagandists address themselves to the question "Who Is An Indian?"

The Indian tribe has the authority to determine its membership. The power of the tribes to determine membership is derived from the origin of an Indian tribe as a separate political entity. Membership may be determined by custom, by law, or by treaty. The tribe may adopt anyone it chooses to adopt; it may terminate membership under certain circumstances. In some tribes membership and inheritance is determined by the bloodlines of the male. In others it is determined by the bloodlines of the woman. In some tribes it is mandatory that in order to maintain membership, the individual must reside on the reservation. The authors state " . . . *there are situations where two full-blooded Indians from different tribes marry, and their children do not have rights in either tribe."*

Most tribes have provisions governing such cases. The tribes alone have the right to decide membership, and there may be situations in which certain persons do not enjoy such membership, depending upon the particular tribe, its customs, traditions, and its laws.

Another statement asserts, that "Indian law of this kind can encourage tribal inbreeding and occasional incest, for some tribes are quite small with most members related." (Page 48.)

This is direct calumny, and is either evidence of abysmal ignorance of Indian cultures, or deliberate misinformation. All the tribes forbid incest, and this extended to remote relatives. Intermarriage between tribes was practiced in many tribes, but the bloodlines were kept distinct between the clans.

Because a tribe is "quite small" does it follow it would permit incest? We would venture to say that there is more incest, child abuse, wife abuse, and moral laxity in the city of Seattle than in all the tribes of the United States.

"Along with the question of who is an Indian went the question of competency." (Page 48.)

Neither is relevant to the other, and cannot be considered in the same light. *Incompetency* was used as a ploy by congress against the alienation of land held by Indian allottees. "Incompetency," as used in Indian law, has several special or restricted meanings relating to particular types of transactions, and particularly to the alienation of land. In *Beck v. Flournoy Live-Stock* and *Real Estate Co.,* the Court of Appeals said . . . "The motive that actuated the lawmaker (congress) in depriving the Indians of the power of alienation is so obvious, and the language of the statute in that behalf is so plain, as to leave no room for doubt that the congress intended to put it beyond the power of the white man to secure any interest whatsoever in lands situated within Indian reservations that might be allotted to Indians." (65 Fed. 30, C.C.A. 8, 1894, App. dism. 163 U.S. 686, See Cohen page 221.)

In *United States v. Nez Perce County, Idaho,* the Federal District Court concluded: "While as applied to Indians the terms 'competency' and 'noncompetency,' or 'incompetency' are used in their ordinary legal sense, there is a presumption, conclusive upon the courts, that until the restriction against alienation is removed in the manner provided by law, either through the lapse of time or the positive action of the Secretary of the Interior, the allottee continues to be an 'incompetent' Indian at least in so far as concerns the land to which the restriction relates." (267 Fed. 495, 497, Dcd. Idaho 1917.)

Despite such restrictions the United States, through the Department of the Interior, deliberately and illegally issued fee patents by the thousands. These were issued without Indian application and in most cases under protest. Once patents were issued, competency was "restored" to the Indian and the allotments were sold to the waiting whites. Millions of acres were lost in this manner. If there were not enough Indian allottees and there was still land left on the reservations, the government declared the land "surplus," and sold it. This is how the white man deliberately and illegally invaded the reservations with the connivance of the United States Government.

In the chapter titled "New Indian Successes," the authors fail to note that there are many Indian successes in all fields of endeavor, that are unknown and rarely mentioned by the "successful" whites. Several years ago it was widely publicized by the news media that the Indians had no professional people in any field. Many self-appointed Indian "leaders" exhorted the public as to the dire lack of educators, doctors and engineers, saying there were none.

In 1970 the American Indian Historical Society issued a call for the First Convocation of American Indian Scholars, which was held at Princeton University. The Convocation was limited to two hundred participants. Several hundred who qualified had to be turned away. This successful Convocation was a milestone in Indian history, showing that there were indeed Indian scholars, engineers, and professionals. The Second Convocation was held at the Aspen Institute for Humanistic Studies. This brought together professionals in education, medicine, the arts, and many other fields of endeavor.

Williams/Neubrech are suddenly alarmed by the so-called Indian successes. Some cases have been won at court, but the tribes have had to make compromises. The effort to wipe out the Indian governments is still continuing, and it is indeed a *Nightmare* for the Indian people. Had it not been necessary for most of us to spend our best years, for many generations, being jumped like a yoyo between the courts and the federal government, we would have more scholars and professionals per capita than any other sector of the population.

The Klamath Indians, the authors say, received quarterly per capita payments from timber sales which "were completely unearned, and were made strictly on the legal basis of tribal membership." (Page 51.)

Is it assumed that this was illegal? Is it a crime to receive income from an asset which you own? To whom should this income be paid, if not to the owners? That some of the Klamaths spent their funds unwisely is probably to be deplored. But it was and is their money, and theirs to do with as they choose. If a white person is improvident, it is not made the subject of a vast study, or criticism by the likes of Williams and Neubrech. We have personally known several remittance men, who went through their fortunes like the proverbial ball of lightning. Perhaps the Klamaths were tired of supporting a cortege of federal leeches and funding the total costs of operating the business of their reservation without their consent.

It is not mentioned that timber rights were sold by the Bureau of Indian Affairs on that reservation to the lowest not the highest bidder. Indeed the timber rights of this tribe have been so mismanaged that the issue has become the subject of open criticism.

"An additional payment of $12,000 each was paid later when the Klamaths won a court battle in which they maintained the $43,000 had not been enough for the land and timber." (Page 51.)

The $12,000 payment received by the Klamaths was not connected in any way to the sale of their reservation that netted them $43,000. It was in payment for land taken from them long before the termination of the reservation. In this case, the Court found that what they had been paid in this prior sale was an "unconscionable amount," and awarded the additional money.

Attempting to villify the Indian people, the authors then promote this fairy tale:

"Another example of Indians not understanding their environment happened in Chaco Canyon . . . They simply overlogged their forests. This degraded their watershed . . . the Indian destroyed much of the ground cover . . . which resulted in lowering the water table. The water rushing through the canyon caused erosion. Tree rings show that a drought hit this country in 1276 A.D. and lasted twenty-four years. But the same tree rings show that the Indians had

been forced to leave Chaco Canyon more than a hundred years earlier, in 1140." (Page 57.)

The erosion of the land in Chaco Canyon was not alone the "overuse" of land. Floods did not occur because of "overuse of land." These were relatively small populations, using the land with care and respect. The notion that they destroyed the land is not only far-fetched, but incapable of authentication.

How did the "super race" handle like situations with their superior knowledge of "the dynamics of forest or rangeland," and their knowledge of conservation?

Consider the dust bowl of the midwest. Let us not forget the land in Oklahoma and Arkansas, forcing people to move out of their homes into other states. What caused the dust bowls if not overuse of the land!

On the other hand, it is well authenticated that the Indians practiced conservation. They fertilized the land and rotated their crops on the east coast. The ignorant early colonist thought that farm land lying fallow was abandoned. It had been left to "rest." The Plains Indians burned the prairie to produce new lush grass and clear out rogue vegetation. Indians on the west coast practiced controlled burning to keep the forests clear of underbrush and avoid forest fires. Other areas were burned, to produce new growth of plants that were used in the production of baskets, cordage, clothing and food. The Indians knew ecological protection, conservation and land dynamics. They knew agriculture. They knew the elements of propagation, cross-breeding, seed selection. Corn was developed by Indians long before the white invasion. Many varieties of plants were planted, tended, irrigated, fertilized, harvested, and stored. They knew how to dry and concentrate foods.

With all this misinformation about the drought in 1276, erroneously said to have been caused by the Indians of Chaco Canyon, it is a fair question to ask, what Indians caused the drought of 1977?

Reference is made to the bald and golden eagles, two species classified as endangered. (Page 60.)

The Indians use a minimal amount of feathers from these birds, and it is certainly not the Indian people who have caused the reduction in that population. But in California, (and similar events occurred elsewhere), a prominent rancher was hailed into court for killing several eagles. He was acquitted by a jury. In Oklahoma, Indians were arrested for possession of feathers that were many years old, had been handed down from generation to generation. They received jail sentences.

138

"Today, taxation without representation is a fact for nonIndians owning land within the original boundaries of some reservations." (Page 62.)

"When an Indian gets his land declared 'Indian trust land,' he pays no taxes on it. Yet the law in many states declares that the city or county must still provide services to the 'trust land Indians,' (such as fire protection), the same as for other citizens who pay taxes." (Page 63.)

Land held in trust status for Indian tribes are exempt from local and state taxation, because the federal government exercises jurisdiction by virtue of the Indian treaties and its trusteeship as provided for in the treaties.

In *Mason v. United States* (461 F. 2nd 1364, Ct.Cl. 1972), the Court held that the United States as trustee, must protect the Indian against foreclosure and taxation.

In *Choate v. Trapp*, the Supreme Court held that the exemption from local taxation was a "vested property right" which Congress could not repeal consistently with the Fifth Amendment (224 U.S., 665, 1912).

There are legal and logical reasons for taxing nonIndians and nonIndian businesses on the reservation:

1. Persons owning property in one state, and residing in another state, pay taxes in the former state where they are not allowed to vote, as well as paying taxes in the latter state, where they vote.

2. Persons living in France (for example), owning property in France, are not citizens and hence can't vote in France. But they are required to pay taxes.

3. NonIndian owners of allotted land purchased from Indians, and not members of the tribe, are not "citizens" of the tribe, hence cannot vote. They pay taxes on their property.

4. All persons pay taxes on property and business wherever they live or conduct business.

5. Indians pay taxes wherever they own property, whether they vote or not in that state, county, or city. They also pay use taxes, sales taxes and indeed any taxes paid by other citizens, off the reservation.

6. Businesses pay taxes, including use and property, wherever they conduct business, whether they can vote there or not.

7. NonIndians have no right to vote on Indian reservations, not being members of the tribe. The right of the tribe to tax has been affirmed in many Court decisions.

139

Further, the charge of "discrimination" is inapplicable, not capable of confirmation or authentication. The issue of "taxation without representation" is not applicable, as above shown. When we say the relationship between the Indian tribes and nations with the federal government is "unique," this is not a mere turn of the phrase. This relationship is unique because of the status of the Indian tribes as descendants *and heirs* of the nations and tribes which made treaties with the United States, were the original owners of the land, whose land is now the whole continent upon which these people who complain about "taxation" now reside.

Americans need to become accustomed to the concept of this very special and unique relationship. Indian tribal constitutions are approved by the Interior Department. Indian tribal government is at best superior to governments having jurisdiction over the counties and states. At worst, it is still more democratic and more responsive to the needs of the people than are most if not all other governments.

Any complaints based on tribal or reservation ordinances or actions, can easily be discussed with the tribal officers, adjusted through the tribal governing body, and negotiated with the same government.

Another complaint is that services being given to Indian tribes and reservations are not being paid for through taxes. Such services are mentioned as police protection, fire protection, and education. A little common sense and access to the facts would dispel this false charge.

The federal government has been and is granting millions of dollars to the states for such services, and within these amounts are sums providing for services that are to be made available for Indians. Funds are allocated on the basis of servicing Indian programs. These include programs such as: school support through the Johnson O'Malley Act and Title IV education grants, employment training and placement through the Department of Manpower program (Comprehensive Employment Training Act), police training and support through the Law Enforcement Act (LEAA), and at least a dozen more programs funded by the federal government, including the states' revenue sharing funds. Through such programs the states and counties receive enough additional money for Indian support, because it is stated in the proposal that funds will include services for Indians.

There are some schools and other institutions in the states that are committing frauds on the federal government, in fact, in order to obtain the additional "Indian" money. In education, for example, school districts are taking a census of Indians in their area, so that they may qualify for receiving additional funds. Some districts are falsifying their census reports, so they may receive federal funds for "Indian" populations.

In the state of California, when Johnson O'Malley funds became available, the state applied and received considerable funds.

In the 1960s, an investigation was made concerning the use of these funds. It was found that instead of being utilized for support services for Indian children, the schools were buying busses, providing services for all pupils, spending funds on travel having nothing to do with the program, and misusing the funds in many other ways. Thus, the state decided to eliminate the whole program. In the 1970s, however, the program was re-instituted. Another investigation showed that again these funds were misused, in the case of at least two school distiicts in New Mexico.

These complaints are therefore invalid, inapplicable, and specious. They are being advanced by provocateurs against the Indian tribes, all of which is propaganda to incite the people against the tribes.

As noted in the Indian Policy Review Report (Page 169):

The most outstanding feature of any analysis of taxation and the comparative benefit-burden discussion is the near total lack of any hard data. To the extent it has been developed it supports the conclusion that States are deriving more direct cash benefits from the Indian presence within their State than they would derive from the Indians themselves if federal recognition were withdrawn and the states allowed to impose taxes without restriction.

A 1976 study of the Yankton reservation in South Dakota commissioned by the Ninth District Federal Reserve Bank reflects a total direct federal program expenditure of $3,164,117, compared to a total direct state expenditure of $1,214,701. The figure for the state is inflated, however, because many of these state expenditures actually involved federal pass-through moneys.

The program moneys expended by the state which did not involve at least some federal pass-through, total only $449,329 and of this sum more than $3,000,000 was spent on highway construction. By contrast, the St. Paul's Indian Mission at Yankton spent well in excess of $500,000. The great bulk of the moneys expended on behalf of services at this reservation passed directly into the adjoining nonIndian community.

The most thorough statewide analysis the Commission was able to find dates from 1973 for the State of Arizona. This study reflects a similar Federal-State expenditure ratio with corresponding cash out-flow from the reservations to the local nonIndian community.

"Equal rights are being denied nonIndians . . . This is one of the most bitter fights today between Indian activists and nonIndians. It goes further than civil and criminal rights. Indian sovereignty sought for reservations would mean control over water, coal and other mineral resources." (Page 62.)

The Indians' right of self-government is an inherent right which has never been extinguished. From the beginning, the United States has recognized the Indian tribes as "distinct, independent, political communities, retaining their original natural rights." It is a settled doctrine of international law that a weaker power does not surrender its independence, its right to self-government, by associating with a stronger, and taking its protection."

In *Barta v. Oglala Sioux Tribe* the Chief Judge delivered the opinion of the court: " . . . Here there was a right of the American Indians to levy this tax on non-members of the tribe using these lands . . . Inasmuch as it has never been taken from it, the defendant Oglala Sioux Tribe possesses the power of taxation which is an inherent incident of its sovereignty. The tribe has seen fit to give an orderly implementation which, among other things, has specifically provided for the levy of taxes. Such action was taken in accordance with the provisions of the Indian Reorganization Act of 1934." (48 Stat. 987, 25, U.S.C.A. 476.)

There are some cases in which the levy of taxes was claimed to be in violation of the defendants' constitutional rights under the Fifth and Fourteenth Amendments of the Constitution. In the *Slaughterhouse* Cases, the Court said that the Fourteenth Amendment "places limitations on legislative actions by the states. The Indian tribes are not , however, states and these Constitutional limitations have no applications to the actions, legislative in character, by Indian tribes. Neither may the Fifth Amendment be invoked against any legislative action of the Indian tribes:'(Talton v. Mays, See Cohen, 1942 edition.)

In *United States v. Seneca Nation of New York Indians,* (294 F. 946; D.C.W.D., N.Y., 1921), it is stated, "Where, however, the United States Constitution levies particular restraints upon federal courts or upon Congress, these restraints do not apply to the courts or legislatures of the Indian tribes."

The authors of *Nightmare* err if they believe that it is "just a small group of activists" who are opposing the demands, the unjustified charges, and the ignorance of the nonIndian establishment respecting the treaties and statutes that protect the Indian tribes. All the tribes and nations oppose this savage offensive against the people. We have experienced such "bitter fights" for more than two hundred years, and we are ready. Indian sovereignty is not "sought" by the Indian nations. It is a fact; it is legal; it is written into the statutes and laws of the land; and it is part and parcel of the laws governing nations the world over.

"Indian sovereignty sought for reservations would mean control over water, coal and other mineral resources." (Page 62.)

Secretary of the Interior Albert Fall attempted to rob the Indians by opening Executive order reservation lands for exploitation of minerals, as above narrated. The Courts defeated him. The *Winters Doctrine,* enunciated in 1908, determined that, "When the Indians made the treaty granting rights to the United States, they reserved the right to use the waters of the Milk River, at least to an extent reasonably necessary to irrigate their lands. The right so reserved continues to exist against the United States and its grantees, as well as against the state and its grantees." (*Winters v. United States* 207 U.S. 564 C.C.A. 9, 1908.)

The Winters Doctrine recognizes that tribal sovereignty and reserved water rights are property rights vested in the Indian nations. In many cases following the ruling in *Winters,* this doctrine is upheld.

A treaty (See *United States v. Shoshone Tribe*) was made, in which there was a provision that lands "set apart for the absolute and undisturbed use and occupation of the Shoshone Indians," was held to convey to the Shoshones full mineral and timber rights. The many acts relating to minerals on Indian reservations agree that the tribes have sovereignty over the minerals on their land. As one act states, extending "to the center of the earth." (Act of July 1, 1902, 32 Stat. 641.)

The Indian tribes are not "seeking" sovereignty. We have sovereignty, and its concomitant rights to self-government, self-determination and jurisdiction over our lands and resources.

"The writers of the treaties looked forward to the day when Indians and their land would be part of the United States, not individual nations within the country's boundaries," it is stated.

There is no such sentiment expressed in any of the treaties, nor in any of the statements of the Presidents of the United States when they were making speeches to such tribes as the Seneca, promising them independence and their lands "forever."

The writers of the treaties probably did look forward to the *extinc-*

tion of the Indians as a people. But there is no evidence in the treaties that the *Indians* looked forward to relinquishing their sovereignty. They were and are indeed a part of this land known as the United States, and have fought in three wars with honor to prove it. There is nothing in this relationship between the Indian tribes and the federal government which denies the Indian people their status as the original owners of the land who signed treaties with the government, ceding most of their land so that this country might be settled, so that the corporations might make huge profits, and so that people like Williams and Neubrech could with impunity insult their race, their culture, and their rights.

"The judges who grant increasing rights may sincerely feel the decisions they are making are sound law. But one point seems beyond argument—even if these decisions are 'sound law,' they are poor national policy . . . because they are based on racial discrimination damaging to all concerned as well as being contrary to the ideals of our nation." (Page 65.)

It would not be the first time that flag-waving, pompous, self-gratifying "upholders of the Constitution" have used the words of human rights to disguise racist and reactionary actions. Wasn't the name of a foremost advocate of that irrational method one by the name of McCarthy? The use of McCarthyist tactics fills the *Nightmare.* How can the observance of justice, and the adherence to the sacred precepts of the law, so highly vaunted by the United States as an example of Democracy at its best, be "damaging," or "discriminatory" to the dominant white establishment? These decisions of the court are certainly not based on racial discrimination. But if racial discrimination means that the courts are denying full control over natural resources, land, and this country's assets to the corporate powers, then the words themselves are meaningless. These two McCarthyites of the Northwest are really saying that the courts are discriminating against the corporate powers. Even ordinary logic hangs its head at reading such statements. Yet, there are some nonIndians, and even some Indians who are taken in by such a rationalization of irrational concepts.

"California has 76 Indian reservations, but the treaties which formed them were not ratified by Congress at that time. This means that the Indians of California could bring a suit similar to the one in Maine. They could claim that all the land they gave up was taken from them illegally." (Page 68.)

There were 18 unratified treaties in the state of California, and one agreement. There are no reservations in this state created by treaty. Reservations in California are statutory reservations and executive order reservations.

There have been two cases against the United States brought by the Indians of the state, for payment of all the land in California illegally taken from them. Considering the genocide practiced against the Indians of California, all of which is documented and fully authenticated, and the land taken from them first by the Spanish, then by the Mexicans and finally by the United States, it is a small payment for the whole gold-filled, metal-filled, richest soil in the continent. In each of these treaties made with the succeeding countries, the rights of the Indians were protected; they were judged to have possession and occupancy of the land, and were accorded citizenship.

About Vermont, the *Nightmare* authors assert, *"The Indians migrated through the area, fishing and hunting as they moved along."* (Page 70.)

Certainly the Vermont Indians "migrated" through their country. All Indians migrated from one area to another, within the confines of their own land. They had established summer and winter homes. These are well known facts. It is a fact as well, that their land was taken from them. It is a fact that they have no reservations. And it is a fact that these Indians, languishing in poverty since the white Europeans took their land and resources, should have a portion of the land that was theirs for thousands of years.

The *Nightmare* men state that "it may be good law, but it is poor national policy." A more flagrant distortion of democratic thought, justice, and the laws under which all civilizations live, cannot be imagined. Was it "national policy" that brought the gold miners, who should be characterized as beasts, when they murdered Indians in the gold country of California by various means. First, by shooting, then by hanging, then by sequestering them on an island in the northwest (Tolowa and Karuk Indians), leaving them there to die of starvation, thirst, and sickness? Was it national policy to leave arsenic-laced food where starving MiWuk Indians could find it, and then die so that the bodies of children were piled on top of adults till humanity found it intolerable? Or, when smallpox-laced blankets were left for the Maidu and MiWuk Indians who were dying of exposure in the land where they had lived for thousands of years, their homes destroyed, their food stores burned, and their clothing thrown into the fire?

145

It is not conscience, or the idea of guilt for wrongs done a century or two ago that motivates the courts today. It is the law. It is justice under the law. In a decision on the California claims case, one judge wrote, "It is not a moral question, that of adjudicating the claims of these Indians. It is a question of extinguishing their title to the land."

The authors of *Nightmare* pretend horror and surprise at "increasing" rights granted to Indian tribes. The rights of Indians have, in fact, decreased. But even the most primitive and simple of these rights, and the laws regarding them, have been ignored by the dominant establishment.

The Indians have the right to govern their lands, their natural resources, criminal and civil jurisdiction, the right to tax, the right to expel trespassers and indeed to decide who shall be permitted on their land. They are not subject to state jurisdiction.

We have attempted to respond to questions of law and justice in this chapter. What emerges, in a thorough examination of the *Nightmare* concepts of racial convenience and ethnocentric precepts, is that the authors, as spokesmen for the corporations, are proposing the abrogation of the Indian treaties.

That is at the root of all the verbiage, the calls to end "discrimination" against nonIndians, the charges that Indians may get all the fish, all the natural resources. Even these two authors couldn't possibly believe that. Or they would be greeted with derision by all thoughtful people.

What is intended by Neubrech, Williams, the state governments, and their spokesmen in the congress such as Lloyd Meeds, is a statute passed by the United States Congress that would take this country back into the dark ages, that would deny the Indian tribes their rights to self-government, and would in fact and in deed plunge the people into the desolation of poverty.

In Missouri, there are anthropologists who are writing learned books about the Indians who "formerly inhabited that state." Of course it is safe to write about them with sadness and regret. They are no longer in existence, having been wiped out by states and settlers who stole their lands, wrecked their culture, and either eliminated them from the face of the earth, or forced them to go underground in hiding with other tribes in other states.

The loss of a race, of a culture, of a language, and of a people, is a loss to all humanity. That is what will result if the attempts of individuals like Neubrech and Williams are successful. Make no mistake about it. These people want a change in the concepts of democracy and a change in the laws to conform to that McCarthyist concept.

As Delfin Lovato, head of the All Indian Pueblo Council said, "We will not be extinguished; we will not give up our sovereignty; we will refuse to be exterminated and our race reduced to pieces in a museum glass cage."

CHAPTER 4

References

References to statements by military personnel may be found in these papers, as well as conditions of Indians of the area:

Ex. Doc. No. 76, 1856-57, ch. iv.

Military reports. Sen. Docs. 1856-57, vol iii, pp. 147-203.

Papers and Correspondence, with affidavits. House Mis. Doc. No. 47, 1858-59, vol. 1.

Report of J. Ross Browne on Indian Wars of Oregon. Ex. Doc. No. 38, 1857-58, vol. ix.

Report of J. Ross Browne on Indian Reservations of the Northwest, Ex. Doc. No. 39, 1857-58, vol. ix.

The history of the Government connections with the Indians is a shameful record of broken treaties and unfulfilled promises.

"The history of the border white man's connection with the Indians is a sickening record of murder, outrage, robbery, and wrongs committed by the former, as the rule, and occasional savage outbreaks and unspeakably barbarous deeds of retaliation by the latter, as the exception."

" . . . however hard it may be for good statesmen and good men to agree upon the things that ought to be done, there certainly is, or ought to be, no perplexity whatever, in agreeing upon certain things that ought not to be done, and which must cease to be done before the first steps can be taken toward righting the wrongs, curing the ills, and wiping out the disgrace to us of the present condition of our Indians."

A Century of Dishonor
Helen Hunt Jackson
1881

THE TRIBES TODAY: AN OVERVIEW

The 1970 census places the Indian population at less than one million, a figure generally conceded to be inaccurate. This is due to the fact that most reservations were not adequately counted. In some areas, Indians were counted as Spanish, because of their Spanish surnames. However, many Indians have Spanish, Portugese, or Mexican surnames. As only one more indignity suffered by the native people, many of the original names have been either anglicized or hispanicized. A rough but educated guess of the Indian population today would be closer to three million, growing faster than any other sector of the population, but still a small minority compared to other groups. Previous estimates of Indian population have also been grossly inaccurate. This was done deliberately, in order to minimize the effects of genocide, disease, and war. The figure before white contact has been placed at approximately 800,000. But in the last few years the contention of the Indian people themselves has been given credence. Scientific surveys now estimate that the native population in the area north of Mexico (the United States, Canada and Greenland) was probably twelve million.

As the American Indian Policy Review Commission noted:[1]

Reliable statistics on Indian affairs that could be the basis for charting conditions, planning programs, and measuring progress do not exist. The reasons for this inadequacy range from the simplest to the most complex. The basic reason is that there is no clear-cut, generally accepted definition of "an Indian." Without this basic definition, the development of further statistical descriptions is very difficult. Defining the problems of various categories of Indians (urban, rural, women, men) becomes a complex task, particularly at census time when some Indians are not identified or even contacted to fill out census forms, or are not familiar enough with English to do so.

The task is made more difficult by the fragmentation of jurisdiction over the people who are classified as Indians. Health services, agricultural and other developmental assistance, business loans, housing aid, land development, and other programs, though all directed to Indians, are handled by different federal agencies with widely dissimilar interpretations of eligibility criteria.

This results in a diffusion, not only of effort, but of information, Data that would yield statistics reflecting the Indian condition are scattered among many federal agencies, with far-reaching and unfortunate results. Not only are data difficult to obtain, but they are often incomplete or unrepresentative.

Other sources of information show the same negligence and inconsistency. For example, of approximately 18,000 reference cards on Indians in the Library of Congress, only 16 point to statistical information; only 11 can be found under the heading of census; and none deal with population or income.

Other sources are similarly inadequate. As another example of federal irresponsibility, the most recent reports of the Commissioners of Indian Affairs contain only 15 double-spaced pages, with only four statistical tables, dealing only with awards, budgets, funding, and income from leases. In contrast, a hundred years ago the annual report of the Commissioner was a 619-page book summarizing policy decisions and situations in each field of jurisdiction, containing tables with information on population, education, agriculture, trust funds, trust land sales, and liabilities, in addition to miscellaneous reports. It is true, as more careful examination has shown, that some of these annual reports manipulated and falsified the figures for various self-serving reasons, but there was at least a body of statistical information that one could at least examine. This distressing situation creates not only the most extreme difficulty in determining Indian needs, but results in misunderstanding Indian issues and problems.

Only eight years ago, the American Indian Historical Society attempted to obtain a complete listing of Indian tribes in the United States. The researchers, who were sent to Washington, D.C. for that express purpose, were shuttled from one department of the Bureau of Indian Affairs to another. Finally, they were told the information was not available in the national office. Only the area offices have the data, they were informed. A listing of area offices was provided, and no more. To contact all the area offices was a difficult and often frustrating task since these offices seldom if ever have the capacity (or even the courtesy) of answering queries and providing information. Some state commissions on Indian affairs now publish annual reports including the names and addresses of tribes, the land under tribal jurisdiction, and estimated population. The accuracy of these statistics has been questioned. The tribes themselves maintain enrollment records, but assembling these records has been neglected.

Some years ago, the Bureau of Indian Affairs installed a computer system. To obtain information from the computers requires still another procedure, a long wait, and usually the information is not current. The irresistible fact is, that if one asks a Bureau official "How many tribes do you have jurisdiction over, and what are their names and current addresses?" that official would be unable to answer. One is sent to the area offices.

It's not illogical to ask: If the Bureau of Indian Affairs, which has been functioning for one hundred and twenty-eight years, can't answer these most elementary questions, what have they been doing all these years?

How can the tribes be expected to maintain contact with one another, exchange information and ideas, build up a national front, and indeed function as a national people? While the American Indian Policy Review Commission has succinctly pointed out the failure in developing statistics, the report fails to note the profound neglect that is represented by this failure. Even this report fails to understand that this very simple fact has resulted in continuing fractionation in Indian affairs.

Who is an Indian? How should a census of Indian population be made, and what criteria should the census use in enumerating the Indian population? These are questions that have plagued local and state agencies, as well as those who must deal with individuals and groups claiming benefits under Indian programs. Each agency has its own definition of "Indian," for purposes of services or benefits under statutes governing that program. Bureau of Indian Affairs regulations, for approving financial aid in education, have certified those who are one-fourth or more "Indian blood quantum." The federal criteria for defining "Indian" are inconsistent. The states also, under certain programs serving Indians, are eligible for financial aid in such areas as education, welfare, and employment training.

But the states are even more inconsistent than the federal government, as reported by the Review Commission. The report observes, "state guidelines for deciding who is or is not an Indian, are even more chaotic" than the federal government.[2]

The Commission contacted some states with large Indian populations to determine what criteria they use in defining an Indian. Two states accept the individual's own determination. Four states accept individuals as Indian if they are "recognized in the community" as Native Americans. Five states use residence on a reservation as a criterion. One state requires one-quarter Indian blood quantum, but generally the individual is not required to substantiate his claim. Another state uses the Census Bureau definition that Indians are those who say they are. The Census under preparation for 1980, at this writing, has no special criteria for deciding the claim of an individual that he/she is an Indian.

The federal bureaucracy is so entangled in its own web of mismanagement, that a memorandum issued by the Department of Health, Education and Welfare in November, 1977, instructed the agency's field officers how to determine who is an Indian for purposes of receiving benefits in various programs directed by HEW. The memorandum came after the Indian Policy Review Commission report was published raising this very question of inconsistency and chaos. During the Commission hearings, Indians testified that only a tribe has the right to decide who is an Indian. But statutes passed by congress in areas of Indian affairs consistently ignore this most basic concept of Indian self-government. Supreme Court decisions confirming the right of the tribes to decide their membership are ignored.

This question goes to the very heart of Indian self-government and self-determination. But the executive, legislative and judicial branches are in a state of confusion regarding this most elementary aspect of Indian affairs. Violations are committed by the congress; violations are carved into agency directives; and violations are persistently perpetrated by the Department of the Interior.

In recent years it has become fashionable to claim to be an "Indian." The tracing of genealogy has become a lucrative business, since so many wish to claim "Indian blood." It must be reiterated, however, that only the tribe has the right to decide this matter.

These conditions continue to erode Indian tribal rights, their unique status in federal-Indian relations, their rights under treaties, and the efforts of the tribes to develop viable economies. The process of "relocating" Indians in the cities with the promise of job opportunities, that began in the 1950s and has continued to this day, served to separate the Indians from their tribes, spilling them into the city ghettos. Every large city, nearly without exception, now has an Indian Center. But the role of the urban Indian, of the Indian Center, and the native populations forced to reside outside of the reservations, is muddied because of misunderstanding and lack of information about Indian tribes generally. This misunderstanding is shared by both Indians and nonIndians. An Indian Center is not a tribal entity, possessing tribal sovereignty and self-determination. That is not to say that such "urban Indians" are not entitled to special services. They are in an urban environment through no fault of their own, and the federal government retains responsibility for each individual so placed.

The problem is multiplied by the influx of thousands of Indians into the cities. An estimate of Indian population in the state of California, for example, notes that there are approximately 150,000 natives in the state. Of these, fully 50 percent are from out of state, with membership in tribes other than those of California. But the cities and county officials of California can only see the stereotype of an Indian, and they act accordingly. For example, when the city of Los Angeles finally took note of the "Indian problem" and decided to select an Indian to serve on its Human Rights Commission, they selected an Oneida, whose tribal membership is in Wisconsin or New York. Los Angeles sits in the midst of the most concentrated tribal groups in the state. There are twenty-nine functioning Indian tribes in that area, with their own reservations, their own tribal government, and continually preoccupied with problems and issues peculiar to that state and that area. The leadership in southern California is exceedingly capable. But there was no consideration of selecting an Indian of a California tribe for that position.

There is a tendency to find some all-embracing formula for deciding who is an Indian when legislation is drafted, or when regulations are formulated in which a qualifying decision should be made as to who is eligible to benefit. It is believed, by many well-meaning people, that if only one formula could be found and adopted, all would be well. This is not so, and defeats the very purpose of Indian self-government.

Exception is taken, therefore, to the statement previously quoted, made in the report of the Indian Policy Review Commission that "there is no clear-cut, generally accepted definition of 'an Indian.' Without this basic definition, the development of further statistical descriptions is very difficult." The Indian tribes see no difficulty in this matter. The solution is very simple, it's legal, and accepts the position that the tribes do indeed have the right to self-government. Both legislation and regulations should have the following qualifying statement: "An Indian, in order to receive benefits and services under this statute, must be certified as such by his/her tribe; an enrollment statement shall be sufficient for purposes of certification." The objection may be raised: what is to be done in such areas as California, in which the tribe has been dissolved through genocide. Or, if a tribe has been terminated. In such cases, the tribe is generally reconstituted; some form of government exists or is reinstituted (or should be); and in any case, tribes ought not to be disqualifed,following termination, from services available to the members or financial aid in education (as only two examples).

The point is, there is no Indian entity without a tribe or nation.

To conclude, only the tribe has the right to determine who is an Indian. As the Indian Policy Review Report stated: "The tribe's power to determine its own membership, that is, individual identity as an Indian, has been repeatedly recognized by the courts; the power derives from the tribe's status as a political entity. The tribe's power over its own membership is the starting point for any discussion of Indian identity."[3]

Clearly, any political or social entity functions through a governing body. Tribal government has necessarily changed through the years since white contact. It is instructive to note the progress of such changes.[4]

In the first several hundred years of contact, tribes were for the most part able to retain their traditional governing systems. These were highly diversified, ranging from the sophisticated confederacy of the Iroquois, which became an example for the framing of the United States federal government in its formative years, to informal structures of consensus by all the people. Most western governments are formalized institutions with complicated, structured laws and regulations largely related to concepts of private property.

Indian societies and tribes did not understand private property as a concept in law. Nor was the idea of privately held property even known. Members of a tribe had certain areas reserved to them; all participated in hunting and fishing areas; and trespass was uniformly punished, without written laws. The sale of land was unknown, and after contact, was forbidden by religious precept. Indian nations and tribes were governed by traditional chiefs and headmen. The religious sector of the society had a vital role to play, mainly through the moral and spiritual respect accorded them by the members. There were many different systems for maintaining law and order. Some nations had systems of repayment for crimes, instead of the modern system of incarceration. Others had warrior societies performing various roles other than "going to war." By far most Indian nations made use of popular pressure to enforce laws, and to deal with offenders. Thus, the famed case of *Ishi*, which has been popularized in a book, is not at all what the author believed Ishi's status to have been. He was found in central California, starving and sick. But Ishi was an offender against tribal law. His offense was stealing food at a time of famine. The laws of that tribe provided that the offender should be driven out of the tribe.

The first three-quarters of the 18th century nearly destroyed the traditional Indian governments. Removal, exploitation of the tribes by competing European governments that were often engaged in war, a new and alien economy that pitted tribe against tribe in a system of intense competition, and finally the reservation era, reduced the traditional governing bodies to shadows. The problem became one of mere survival.

In the latter half of the 19th century, there was a strong movement towards assimilating the Indian into the general population. Religious groups, military establishments and humane societies striving to save the Indian for civilization, competed for control of Indian tribes, Indian governments, Indian lands and influence over Indian religious life.

Federally controlled Indian police appeared at this time. Courts of Indian Offenses were formed. Indian agents, as part of the assimilation process, acted to further erode and undermine the remaining power of tribal authority and traditional leadership. However, neither the Indian police nor the courts were successful in eradicating the influence of traditional Indian culture. The combination that evolved was a curious mixture of western style law and tribal custom, because the Indian police and the Courts of Indian Offenses exercised jurisdiction over both Indians and nonIndians. In some areas, nonIndians created the principal problems faced by the Indian police and courts. In Oklahoma, as only one example, most of the police effort was expended in removing nonIndian herds from Indian lands.

Finally, in 1934, when the Indian Reorganization Act was passed, a system was provided for "re-establishing tribal governments," but this was done according to preconceived notions of white experts and the ideas of John Collier, Commissioner of Indian Affairs.

Tribes were to hold regular elections (when elections were unknown, and the tribe was governed by recognized and respected elders and statesmen); constitutions were written and adopted (when the unwritten law was the rule and was strictly adhered to); and the court systems became a mixture of judges who usually acted as juries as well as prosecutors and defense attorneys (instead of the traditional system of determining offenses, in which the culprit generally admitted the offense and was punished according to prescribed rules). A western style of government and court system was established. But the IRA succeeded in ending the infamous Dawes General Allotment Act, which had resulted in the massive loss of Indian land.

The traditional governing systems prevailed, at least in basic form. The Indian tribes still cling to their ancient traditions, not because of unreasonable, stubborn insistence, but because they work better. The governing system instituted under the IRA is still being opposed, as in the Pine Ridge Reservation of South Dakota. The fact is, that if left alone to the processes of natural selection and adaptation to modern life, the tribes would themselves have instituted such forms of governments as would gain the approval of the governed, and be more effective in directing their activities, their economy, and their societies.

Of particular interest is the system developed by the Pueblos of New Mexico. Strong elements of traditional culture remain to this day in most Pueblos, but accomodation has been made possible by a type of dual government. Most Pueblos elect a governing body every year. The head of this council is called a governor. But another governing body exists comprised of religious leaders, and they have their own unique duties to perform. Tribal pressure continues in the form of elders and religious leaders who exert moral and spiritual influence. These two systems of government exist simultaneously and indeed are blended in the unique system of Pueblo government. Other tribes in the southwest, including certain Pueblos, have adopted the Indian Reorganization Act structure of western government.

The governing system of some tribes is as complex as that of the states. The Navajo tribe, as only one example, has numerous agencies, corporations for economic development, an educational department, a community college, boarding schools, an elementary school, a high school, a department of social welfare, public relations officers, an editorial board controlling their newspaper, and a tribal council comprised of seventy-four delegates representing the communities of the Nation. To a lesser degree, the same complex government which includes various agencies and departments, exists in the Choctaw Nation of Mississippi, the Oglala Sioux of Pine Ridge, the Mescalero Apache of Arizona, the Wind River Reservation of Montana, and the Colville Indian Tribe of Washington, to name only a few.

Confronted with the complex and confusing status of Indian government, treaty rights, natural resources rights, and the conflict with the states about jurisdiction over tribal affairs, the general reader asks: Why not just eliminate the reservations and solve the whole problem? Let the Indians be just like everyone else. Such a proposal is self-defeating, and has been proven to be ineffective. Too much experimentation has already been done at the expense of Indian life. The time has come to let the Indians decide their own destiny, undertake their own options, and have the dominant voice over their own affairs.

The foundation for Indian existence, tradition, culture, and the survival of the people is in the land. The reservations contain the only land remaining in Indian control. The very name "reservation" is a misnomer. It was adopted because, in treaties, it was either directly stated or implicit in the conditions of the treaties, that the tribes and nations "reserved for themselves" certain land, which then became reservations. In other cases, particularly in the process of confiscation of Indian land and removal to Indian territory, the United States promised the Indians would have an adequate land base by "reserving" the land for the tribes. However, the Indians themselves, in removing to the new territory, reserved the rights over that territory in place of the homeland they had been forced to relinquish.

Indian land has been subjected to persistent confiscation, either by statute, by amended treaties, or by the illegal stealing or "squatting" on their land. In 1862 the Homestead Act was passed, making land available to settlers. A great part of the "settling" was done on Indian land, then the settler received title without the tribe even being aware of it in most cases. In 1875, the Homestead Act was made available to individual Indians, but very few took advantage of it. When the Dawes General Allotment Act was passed in 1887, a provision was that after the allotments were certified to individual Indians, all "excess land," or land that remained unallotted, passed into the public domain as surplus land. These lands were then opened to settlement through the Homestead Acts. It was not unusual for the tribes to have permitted the "surplus" land to remain unallotted, on the mistaken premise that they would be allowed to hold this portion as tribal land.

In 1875, after congress had ended formal treaty making with the tribes, the total Indian reservation land base stood at about one hundred and sixty-six million acres, or about twelve percent of the land in the continental United States. By 1887, with the passage of the General Allotment Act, the Indians lost more land. They now had less than one hundred and thirty-seven million acres. By 1934, Indian land holding amounted to only fifty-two million acres. It is estimated that this is approximately the figure today. Under the Allotment Act, one hundred and eighteen reservations were allotted. Forty-four of those were opened to homestead entry under public land laws. In addition, approximately thirty-eight million acres of land were ceded outright to the government, and the proceeds of sales distributed in per capita payments or agency funds. Another twenty-two million acres of so-called surplus tribal lands existed after the allotments were made and reservation land opened for settlement by nonIndians. Today the tribes are seeking to regain their land, even if it means buying back their own property, much of which had been taken illegally, or stolen outright by various means.[5]

The tribes endure. The people endure. Tribal culture and tradition continues. As the United States Congress itself recognized, in passing the Indian Self-Determination and Education Assistance Act of 1975:

". . . the Indian people will never surrender their desire to control their relationships both among themselves and with nonIndian governments, organizations, and persons.

"The Congress declares its commitment to the maintenance of the Federal Governments' unique and continuing relationship with and responsibility to the Indian people through the establishment of a meaningful Indian self-determination policy."

There is a current, sharpening controversy over Indian tribal jurisdiction. It has its foundation in the sale or illegal acquisition of Indian land by nonIndians. Allotted land could be sold. Some tribal land was leased, with leases running as long as ninety-nine years. But the tribal boundaries were retained, and ultimate control over land use and jurisdiction remains in the tribes.

The devastating story of government mismanagement and illegal confiscation of Indian land has brought the tribes to such a pass that they are now confronted with a racist movement against tribal government, against tribal self-determination, and against tribal rights to their own natural resources.

A glance at the situation existing in some representative tribes is informative. The following figures deal with various types of reservation land. *Tribal land* is land held by the tribe in common. *Allotted land* is that held under the General Allotment Act and may be owned either by Indians or nonIndians. *Federal land* is acreage held by the federal government, reserved for the United States for such purposes as government buildings, posts, or military facilities. All land, whether allotted or tribally owned, is considered to be under the jurisdiction of the tribe and within the tribe's reservation boundaries unless the title has been extinguished and the land is entirely out of reservation boundaries. Some tribal and allotted land is off reservation. These figures are the result of a survey taken by the American Indian Lawyer Training Program. Another listing and description of the tribes exists, published by the United States Department of Commerce in 1972. The information therein is in many cases inaccurate and not dependable.

Below is a listing of representative tribes. Many of these tribes have jurisdictional controversies with the states or counties. Note the land held in the various types of ownership. Also note the numbers of nonIndians now residing on Indian reservations. It is these individuals who, through misconception and indeed misinformation about their status, are now organizing the offensive against the Indian tribes, with the aid and support of the huge corporations hungry for Indian land and resources. Regarding the figure on "Indian residents," it should be understood that this does not represent the total tribal enrollment, which is many thousands higher in various tribes. It represents only those who reside on the reservation. The economic poverty of the reservation precludes numbers of members from living there; jobs must be found elsewhere, and often the members work near the reservation. Wherever available, the enrollment figure is given.

It should also be noted that these figures can be expected to change. Some conditions making for change are: developing economic opportunities on the reservation, young people coming home from school to take part in the tribe's government and activities, new births which increase population figures, and the addition of land to tribal reservation holdings through purchase or return to tribal status following litigation.

Some tribes do not have "allotments," as will be seen. Others have both tribally held land and "assignments," made by the tribal members themselves and held by families or individuals.

The tribes described below are fairly representative of the situation among the Indians today:

Acoma Pueblo, located in Valencia County, New Mexico. Tribal land: 245,358 acres. Allotted land: 320 acres. Indian residents: 2,129. NonIndian residents: 26. Traditional form of government. No written constitution. Governing body composed of a council whose members are appointed by the tribal religious leaders. A governor and one or more lieutenant governors are appointed annually to serve as executive officers.

Assiniboine and Sioux Tribes, Fort Peck Reservation, located in Roosevelt County, northeastern Montana. Tribal land: 276,474. Allotted land: 567,320 on reservation. Federal land: 22,791 in public domain and 86,597 on reservation. Indian residents: 3,812. NonIndian residents: 6,461. A 12-member elected tribal council and a chairman operate under a non-IRA constitution.

Blackfeet Tribe, located in northwestern Montana. Tribal land: 176,311 acres. Allotted land: 720,311 acres. Federal land: 9,176 acres. Indian residents: 5,676. NonIndian residents: 1,676. An IRA tribe, with a 9-member elected tribal council and chairman.

Omaha Tribe, located in east central Nebraska. Tribal land: 10,877 acres. Allotted land: 16,516 acres. Indian residents: 1,362. NonIndian residents: 2,293. Organized under IRA, with an elected tribal council which in turn elects its officers including the chairman.

Cheyenne River Sioux Tribe, located in northwestern South Dakota. Tribal land: 925,429 acres on reservation; 1,087 acres off reservation. Allotted land: 470,767 acres on reservation; 2,934 acres off reservation. Federal land: 3,914 acres on reservation. Indian residents: 4,658. NonIndian residents: 3,795. Organized under IRA and governed by a 15-member elected council and an elected chairman, secretary, and treasurer.

Coeur D'Alene Tribe, located in northwestern Idaho. Tribal land: 19,756 acres. Allotted land: 49,573 acres. Indian residents: 450. NonIndian residents: 2,742. Operates under a tribal constitution adopted in 1949, amended in 1960, with a 7-member elected council. Not an IRA tribe.

Colorado River Indian Tribe, located in western Arizona and eastern California. Reservation acreage as tribal land: 220,038 acres in Arizona; 42,696 in California. Allotted land: 5,958 acres in Arizona. Indian residents: 1,673. NonIndian residents: 3,672. Organized under the IRA, tribal constitution revised in 1975. Governing body composed of 9 elected members.

Colville Confederated Tribes, located in Ferry and Okanogan Counties, northcentral Washington. Tribal land: 947,509 acres on reservation. Allotted land: 57,725 acres on reservation; 2,756 acres in public domain. Indian residents: 2,909, with an enrollment of 5,837 according to BIA data. NonIndian residents: 1,495. Operates under the IRA and has a constitution.

Confederated Salish-Kootenai Tribes, Flathead Reservation, located in northwestern Montana. Tribal land: 564,733 acres, on reservation. Allotted land: 50,976 acres on reservation. Federal land: 1,017 acres on reservation; 723 acres off reservation. Indian residents: 2,910. NonIndian residents: 12,831. Organized under IRA,

160

with a governing body composed of 12 elected Salish and Kootenai members.

Confederated Tribes of Warm Springs, located in northwestern Oregon. Tribal land: 480,196 acres. Allotted land: 84,118 acres. Indian residents: 1,922. NonIndian residents: 185. Organized under IRA with an elected tribal council and chairman. Chiefs of the three bands present on the reservation, and 8 representatives comprise the 11-member body. The three bands are known as the Warm Springs, Northern Paiute, and Wasco Confederated Tribes.

Crow Tribe, located in southern Montana. Tribal land: 361,901 acres. Allotted land: 1,205,926 acres. Federal land: 1,401 acres. Indian residents: 4,269. NonIndian residents: 2,469. Organized under IRA, with a 10-member council including a tribal chairman. A general council of all members meets four times a year.

Cochiti Pueblo, located in Sandoval County, New Mexico. Tribal land: 776 acres. No allotted land. Indian residents: 544. NonIndian residents: 245. Functions under a traditional form of government without a written constitution. Political affairs controlled by the governor or chief executive officer and a council composed of former governors. Cochiti Dam, now nearly completed, will change the situation in that Pueblo. A new huge housing development has also been constructed and it is anticipated that as many as 45,000 nonIndian residents will come into the area.

Jemez Pueblo, located in Sandoval County, New Mexico. Tribal land: 88,860 acres. No allotments. Indian residents: 1,756. NonIndian residents: 195. Operates under a traditional form of government without a written constitution. Authority over secular matters in a 12-member council and a governor who serves as chief executive officer. The governor is appointed annually by the tribal religious leaders acting in conjunction with the council, whose members are all former governors.

Laguna Pueblo, located in Bernalillo, Sandoval and Valencia Counties, New Mexico. Tribal land: 413,229 acres. Allotted land: 4,006 acres. Indian residents: 3,258. NonIndian residents: 199. Has a constitution under the IRA. Governing body is a council of 21 elected members. Twelve are representatives elected by the individual villages of the Pueblo. The other 9, designated as staff officers, are elected at large. The chief executive officer and head of the staff is the governor, who also serves as a member of the council.

Nambe Pueblo, located in Santa Fe County, New Mexico. Tribal land: 19,073 acres. No allotted land. Indian residents: 383. NonIndian residents: 666. Traditional form of government, no written constitution. Political affairs controlled by the governor or chief executive officer and a council composed of ex-governors. Each year a new governor and his staff of four assistants are appointed by tribal religious leaders acting in conjunction with the council. They are currently drafting a written constitution.

San Ildefonso Pueblo, located in Santa Fe County, New Mexico. Tribal land: 26,192 acres. No allotted land. Indian residents: 304. NonIndian residents: 684. Traditional form of government, no written constitution. Political affairs conducted by the governor or chief executive officer, and a tribal council of 14 members. Governor is appointed to a two-year term by tribal religious leaders and the council, which consists of former governors.

San Juan Pueblo, located in Rio Arriba County, New Mexico. Tribal land: 12,236 acres. No allotments. Indian residents: 1,666. NonIndian residents: 3,275. Functions under a traditional form of government, no written constitution. Political affairs controlled by the governor or chief executive officer and a council composed of ex-governors. Tribal religious leaders in conjunction with the council appoint a new governor annually.

Zuni Pueblo, located in McKinley and Valencia Counties, New Mexico. Tribal land: 406,191 acres. Allotted land: 2,213 acres. Indian residents: 5,975. NonIndian residents: 399. Organized under IRA with a constitution. Governing body is an elected council composed of 8 members with a governor as chief officer.

Eastern Band of Cherokee Indians, located in western North Carolina. Tribal land: 56,557 acres. Federal land: 129 acres. No allotted land. Indian residents: 5,500. NonIndian residents: 500. Organized under IRA, also chartered by the state of North Carolina. Governed by a 12-member council elected by the members, and by a principal chief and vice chief, who are elected to four-year terms.

Flandreau Santee Sioux Tribe, located in southeastern South Dakota. Tribal land: 2,180 acres. No allotted land. Federal land: 176 acres. Indian residents: 55. NonIndian residents: 6,956. Operates under IRA and a constitution approved in 1946, amended in 1967. Two trustees, a secretary-treasurer, a vice-president, and a president serve as the governing body of the tribe. All are elected.

Fort Mohave Tribe, located in western Arizona, California, and

162

Nevada. Tribal land: 41,884 acres. No allotments. Indian residents: 374; tribal enrollment, 433. NonIndian residents: 850. Organized under the IRA. Tribal constitution adopted in 1957, revised in 1976, currently pending approval by the tribe and the Interior Secretary. Governing body composed of 7 elected members.

Gros Ventre-Assiniboine Tribe, Fort Belknap Reservation, located in Blaine County, Montana. Tribal land: 175,412 acres. Allotted land: 457,536 acres. Federal land: 25,530 acres. Indian residents: 1,603. NonIndian residents: 246. Has a 12-member elected council and a tribal chairman. Operates under a tribal constitution (IRA) and a law and order code.

Hopi Tribe, located in northeastern Arizona, in Coconino and Navajo Counties. This tribe has been locked in a dispute with the Navajo Indian Nation for some years. An executive order of 1882 granted the Hopi Tribe 2,600,000 acres of land in northeastern Arizona, entirely surrounded by the Navajo Reservation. The Hopi are currently living on 650,000 acres, the remainder being occupied by the Navajo. Conflicting tribal claims to land have led to a series of ownership and boundary disputes. A 1963 court order provided for an area of joint-use land and the negotiation of disputes. However, the case was not settled until 1977, when it was decided in favor of the Hopi, and the Navajos were to vacate the land. Other land was to be made available for those Navajos dispossessed. The issue, however, in late 1977, while being settled legally, has still not been resolved.

Indian residents: 5,673, with a total enrollment, according to Bureau of Indian Affairs estimates, of 7,500 to 8,000. NonIndian residents: 214. There are no allotments. Government: each Hopi village is organized independently, having either an elected governor or a hereditary village chief. The first tribal constitution was adopted in 1935. A tribal council was elected in 1955 for the first time. The tribe is a member of the Indian Development District of Arizona, through which it obtains planning and development funding assistance. Lately, it has received various grants from the federal government for economic devlopment. There is strong division in the tribe at present, between the Hopi traditionalists and the more modern group represented by the tribal council.

Hualapai Tribe, located in central Arizona. Tribal land: 992,523 acres. Allotted land: 650 acres. Indian residents: 703. NonIndian residents: 80. Organized under the IRA. Governing body consists of 9 elected members. Their constitution has been recently revised.

Jicarilla Apache Indian Tribe, located in Rio Arriba and Sandoval

Counties, New Mexico. Tribal land: 742,315 acres. No allotted land. Indian residents: 1,976. NonIndian residents: 494. Operates under IRA. Has an elected president and vice president and an elected council composed of 8 members.

Lake Superior Band, Chippewa Tribe, at Keweenaw Bay Reservation. Located at Upper Peninsula, Michigan. Tribal land: 1,664 acres. Allotted land: 8,124 acres. Federal land, 4,016 acres. Indian residents: 758. NonIndian residents, 6,000. Organized under IRA with a tribal council composed of 12 elected members.

Lummi Tribe, reservation includes the Lummi and Nooksack tribes, located in Whatcom County, Washington, in northern part of the state. Tribal land: 289 acres. Allotted land: 6,951 acres. Indian residents: 1,305. NonIndian residents: 905. Operates under a constitution approved in 1970, not under IRA. Eleven elected council members and a tribal chairman govern the tribe.

Mandan, Hidatsa and Arikara Tribes, at Fort Berthold Reservation, located in northwestern North Dakota. Tribal land: 57,954 acres on reservation, Allotted land: 360,438 acres on reservation; 2,560 acres off reservation. Federal land: 164 acres on reservation. Indian residents: 3,051. NonIndian residents: 209. An IRA tribe, with an 11-member elected business council. Adult members who reside on the reservation are qualified to vote and are eligible to be candidates for the council. Tribal chairman is elected by the council.

Menominee Tribe, located in northeastern Wisconsin. Tribal land: 220,000 acres. No allotted land. Recently restored to federal recognition (1975). Was an IRA tribe before termination. Indian residents: 2,707. NonIndian residents: 301.

Mescalero Apache Tribe, located in Otero County, New Mexico. Tribal land: 460,384 acres. No allotted land. Indian residents: 2,253. NonIndian residents: 257. Organized under a constitution adopted through IRA. Governing structure consists of an elected president, vice president and an 8-member council.

Mississippi Band of Choctaw Indians, Choctaw Reservation, located in southern Mississippi. Tribal land: 17,441 acres. Allotted land: 10 acres. Federal land: 229 acres. Indian residents: 2,437. NonIndian residents: 125. Under IRA, constitution approved in 1945 with a governing body of 16 elected tribal members and an elected chief. A general council of all members meets four times a year.

Navajo Tribe, located in northeastern Arizona, New Mexico and Utah. Tribal reservation acreage in the three states: 12,956,278 acres. Allotted land: 716,913 acres. Federal land: 324,350 acres.

Indian residents (1973): 125,520. NonIndian residents: 7,355. The Navajos at this writing do not have a written constitution and are not organized under the IRA. The tribe operates under a law and order code, governed by a council of 74 delegates and an elected tribal chairman and vice chairman. The delegates are elected by their Navajo communities. The tribal government is now being reorganized, and a reapportionment of delegates is anticipated based on the changing population. Total enrollment figure not available.

Northern Cheyenne Tribe, located in Rosebud and Big Horn Counties in Montana. Tribal land: 287,696 acres. Allotted land, 146,043 acres. 680 acres in public domain. Indian residents: 2,959. NonIndian residents: 443. Organized under IRA. Tribal council of 15 elected members and a chairman who is elected by the council.

Oglala Sioux Tribe, Pine Ridge Reservation, located in southwestern South Dakota. Tribal land: 485,365 acres in South Dakota; 397 acres in Nebraska. Allotted land: 1,160,973 acres in South Dakota. Federal land: 74,691 acres in South Dakota; 155 acres in Nebraska. Indian residents: 12,515. NonIndian residents: 3,941. Organized under IRA, governed by a 21-member council including a chairman and four other officers.

Papago Tribe, located in southern Arizona. Tribal land: 2,813,497 acres. Allotted land, 41,003 acres. Indian residents: 8,707. Tribal membership enrollment: 13,000. NonIndian residents: 303. Organized under the IRA. Council is composed of 22 elected members. The Sells, San Xavier and Gila Bend Papago reservations are all governed by the same council and utilize the same tribal facilities such as the tribal court. Their constitution was adopted in 1937.

Pima Indian Tribe, Salt River Indian Reservation, located in Maricopa County, Arizona. Tribal land: 24,859 acres. Allotted land: 24,435 acres. Indian residents: 2,809. NonIndian residents, 84. Organized under the IRA, its constitution recently revised. Governing body consists of 9 elected council members.

Pima-Maricopa Tribe, located in south central Arizona. Tribal land: 274,522 acres. Allotted land: 97,408 acres. Indian residents: 6,405. NonIndian residents: 264. Organized under the Indian Reorganization Act, has a constitution adopted in 1936, revised in 1960. Governing body consists of 17 elected council members.

Quinault Indian Nation, located at Grays Harbor and Jefferson Counties, Washington. Tribal land: 5,105 acres. Allotted land: 124,279 acres. Indian residents: 1,153. NonIndian residents: 303. Operates under a tribal constitution adopted March 22, 1975. All members of the Quinault Nation, including adopted members, comprise a general council which meets annually. Regular business of the tribe is conducted by a business committee composed of the president, vice-president, secretary-treasurer and 7 elected council members. According to BIA records, there are 1,424 enrolled members.

Rosebud Reservation, located in southcentral South Dakota. Tribal land: 453,355 acres. Allotted land: 476,320 acres. Federal land: 28,797 acres. Indian residents: 8,410. Nonindian residents: 16,470. Organized under IRA, constitution approved in 1935. Thirty elected council members. Council president and executive committee serve as a tribal chairman and administrative leadership.

Seminole Tribe, located in southern Florida. Tribal land: 79,014 acres. No allotted land. Indian residents: 998. NonIndian residents: 27. Organized under the IRA, tribal constitution adopted in 1957 with five elected tribal council members.

Shoshone and Arapahoe Tribes, Wind River Reservation, located in west central Wyoming. Tribal land: 1,787,382 acres. Allotted land: 97,890 acres. Federal land: 1,296 acres. Indian residents: 4,677. NonIndian residents: 11,938. The two tribes have a 12-member tribal council, 6 of whom are Shoshone and 6 are Arapahoe. There are two tribal chairmen. The general council of the tribes' members meets once a year. They are not organized under IRA. There is no constitution, and though the tribes do have law and order codes, they depend primarily on the Code of Federal Regulations (Title 25: Indians).

Shoshone-Bannock Tribes, Fort Hall Reservation, located in southeastern Idaho. Tribal land: 244,288 acres. Allotted land: 237,563 acres. Federal land: 41,343 acres. Indian residents: 2,256. NonIndian residents: 1,342. Organized under IRA, with a constitution approved in 1936. Tribal government consists of the Fort Hall Business Council, composed of 7 tribal members elected for two-year terms.

Shoshone and Paiute Tribes, on Duck Valley Reservation, located in Owyhee County, Idaho, and Elko County, Nevada. Tribal land: 145,545 acres in Idaho; 144,274 acres in Nevada. No allotted land. Indian residents: 1,007. NonIndian residents: 119. Operates under IRA.

Southern Ute Tribe, located in southwestern Colorado. Tribal reservation acreage: 303,127. Allotted land: 4,003 acres. Indian residents: 792. NonIndian residents: 3,334. Operates under the IRA with a constitution and 6 elected council members.

Sioux Tribe, Crow Creek Reservation, located in southcentral

South Dakota. Tribal land: 39,854 acres on reservation. Allotted land: 65,693 acres on reservation; 144 acres off reservation. Federal land: 19,120 acres on reservation; 130 acres off reservation. Indian residents: 1,479. NonIndian residents: 442. Constitution provides for election of 6 tribal council members from three districts of the reservation. A president is elected at large.

Sioux Tribe, located on Standing Rock Reservation in an area bordering North and South Dakota. Tribal land: 96,173 acres in North Dakota; 266,897 acres in South Dakota. Allotted land: 198,882 acres in North Dakota; 277,132 acres in South Dakota. Federal land: 3,848 acres in North Dakota; 6,407 acres in South Dakota. Indian residents: 5,159. NonIndian residents: 5,300. Organized under the IRA, governed by a 14-member elected council, whose chairman is the administrative head of the tribe. Constitution recently revised.

Sisseton-Wahpeton Tribe, Lake Traverse Reservation, located in northeastern South Dakota. Tribal land: 200 acres in North Dakota; 7,870 acres in South Dakota. Allotted land: 2,392 acres in North Dakota; 95,917 acres in South Dakota. Federal land: 72 acres in South Dakota. Indian residents: 3,241. NonIndian residents: 11,309.

Spokane Tribe, located in northeastern Washington. Tribal land: 105,960 acres. Allotted land 30,965 acres. Federal land: 3,122 acres. Indian residents: 1,008. NonIndian residents: 209. Organized under IRA, with a business council composed of 3 elected councilmen, but in August, 1972, the constitution was amended establishing a 5-member business council, elected for staggered terms.

Suquamish Tribe, Fort Madison Reservation, located in Kitsap County, Washington, Tribal land: 61 acres. Allotted land: 2,658 acres. Indian residents: 161. NonIndian residents: 3,000. Under IRA.

Swinomish Tribe, located in Skagit County, Washington. Tribal land: 313 acres. Allotted land: 3,117 acres. Indian residents: 389. NonIndian residents: 403. Operates under IRA, with election of an 11-member Swinomish Indian Senate. Members are elected to 5-year staggered terms.

Tulalip Reservation, comprised of Snohomish Tribe, (although other tribes are represented in the membership) located in Snohomish County, Washington. Tribal land: 5,919 acres. Allotted land: 3,413 acres. Indian residents: 502. NonIndian residents: 1,034. Organized under IRA.

Turtle Mountain Chippewa Tribe, located in north central North Dakota. Tribal land: 8,206 acres on reservation; 27,419 acres off reservation. Allotted land: 24,774 acres on reservation; 16,473 acres off reservation. Federal land: 477 acres on reservation; 40 acres off reservation. Indian residents: 4,581. NonIndian residents: 347. Organized under the IRA. Has an elected council of 8 members with an elected chairman.

Uintah-Ouray Tribes, at Fort Duchesne Reservation, located in Uintah, Duchesne, and Grand Counties, Utah. Tribal land: 992,528 acres. Allotted land: 19,634 acres. Indian residents: 1,663. NonIndian residents: 8,329. Operates under IRA, with a 6-member tribal business committee and a tribal chairman.

Umatilla Tribe, located in northeastern Oregon. Tribal land: 16,209 acres. Allotted land: 69,142 acres. Indian residents: 787. NonIndian residents: 2,876. Tribal constitution approved in 1949, providing for a 9-member elected board of trustees, elected by the general council. The general council, composed of all tribal members, delegates powers to the board. Authority for formation of a tribal court and court of appeals is provided by a law and order code.

Ute Mountain Tribe, located in southwestern Colorado. Tribal land: 555,270 acres. Allotted land: 8,979 acres. Indian residents: 1,299. NonIndian residents: 77. Organized under the IRA, tribal constitution adopted in 1938. Has a council of 7 elected members. A general council of all members over the age of 18 also governs the tribe.

Walker River Tribe, located in west central Nevada. Tribal land: 313,670 acres. Allotted land: 8,751 acres. Federal land: 964 acres. Indian residents: 452. NonIndian residents: 140. Organized under IRA with an elected tribal council of 7 members and an elected tribal chairman.

White Mountain Tribe, Fort Apache Reservation, located in eastern Arizona. Tribal land: 1,664,972 acres. No allotted land. Indian residents: 8,077. NonIndian residents: 1,335. Organized under the IRA, with a constitution adopted in 1934. Governing body composed of 11 elected members.

Winnebago Tribe, located in east central Nebraska. Tribal land: 3,670 acres. Allotted land: 24,498 acres. Indian residents: 1,353. NonIndian residents: 1,404. Operates under IRA with 9 elected council members, constitution adopted in 1936, amended in 1968.

Yakima Indian Nation, located in Yakima and Klikitat Counties, Washington. Tribal land: 842,978 acres. Allotted land : 274,988 acres. According to the American Indian Lawyer Training report, there are 1,298 tribally owned acres in public domain; and 20,504 acres of allotted land in public domain. Governed by a council composed of 14 members and two alternates elected at-large. All council members and the tribal chairman serve four-year terms. Indian residents: 5,210. NonIndian residents: 17,714.

Yankton Sioux Tribe, located in southeastern South Dakota. Tribal land: 11,687 acres. Allotted land: 22,370 acres. Indian residents: 1,227. NonIndian residents: 5,705. Governed under a constitution and by-laws adopted in 1932 and revised in 1961, under a business and claims committee composed of 9 elected members including a chairman.

It has been noted above that there are no reliable statistics for the Indian tribes and population. There are no current statistics for the *number* of Indian tribes either. However, to obtain some sort of a view of the numbers of reservations, and generally where the Indian people are, the following is submitted. (Data was extracted from the Commerce Department survey of 1972, the American Indian Lawyers Training Program of 1976, and state reports.)

The state with most reservations is California, with eighty reservations having as little land as six acres, and as much as 89,000 (Hoopa). Nevada has twenty-four reservations. New Mexico has twenty-four reservations. There are twenty-two reservations in the state of Washington, and ten in the state of Wisconsin. South Dakota has nine reservations; and North Dakota five. According to the U.S. Commerce Department there are 291 reservations, some of which are state reservations (minimum) and most of which are federally recognized. Alaska has a special situation, since the settlement of the Alaska Native Claims case. According to recent figures, there are thirteen native corporations in that state, and approximately one hundred and seventy-one villages divided into the corporations. The thirteen regional corporations have "for-profit" status. The village corporations are exempt, nonprofit. Alaska is a subject requiring a complete study of its own, and no effort is made herein for such a study.

The sample study of certain tribes noted above shows that there are quite a few reservations having more than one and sometimes four or five tribes residing on the same reservation. In many cases the tribes have intermarried, and the tribal lines are being obliterated gradually. In other cases, the tribes remain distinct, especially where two formerly antagonistic tribes have been placed on the same reservation.

A tribe-by-tribe analysis of economic conditions is impossible both because of space requirements, and the lack of dependable data. However, a considerable amount of information has been gathered by the American Indian Policy Review Commission, and the following brief summary relies on this data.

Farming. According to 1974 Bureau of Indian Affairs statistics, 2,440,172 acres (4.7 percent) of all Indian trust land, were classed as agricultural. Of the almost two and a half million acres, 29 percent were irrigated and 71 percent were dry farm. While the size of Indian agricultural land seems small, the value of products grown was considerable: $339,919,780.

However, 73 percent of this value was produced by nonIndian operators. NonIndian operators usually cultivate 63 percent of all Indian agricultural lands, while Indian operators cultivate only 29 percent and 8 percent remains idle. Explanations for this phenomenon include these reasons: The Indians could not obtain credit. Land ownership patterns brought about by individual allotment of Indian lands and by policy decisions of the BIA in years past, which favored leasing out of Indian land rather than stimulating large-scale tribal development is responsible for most reasons. Some tribes have attempted to break the lease cycle and develop their own tribally operated farm enterprises. This provides a greater rate of return to the Indian community, as well as employment for tribal members.

At Crow Creek, the tribe has brought 1,500 acres under dry farm cultivation, principally alfalfa and winter wheat. Funds were obtained for land consolidation through federal agencies. These funds were insufficient for continuing development.

The Umatilla farm enterprise manages the tribal farm lands. They obtained a federal loan for purchase loans, spraying, fertilizer, and related expenses. The farm enterprise has generated a net income which exceeds the average net income received by Umatilla lessors.

The Quechan Tribe, with land on the border of California and Arizona in the southern part of California, has what appears to be a successful hydroponic farm, growing tomatoes in a relatively new system which they merchandise commercially.

Rangeland. Rangelands and livestock operations are an important part of the Indian economy. In 1975, the General Accounting Office reported that about 44 million acres existed on Indian reservations. Indian ranchers used about 90 percent of this land. The Bureau of Indian Affairs reported in 1975 that some 15,074 Indian ranching operations accounted for livestock products valued at $74.8 million. However, it was also reported that an estimated 13 million acres, or 30 percent of Indian rangeland are not properly managed and in poor condition because the range has been overgrazed; range improvements have not been effectively used or maintained; and limited use has been made of training and education programs. However, these problems have existed on some Indian reservations for many years. Short-term stopgap measures have been taken to relieve the situation, but the long term problems still remain. An important factor hindering the effective management of Indian rangelands on some reservations is the conflict between tribal and individual Indian desires with respect to accepted range management practices.

About 60 percent of Indian rangeland is located in two arid states: Arizona and New Mexico.

Leasing. The General Allotment Act of 1887 divided a considerable amount of tribally held land into individual Indian allotments. In the years following, support grew for the concept of allowing Indians to lease their lands, mainly because Indians had too little land and no funds. The first general Indian land leasing statute, enacted in 1891, placed a restraint on Indian leasing by permitting Indians to lease their land only if they were unable to farm it themselves by reason of age or disability. However, for all practical purposes, the leasing of allotted land fell prey to the influence of white settlers, and leasing often became the rule rather than the exception.

Allotments made to individual Indians was generally too small for the support of family agriculture. Plots of 160 acres in sparsely vegetated rangelands were completely inadequate for ranching activities. Plots of 40 or 80 acres on irrigable land may have been viable in the late 1800s, but not until properly irrigated, and funds for such purposes was not forthcoming.

The first consequence of this fractionation of ownership out of tribes into individual tracts was a massive loss of land. Between 1887 and 1934, about two thirds or 90 million acres of Indian land passed out of Indian ownership into nonIndian hands. Another major cause of the lack of productive land was the additional fractionation of individual ownership among succeeding Indian heirs. Today, a major portion of lands classified as Indian owned are, in fact, under the control of nonIndians because they have been leased out. Uneconomically sized plots, the lack of capital, and the lack of technical assistance have forced Indian owners to lease their land to others. Despite the current availability of loans from various government agencies, the amounts of such loans are inadequate, and the leasing program has already tied up tribal and individually owned trust land for years to come. Today this situation poses serious obstacles to tribal initiative and economic development. Another serious problem involves the inequitable amounts received by the Indians for leases negotiated by the Bureau of Indian Affairs. A massive fraud was perpetrated against the Indians by way of the leasing activities, and only in the last few years has this begun to give way to more equitable ways of dealing with Indian leasing.

An example may be related of the situation on the Fort Hall Indian Reservation. The tribe engaged the services of Economic Research Associates of Los Angeles, to propose an overall economic development plan. The company found that Fort Hall Indians failed to get equitable income for all agricultural land leased to nonIndian tenants. Typical nonreservation leases in the Fort Hall area averaged 35 percent of gross crop value, while Fort Hall Leases were equivalent to about 2.3 percent of gross crop value.

Another investigation was conducted following this, by the General Accounting Office. This agency found there was a large disparity in lease rates, particularly in irrigated reservation land. Irrigated reservation land was found to rent at an average of $15.36 compared to high quality irrigated nonreservation land. Dry farm acreage rentals were about equal for reservation and nonreservation lands, but there was a substantial disparity found to exist for pasture rental. The GAO report found, however, that "certain intangibles" caused nonIndian lessors to be less willing to pay the same rent for Indian land as for nonIndian land, but these intangibles were not identified.

In 1975, another firm, Farm Management Company, conducted still a third evaluation of leasing at Fort Hall. They calculated the value of cash leases for both high quality and average quality nonreservation land, thus taking into consideration the tangible costs raised by GAO, and compared them to the value of cash leases for the same quality land on the reservation. Theyfound that the average value of cash leases on nonreservation land was $56-$70 for potatoes of high quality. They also found that the average value of cash lease for high quality potatoes on reservation land was $35. Since potatoes are normally rotated with a grain crop every other year, the average cash rent is $56-$70 on the better soils and $17-$24 on the sandier soils. The tribes then raised their standard rent per acre to $35 an acre. This caused the poorer or marginal lands to be abandoned because of lower yields. Finally, this resulted in the tribe receiving less rent than it should for better farmland, and the poorer land was left idle.

The Shoshone-Bannock Tribes at Fort Hall then commissioned an additional study by an economist, Mr. Jack Peterson. His report confirmed the continued inequitable leasing practices. He found that fixed rate rentals on Indian land are substantially less than on nonIndian land; Indian fixed rate rentals are preferred over crop share rental; Indian lessors have no recourse when leases are violated; leases are for uneconomical lengthy periods of time; and lease regulations for proper conservation practices are unenforceable.

According to the Indian Policy Commission report, an alternative to leasing could well be the consolidation of tracts of trust land for farming. With good credit, technical assistance, and modern farming practices, the yields from farming go directly to the tribal members, and the cycle of failure could be broken. Several tribes have proven this can be done.

Once an examination is made of such practical matters as the economic health of a tribe, or the lack of it, and the whole picture of Indian poverty is seen and understood, the issue of tribal self-government should be raised. When one sees the practical results of dependency and violation of statutes, court decisions, and trust responsibility, the controversy over "tribal sovereignty" is viewed only dimly by the Indian, and appears as some sort of abstraction.

The Indians themselves are confronted every day with violations of their rights to self-government. They have been restrained from the development they have a right to expect and are thoroughly capable of, because of violations of their right to govern themselves. The leasing program, the unconscionable length of time for leases, the low prices paid for the leasing of Indian land, and the failure to exercise control over the lands leased, has been done through the mismanagement of the Bureau of Indian Affairs and the Department of the Interior. The Indians themselves, given the chance to make their own mistakes, and accumulate their own successes, could not have done worse.

There are other projects proposed by federal agencies, which the tribes have been encouraged and often induced, to experiment with. But the desires and opinions of the tribal members have not been taken into account. Confronted with a barrage of arguments for such projects, (as only one example), as tourism, the tribes have backed away and surrendered their own good judgment to that of others who are considered to be "experts."

A recent report, funded by The Ford Foundation and the Bureau of Indian Affairs, supports the view that most if not all the tourism projects for the tribes have been grossly inefficient, and finally may be considered as failures. Most of the trouble arises from the fact that Indians must engage the services of nonIndian experts in a field with which they have no experience, and from the lack of adequate funding for this high-risk and high-capital requirement type of enterprise.

The reservations could be made into veritable beauty spots and a source of continuing income for the tribes, were it not for the mismanagement and lack of vision of the federal government. Unemployment ranges from 35 to 70 percent on reservations. Disease is at a higher rate than in any other sector of the population, and the economy, despite the considerable millions of dollars in federal funds brought to bear upon the poor economic conditions on the reservations, has not developed an appreciable change in the life of the Indian in the hogan, in the hut, those living in jerry-built federal houses, or confined to the ghettos of the cities. There are some successes, but these are the exception and not the rule. Indian economic conditions remain the worst in the nation.

Considering the current attack upon the Indian tribes, with the purpose of taking their water and natural resources, it is a matter of continuing to fight for rights in the courts, merely so that the people may survive.

The data presented above describing the land base and population of various tribes reveals some basic reasons for current controversies between the Indians and the states. These controversies involve even more deeply the nonIndians residing on the reservations, and is bearing bitter fruit in the form of a new war against the Indians. Of all the tribes confronted by these problems, the Salish-Kootenai on the Flathead reservation in Montana present a clear example of the effects of two centuries of abuse and violations by the federal government.

Mr. Thurman Trosberg, a member of the Salish-Kootenai Confederated Tribes, expressed the reasons and results of the conflict, when he testified before the American Indian Policy Review Commission in a hearing (April 19, 1976, Missoula, Montana). His statement is given below:

"We have seen, over a long period of time, the gradual erosion of the tribe's resource base. It has been eroded mainly by government, by preemption through and by government, by Interior Department decisions through the Interior solicitor. This has resulted in a gradual attrition of the resource base. These administrative decisions favored the white majority. We are experiencing an interesting phenomenon on the Flathead reservation. We are having a white uprising. This comes about because for the first time the

174

Tribal Council has gotten itself together and has taken steps, legal steps, to stop the further erosion of our resource base and to retrieve some of the losses we have already sustained.

"There are some questions that are clear to us, but not to the white people. Who has jurisdiction over the water and the land underlying the water on the reservation? How does a tribe go about controlling use of their lands for recreation and fishing? Steps have been taken to stop the erosion of the resource base, and to regain some of the losses. And still there is no clear-cut answer, even though we have gone to court.

"The question of jurisdiction, the right of the tribe to decide what shall be done, and to govern its resources and the people, is absolutely bedrock. It's the basis upon which a tribe exists. If we don't have jurisdiction, the power to control the use of and manage our assets, we have nothing.

"If you cast the problem in economic terms the foot race that we have on the Flathead reservation is one in which the white people have gained control of the bulk of the fertile land. They have gained control of the water through the help of congress, but there are valuable assets remaining, particularly in lands needed for development purposes. It is these assets that the white community would like to get their hands on. They are losing their cases in court. To them, it looks like the regulatory and statutory base is stacked against the white community. So they are organizing on a regional and national basis to bring about the end of federal supervision over these assets. They have other arguments involved, such as the tax base. In reality, the productive agricultural lands are already in private ownership. The tribe has only the rocks and the mountains left, although there are some timber assets.

" The ownership was clearly defined in court decisions that the Indians, the tribe, actually control and own the lake bed. But this was contested and we lost the case in District Court, not on judicial grounds, but on political grounds, that it would be a hardship on all those nice people who bought land up there. It would be a hardship now, it is said, to roll back the pages of history and reassert that the Indians have ownership and therefore the whites are in trespass. The judge reasoned that inasmuch as the Indians didn't exercise this authority over their land for fifty years, their authority over the land and their ownership of the land has gone by adverse possession, that they acquisced, in other words. It had just slipped away into private ownership. We don't believe that is the case. The only recourse the tribes have is to go to court and get a clear-cut decision.

" I think that most of the problems can be resolved by the tribes and the state and local governments working together. But it takes cooperation from the white community, and from the tribes. From watching this process operate, I believe the tribes are fully willing to cooperate. I don't see the same measure of cooperation coming from the white community, primarily from the County Commissioners, who of course are no more than spokesmen for the white community.

"Unfortunately, the white people are not informed. They are smart people but they are not informed about Indian law, history, the background for our reservation and the background for our rights. The public education system is the root cause because these things have never been taught, and so there is a tremendous public education job to do to bring the white community up to understand, and accept, not only understand, that there were treaties, that the federal government does have a trust responsibility, and is obliged to carry out these responsibilities as trustees. I think these are simple and specific kinds of concepts. Yet it is very hard to get these simple points through and understood by the white community. You run into a whole set of prejudices; barriers have been built. Communities have been inflamed, and this is why it will take a long time to break through these barriers and sit down and discuss the problems on a face-to-face basis.

"If we are not successful in this effort, it will mean that the goup, a small group that are stirring up this controversy to frighten people of the white community, will be responsible. They are saying that the Indians are out to preempt their rights. This is not the case.

"We have to find a way of overcoming the conflict of interest that exists in the solicitor's office in the Interior Department, so that we can adjudicate resource problems. If you examine the record, you see that most of the resources were lost not by legislation (although some were lost through the Allottment Act), but most were lost by secretarial decisions, and you can give chapter and verse of where this occurred. The Justice Department hasn't been vigorous in championing the Indian cause. I think there is a great deal of sympathy for the Indian cause, but there is no political clout, and that's what you need to change the situation.

" I think we need a statute that sets up an Indian trust commission that is free of the Interior Department, that is free of the Justice Department, a small group of lawyers with sufficient money to hire legal advice, counsel, to carry the Indians' side of the case.

" A halfway measure was taken by the Secretary of the Interior in establishing an Indian Associate Solicitor. But the Associate Solicitor is still under the Solicitor, and he is still under the Interior Secretary. As a consequence they are suffering from a great deal of concentration just now, because they have nearly a dozen substantive questions to be decided. I will lay you ten to one that these questions will never be decided by the Secretary because he has to make a choice between Indians and whites and he will be in hot water if he decides for the white community. He will be in hot water politically, and elections are coming up soon. So here we sit.

" We're really dead in the water as far as getting the Secretary to make these kinds of decisions. In order to avoid this kind of complication I urge that an Indian Trust Commission be established on a cabinet level, in the executive department.

" The solution that has been attempted, that of having the Commissioner of Indian Affairs become an Assistant Secretary in the Department of Interior, is no solution at all. He is still under the Interior Secretary. The Interior Department is a conglomeration of conflict of interest groups, conflicting agencies. You've got the developers and the preservers and in all of this mix you've got the Bureau of Indian Affairs. I never have understood why this Bureau was put into Interior. The people who are running Interior are the people who are exploiting resources, the Bureau of Reclamation, the Bureau of Mines, the Bureau of Land Management. These are the people (to name only a few agencies) who are in the driver's seat. So there isn't a chance that the Indians will ever get equity under that kind of a decision-making process."

These observations from a member of the tribe who is not in the tribal government, were followed by the legal opinion of an attorney who represents six of the largest tribes in the Northwest, Mr. Alvin J. Ziontz:

"Thousands of nonIndians in the western states live on or near Indian reservations. Many drive through Indian reservations almost daily. There are numerous farms and ranches owned by nonIndians on reservations and many towns and cities are located within the boundaries of reservations. Such incursions by nonIndian populations have resulted from the opening of Indian lands by the Indian Allotment Acts which declared many lands within Indian reservations to be surplus to the Indians' needs, and allowed them to be sold to nonIndians; by homestead acts which opened Indian lands for settlement by nonIndians, and by Indian lands going out of trust and being sold to nonIndians.

"Many nonIndians are now deeply disturbed by the prospect of Indian tribal government imposing tribal authority over them in many areas of conduct. Such tribal regulation includes law and order codes, building and zoning codes, water codes and taxing and licensing ordinances. Generally, these codes occupy no different position than the codes and ordinances promulgated by the local states, cities and counties.

"The attack on such tribal authority is made on a number of grounds. The principal ground, however, is that nonIndians should not be subjected to tribal government because they are barred from membership in the tribe, and therefore, from participation in voting and holding office. They are in effect "non-citizens" insofar as tribal government is concerned.

"It is certainly true that a nonIndian may not participate as a matter of right in the affairs of tribal government merely because of his residence within the boundaries of a reservation. He has no voice in the selection of tribal officials or in the establishment of tribal policies. NonIndians who reside outside the reservation but who may frequently pass through the reservation cannot rest their protest on such grounds since they have the same relationship to tribal government as any transient has with respect to the government of the community through which he is passing . . .

" It is clear that under present law nonIndians residing on Indian reservations are non-citizens with respect to the tribe which governs the reservation. This does not affect their status as citizens of the states and counties within which they reside nor as citizens of the United States. They are full citizens of those governments and have full rights of participation. But as to the local tribal government, their position is comparable to the position of non-residents or aliens. Such persons are generally unable to vote, or hold office, or serve on juries or qualify for a variety of activities reserved for residents by state and local laws.

"In addition, numerous benefits are available to residents which are denied non-residents, such as differentials in fees for tuition in state institutions of higher learning. That the non-resident is denied the right to participate in the decisions of the local government, or is subjected to differential treatment, is not in itself a denial of civil rights.

"However, his subjection to taxation and other powers of government without any right to participate in that government, appears to collide with fundamental notions of democracy and due process of law. The Supreme Court has resolved the problem by applying two basic principles: Indian tribes have authority over their reservations, and nonIndians have no right to membership in Indian tribes. Any attempt to give nonIndian reservation residents the same standing as they would have if they resided on the reservation presents a basic dilemma: either tribal government must be open to nonIndian participation or tribal government must be stripped of governmental authority over the reservation. Either solution would be destructive.

" If tribal government is opened to nonIndian participation, it will mean the end of Indian tribes as tribes. Their identity will be lost and the political relationship between the United States and the political entities which have made treaties and agreements with it will be destroyed. Such a proposal is actually one to end Indian tribes and their existence.

" Alternatively, destruction of tribal authority by legislative fiat would mean turning the clock backward. It would prevent tribes from controlling lawlessness on reservations resulting from the unwillingness or inability of local governments to extend adequate law enforcement to the reservations. In some cases, governmental authority of non-tribal governments has been chaotic and confusing as a result of the differing status of land parcels within the reservations. As the United States Supreme Court recently held in *Moe v. Confederated Salish and Kootenai Tribes* (425 U.S. 463, 1976):

" 'Congress by its more modern legislation has evinced a clear intent to eschew any such 'checkerboard' approach within an existing Indian reservation . . .'

" Impairment of tribal authority would, in the long run, benefit no one. It would, on the other hand, strip away those aspects of tribal government which the courts have found to be an inherent aspect of sovereignty which all governments must have to carry out the basic function of maintaining an orderly and peaceful community.

" Thus, the efforts of groups opposing Indian rights and seeking legislation to assist them is based on a fundamental misunderstanding of the nature of those Indian rights.

" There is no constitutional right for a nonIndian to be a member of an Indian tribe. That Indian tribes have authority over their reservations and are entitled to rights, privileges and immunities not granted to nonIndians is a product of their original occupancy of this continent and the commitments made by the United States of America to them on that account. . . . We cannot agree that Indian rights are inconsistent with our system of constitutional law. Indian tribes appear to be in a state of transition at the present time and undoubtedly many problems will be encountered as they exercise their authority. Tolerance, cooperation and good will are required of Indians and nonIndians alike.

" But in the long run, we all must recognize that the principle of self-government is as dear to the Indian tribes as it was to our colonial forefathers. It is in the best interests of our political and social system for Indian tribes to exercise that self-government responsibly and effectively. It is difficult for Indians to escape the feeling that the opposition to such efforts by nonIndians, no matter how phrased, is ultimately racist. Perhaps it is even now too late for words of moderation. But lawyers have a special responsibility to avoid worsening the already serious conflicts between tribal governments and their nonIndian residents and neighbors.''

Summing up the condition of the Native American today, it must be said that it is a crazy-quilt pattern of some successes, some failures, many problems, and general strengthening of the tribal government.

The tribes have more sophisticated leadership now. They go to the courts, and they go to win their cases. They are insisting upon self-government, the development of their economy, education for their youth, and the fulfillment of obligations undertaken by the United States when this country forged its nationhood out of a continent that was owned by the native nations and tribes.

CHAPTER 5
References

1. American Indian Policy Review Commission Report, page 87.
2. Ibid, page 89.
3. Ibid, page 108.
4. See Chapter 3, Policy Review Report.
5. See *100,000,000 Million Acres*, by Kickingbird and Ducheneaux.

"President after president has appointed commission after commission to inquire into and report upon Indian affairs, and to make suggestions as to the best methods of managing them.

"The reports are filled with eloquent statements of wrongs done to the Indians, of perfidies on the part of the Government; they counsel, as earnestly as words can, a trial of the simple and unperplexing expedients of telling truth, keeping promises, making fair bargains, dealing justly in all ways and all things.

"These reports are bound up with the Government's Annual Reports, and that is the end of them."

A Century of Dishonor
Helen Hunt Jackson
1881

Chapter 6

A DISCUSSION
OF SOLUTIONS

There are no easy solutions in Indian affairs, considering the insidious lawlessness of the Interior Department as it continues to manipulate the tribes for the benefit of corporate interests. Every agency of this department is acting to perpetuate the historic violations of the treaties, statutes and Supreme Court decisions. There are more statutes and regulations controlling Indians than any other department of government. There are more judicial decisions concerning Indian affairs than any other sector of the American nation. There is more money expended for Indians than for any other purpose excluding the military. The largest amount of this huge expenditure is for administration, as the evidence shows.

Remedies aimed at solving this unconscionable expenditure for purposes that have been ineffective in changing the situation have been largely federal. Some years ago the federal government attempted to divest the Bureau of Indian Affairs of its huge bureaucracy and bring government closer to the Indian people. This resulted in the fractionating of services into various departments of government. Today, at least nine cabinet-level departments and ten individual agencies have programs affecting Indian people. Obligations for these programs totaled about $1.1 billion in 1974, and increasing geometrically. Programs designed exclusively for American Indians amounted to about $950 million. Indian set-aside programs amounted to $170 million. Five temporary committees are engaged in studies that will have a direct impact on Indian interests.[1]

These figures represent only part of the cost. The Bureau of Indian Affairs alone expends enough money to raise the income of the

Indian appreciably, were these sums apportioned per capita. The delivery system through which the Bureau programs are administered is composed of a central office located in Washington, D.C., twelve area offices representing broad regional divisions, and eighty-two agency offices representing subordinate field installations. There have been seventy-five studies, documenting the inadequacy of this system over the last twenty-five years. The area offices are located in: Aberdeen, South Dakota; Albuquerque, New Mexico; Anadarko, Oklahoma; Billings, Montana; the Eastern agency; Juneau, Alaska; Minneapolis, Minnesota; Muskogee, Oklahoma; the Navajo Agency; Phoenix, Arizona; Portland, Oregon; Sacramento, California, Expenditures for maintaining these regional offices per Indian individual, amount to an average of $1,000 per Indian. Some of the area offices showing most expenditures are: Aberdeen, $1,823 per Indian served: Portland, $3,632 per Indian; Navajo, $1,632 per Indian; Billings, $1,461 per Indian; Albuquerque, $1,449 per Indian.[2]

The American Indian Policy Review Commission has documented that many millions could be saved, if recommendations the Commission has made were put into effect. One of the most important recommendations is the elimination of most of the area offices, which cause laborious interruptions in service, strengthen bureaucratic controls over the tribes, and in most cases impede the efficient delivery of services. The recommendation involves the elimination of the area offices, and the strengthening of the superintendencies which are closer to the Indian people and can be structured into a delivery and technical assistance service. The tribes, however, should determine the nature of such changes and the areas in which they may be made.

Major departments with multiple programs relating to Indians are: Interior; Health, Education and Welfare; Agriculture; Housing and Urban Development; and Commerce. The Departments of Labor, Transportation, Treasury, State, and Defense also have major programs important to Indians. The Department of Justice handles most of the legal problems affecting Indian rights.

Independent agencies with programs affecting Indians include: Federal Energy Administration, Environmental Protection Administration, Federal Power Commission, Commission on Civil Rights, Small Business Administration, Occupational Safety and Health Review Commission, Equal Opportunity Commission, and the Marine Mammal Commission. There are also many temporary commissions whose studies and functions are bound to affect Indian interests.

All these agencies are afflicted with these weaknesses, amounting to guaranteed ultimate destruction of Indian self-government: There is no understanding of federal-Indian relations. There is no understanding of the historic basis nor the present requirements of Indian self-government. Where there is understanding, the violations are built into the statutes governing the activities of these agencies. The regulations implementing the statutes further erode Indian rights and violate the basis for the federal responsibility as trustee for Indian affairs. While the controversy rages over state intrusion and the attempt to usurp tribal authority, the states have authority over the tribes through the programs that are administered by the agencies. No consideration is given, when regulations are published, as to the federal-Indian relationship and the principle of tribal self-government. Thus, federal agencies consistently fail to recognize tribal sovereignty and the unique trust and treaty obligations of the federal government to American Indians.

Of all the agencies and departments of government, the most culpable is the Bureau of Indian Affairs.

The Bureau of Indian Affairs has acted directly to undermine tribal government. Allegations in this regard were documented by the Indian Policy Review Commission, and include the following violations:

1: The Bureau has directly interfered in tribal elections.

2: The Bureau has usurped one of the most basic powers of self-government—the right to determine membership, by conditioning BIA funding on BIA-determined membership qualifications.

3: The BIA has played one tribe against another in competition for funding.

4: The BIA has conditioned funding or delivery of services on the level of cooperation between tribal members and agency or area office employees.

5: The Bureau has failed to respond to tribal requests for legal assistance.

6: The BIA has failed to respond to tribal requests for technical assistance.

7: The BIA has failed to respond to requests for financial assistance.

8: The Bureau has entered into leases or contracts on behalf of the tribe without tribal approval, and often despite tribal opposition.

9: The Bureau has failed to assist tribes in asserting their sovereign powers.

10: The Bureau acted specifically to diminish tribal exercise of powers of self-government.

11: The Bureau has terminated tribal employees from area offices without notification to the tribe.

12: The BIA has allocated judgment funds without approval of the tribal council, its governing body.

13: The BIA has displayed nepotism and favoritism in agency office hiring practices.

14: The Bureau has withheld information on tribal trust resources from the tribe.

15: The Bureau has advised tribal members to sell their land to qualify for state welfare.

16: The BIA has failed to act upon tribal requests for Secretarial approval of contracts.

17: The Bureau is accused of failing to act upon tribal requests for Secretarial approval of tribal constitutions, constitutional amendments, ordinances, resolutions, and charters.

18: The BIA has mismanaged tribal trust assets and resources.

19: The Bureau is accused of obstructing tribal negotiations with federal agencies.

20: The Bureau has discouraged tribes from contracting Federal programs which would obviate Bureau services.

21: The Bureau has distributed Federal program moneys in an arbitrary manner, relying upon the broad discretionary power of the Secretary.

These twenty-one indictments are based on hard evidence presented by Indian complainants during Commission hearings. There are affidavits to the effect that such lawless actions have been committed by officials of the Bureau of Indian Affairs. The allegations have been substantiated.

Each of the indictments is evidence of violations of treaties, violations of statutes, and violations of Supreme Court decisions. But such illegal practices have been customarily viewed as mere administrative weaknesses. They should, however, be considered as acts subject to Grand Jury investigation, followed by criminal indictments, in most cases. If some Bureau officials and petty civil service employees were sent to jail for such offenses, the criminal practices might be stopped. Properly viewed, the practices enumerated in the twenty-one indictments are at least as illegal as the offenses committed in the Watergate cases.

The insidious influence and the power of the Bureau of Indian Affairs is seen in a number of ways. Here is one method, by which the tribes are rendered powerless to act as governing bodies.

Factions are instigated in certain tribes by Bureau officials. When elections come along, the Bureau supports "their" faction. When the election fails to give a clear-cut majority to any candidate, or, if the anti-Bureau candidate is elected, the BIA supports their faction in objections to the election. On the other hand, if the anti-BIA faction is deprived of their electoral rights, and places a formal complaint against the final decision, the Bureau officials hold up the processing of the complaint, or pulverizes the tribal government completely by failing to act on anything. Thus, there is no tribal government functioning at all.

Bureau officials, when threatened with loss of their jobs, or limitation of their powers, often react by simply taking over the leadership in Indian affairs either by public statements which they have no right to make, or reporting data that is inaccurate but serves their own personal ends. The problem of divesting the area directors of their power is critical. What the tribes have said they want, are strong superintendencies in the areas where the people live and work, as close to the tribes as possible, so that services may be provided.

There have been support movements involving the American public and the United States Congress on behalf of the Indian people for a hundred and fifty years. One such movement began following the publication of Helen Hunt Jackson's *A Century of Dishonor*. This resulted in passage of the infamous Dawes General Allotment Act. The Meriam Report of 1928 resulted in changes in the delivery of health services to Indians and focused widespread attention on the abysmal failure of education of Indians. Some changes came about, and the legislation that resulted was the Indian Reorganization Act, bringing an end to the Allotment Act, as well as violations of Indian self-government. The broad, largely white-dominated movement of the 1920s, headed by John Collier and his Indian Defense League, raised some of the most serious questions affecting the American Indians, and formulated the I.R.A.

It is noted, in the Indian Policy Review Commission report, that Indians fear new legislation. A review of Indian legislation shows that this fear is well founded. All legislation thus far has resulted in some positive actions taken by the federal government to end abuses. It has also resulted in further strangling the Indian tribes and reducing their capacity for self-government.

The Indian Reorganization Act (25 U.S.C. 476) authorized tribes to reorganize and adopt constitutions and bylaws, *subject to the approval of the Interior Secretary*. Tribal ordinances, funds, and contractual arrangements *must have the approval of the Interior Secretary*. The right and power of Indian tribes to form their own governments exists independently from federal statute. This was well-recognized at the time the Indian Reorganization Act was

185

enacted.[3] But, due to the federal policies which had been pursued in the latter half of the 19th century and the first half of the 20th century, many of the traditional instruments of tribal governments had been drastically weakened and some lost for good. This Act, which was intended to strengthen Indian tribal government, has been an impediment to their governmental functions. The Interior Department has, for many years, denied that tribes could exercise any jurisdiction over nonIndians even though there was no clear statute and no judicial decision to confirm the Department's position.[4]

Because Indian tribes had no financial means to structure an effective law and order system, the congress has responded by enacting Public Law 83-280, which provided for the transfer to the states of major components of the jurisdiction that the federal government had assumed with respect to Indian tribes. Tribal consent was not provided for in the act, which allowed the states to assume control over such areas as crime and justice. The states, on their part, undertook jurisdiction over many other areas of tribal government, such as jurisdiction over hunting, fishing, trapping, and the alienation or taxation of trust property. This was specifically forbidden in the act. Public Law 280 is a major incursion on tribal sovereignty and self-government; it is a failure of federal policy. Its simple existence is an affront to tribal sovereignty and to the historical relationship between tribes and the United states, which deliberately excludes state jurisdiction.[5] The act is also a factual failure. It was premised on notions of fostering the individual assimilation of Indians. This has not been achieved. It was to provide adequate and just law enforcement and other services on Indian reservations. This has not been achieved. Oppressive BIA paternalism was to have been removed. This too has been a complete failure.

Another act has been passed, therefore, to permit retrocession of those tribes which have had Public Law 280 inflicted upon them. Under this legislation, some tribes have succeeded in returning jurisdiction to their tribal government. It remains to be seen how effective this legislation will be. One thing is clear, however, there is no explanation to the tribes of the retrocession process. In some cases, the tribes have no means for developing their own law and order system, and so feel that this service should be acquired wherever possible, no matter what the consequences.

When the struggle for civil rights reached its fever pitch, the legislation that resulted embraced the Indian people, and became known as the Indian Civil Rights Act of 1968, through Title II of the Act.[6]

Through the Indian Civil Rights Act, abuses have proliferated and tribal self-government has been further amputated. The courts have taken jurisdiction over a nearly limitless range of complaints including election disputes, apportionment of voting districts, membership rights, conduct of tribal officers in their official dealings which may exceed the authority vested in them under tribal constitutions, orders of tribal councils excluding certain nonmembers from the reservation. There is confusion as to the reach of the courts' jurisdiction. Indeed it was not the intent of congress when it enacted the 1968 act to make federal courts general overseers of tribal government. Under the act, jury trials must be held whenever the defendant requests it. No matter how short the potential jail sentence, a defendant before a tribal court is presumed to be entitled to a trial by jury.

Tribal courts presently handle a caseload in excess of 80,000 a year. If jury trials were liberally sought, the tribal judicial system would break down.[7]

As only one more instance of the perverse actions imposed upon the tribes through the Civil Rights Act, is the refusal of some courts to give full faith and credit to rulings of the tribal courts. Some courts do. Some courts don't. But the refusal of some states to recognize the orders of the tribal courts and the laws of the tribes is clearly harmful to both the tribes and the states. On the other hand, the tribes generally recognize lawful orders of state courts when an appropriate request is made. Thus, in these and various other provisions, the Indian Civil Rights Act has harmed instead of helped the Indian people.

The Indian Self-Determination and Education Assistance Act was enacted to strengthen tribal government, provide funds for this purpose, and promote the development of Indian education. Fulfilling the conditions of the act, however, have proved to be more of the same abuses of federal power, and presumptions of authority not provided in the legislation. For example, the Office of Management and Budget has decided that the population formulas used for the administration of part of this act be based on 1970 census data population estimates. Objections of the Indian people have been unavailing. These population estimates are grossly inaccurate, and the problem is only magnified in 1977. Other regulations involve determination of the "eligible service population." Administrative regulations decided that the service population should be restricted to Indians living on trust property. Many Indians reside off the reservations because they work in nearby cities. The shortage of adequate housing on reservations and the high rate of unemployment on most reservations, force Indians to seek employment and housing elsewhere. The capacity of the tribal government to provide its members with services such as health care is severely limited by these administrative regulations which penalize the tribal government for its off-reservation service population.[8]

The Review Commission report lists two hundred and six recommendations for essential change. Of these recommendations, approximately fifty require legislative action for new laws or amendments to such acts as the Indian Reorganization Act and the Indian Self-Determination Act. Quite possibly, the congress, if it enacts legislation based on the Commission's recommendations, will combine many of the proposals. What is feared by most Indians is that new legislation will contain further emasculation of tribal self-government. After all, evidence clearly shows that this invariably has occurred. What is to prevent its happening again?

There are two elements of control to which the Commission has not given adequate emphasis.

First: While the Policy Review Commission has had the benefit of Indian testimony and proposals for change, the recommended legislation should be submitted to the Indian tribes at the time they are introduced, and no legislation ought to be allowed to pass without discussion by the tribes in which all members are shown to have been invited to participate. Indians should be given an opportunity to testify at hearings held on any legislation, at government expense. Tribal referendum procedures should be developed for approval or disapproval of legislation specifically designed for Indians. Opposition can be heard immediately, that the tribes are demanding rights not held even by the states. However, the states participate in proposed legislation through their congressmen in the Senate and House of Representatives. Indian tribes, althrough promised in at least two cases that they would have congressional representation, do not have such representation. The states also have influence beyond imagination on legislation proposed in the congress, and the states even initiate legislation which their congressmen faithfully carry out.

Two such incidents come to mind. The state of Maine directed its congressional delegation to work for ending the pending Indian court cases through congressional legislation. The State of Washington instructed its congressional delegation to void court decisions protecting Indian fishing rights and impose state jurisdiction over the tribes through congressional legislation.

Thus, unless the federal government elects to fulfill its promises to the tribes, solemnly made in at least two treaties, that they may have congressional representation, the only recourse left is by referendum of the members of the tribes on any legislation proposed on behalf of the Indian people.

Second: There is no clear statutory requirement making a monitoring of Interior and other agency regulations possible. The agencies pass regulations, have them printed in the *Federal Register,* and after thirty days of such publication, the regulations have the effect of law. Since these departments, as has been extensively documented, have a history of violation of laws and court decisions, they must be monitored and no regulations passed unless the tribes have an opportunity to act upon them. This opportunity should not be restricted to merely making "observations" on the regulations. These are usually ignored. A consultative status is ineffective and undesirable, and violates tribal self-government. The tribes should have the right to approve or disapprove such regulations.

There is no vehicle, no structure, no statute requiring the Interior Department to abide by the statutes and the court decisions. A Commission or independent agency should be established (a Trust Counsel Authority has been recommended) which would place a mandatory restriction on Interior actions and regulations in Indian affairs, and violations should be followed by legal investigation and penalties.

The Trust Counsel Authority recommended by the Policy Review Commission, therefore, would be relegated to virtual impotency unless violations are punishable by law.

One question always emerges, when the tribes are confronted with proposed changes in administration, commissions to be established, and personnel named to various departments. That question is: who will be named to the commissions; who will have the right to decide the proposals in administration; who is the individual or individuals to be named to the departments? And who will make the nominations, as well as the decisions on such personnel?

As to proposed statutes and regulations: If the referendum is too bulky for handling, then there are several Indian organizations that have proven reliability and talent. One is the Institute for the Development of Indian Law. Another is the National Congress of American Indians. Certainly discussion should take place with these Indian institutions, at least. At the same time, it should be clearly understood that they will contact their constituencies for approval or disapproval.

As to personnel: Two instances of decisions violative of Indian self-determination are recent occurrences. One involves the personnel named to the American Indian Policy Review Commission itself. Most of the tribes in the nation objected to the personnel who were finally accepted. The complaint was that the Indians chosen for these positions were not representative of the largest tribes, those with the most severe issues (such as water rights) and Indian tribal suggestions were generally overlooked. As has been said "Someone" had his hand on our shoulders, so that the Commission report came out as strong advocacy for Indian rights, despite this improper, highly questionable procedure.

Another case occurred recently, when the tribes were asked for nominations for the position of Assistant Secretary for Indian Affairs a new position established in the Department of the Interior which replaces the office of Commissioner of Indian Affairs. Most of the tribes contacted nominated Mr. Mel Tonasket, a Colville Indian. Fourteen tribes nominated Mr. Forrest Gerard. Mr. Gerard was nominated and finally approved by the Select Committee on Indian Affairs. Probably "Someone" had His hand on our shoulders as well, because thus far, Gerard has shown he intends to be an advocate for Indian rights. Whether he will be allowed to do so, because of the continuing presence of the Bureau of Indian Affairs within Interior, is questionable. What went wrong in both these instances?

In the first instance, the naming of Indians to sit on the Policy Review Commission was a political determination made behind closed doors. Those were named who were considered to be "safe" as to causing any trouble for the congress. A reading of the minutes of the Commission when names were submitted for the task forces working with the AIPRC confirms this. Both the congressmen and the Indian commissioners jockeyed back and forth, each urging the nomination and approval of favorites.

In the second instance, the method of obtaining tribal nominations became one of popularity contest status. There was no discussion dealing with abilities and experience of the candidates. A notice was sent in the form of a memorandum, and the tribes were left to make whatever nominations they chose. The final choices, between the six or more candidates, did not result in a notification of the candidates' experience, record, history, or commitments.

Should the congress set up commissions without adequate and efficient participation by the Indian people themselves, the results will be just as disastrous as past experience shows.

In the same vein, the Policy Review Commission recommends that a new agency be set up, free from the Interior Department, answerable to the Executive. Will a new agency end the conflict of interests? Who will name the administrators? What is to prevent such administrators being mere adjuncts of Interior? Can the Bureau of Reclamation and other agencies now within Interior be compelled to observe the treaties and the statutes guaranteeing Indian sovereignty and self-government?

An issue of paramount importance, one that will determine the life or death of the Indian people, is that of Indian water rights. The recommendations in this case have been carefully considered with the consultation of the Indian tribes, and the help of experienced attorneys. These recommendations are noted herewith, as proposals for change having a priority rating. Other proposals are condensed in order to show the general direction of the Policy Review Commission's handling of proposed changes.

The Commission recommends, in addressing the issue of Indian water rights, that:

The Secretary of Interior allow the tribes having legal rights over water to develop their own water codes designed to regulate all forms of water usage. (Allow? "not interfere" would have been more appropriate.)

That Congress enact legislation to provide for an Indian trust impact statement any time federal or state projects affect Indian water resources.

The Secretary and the Bureau of Indian Affairs take the following actions or provide tribes with the financial capability to:

1: Inventory all tribal water resources.

2: Complete land use surveys particularly, to determine lands which are irrigable or which can use water for other beneficial uses.

3: Conduct adequate engineering studies of Indian water resources necessary for litigation.

4: Make available to the tribes funds to conduct legal and engineering research regarding particular water resources and to proceed with litigation where necessary.

That congress investigate litigation in the San Juan River Basin, the Rio Grande Basin, and the Colorado River Basin, and it likewise investigate the *Walton* cases, the *Bel Bay* case, and the *Big Horn* case to ascertain the scope of the federal conflicts of interest.

That congress amend 42 U.S.C. 666 known as the McCarran amendment, to specifically exclude Indian water rights from its provisions.

The Secretary of the Interior direct the BIA to work with Indian tribes and the Bureau of Reclamation to (1) identify those Indian lands served by BIA irrigation projects which would most benefit from IMS; and (2) plan and provide guidance to implement IMS on those lands.

A digest of most important recommendations of the American

Indian Policy Review Commission is provided below. The recommendations are published within each chapter of the report, and a summary is given on page 11 of the report. This digest is based on the summary:

On Contemporary Conditions, the recommendations are:

1: Congress require the Assistant Secretary of Indian Affairs to prepare a comprehensive annual report.

On Trust Responsibility:

1: Congress reaffirm and direct all executive agencies to administer the trust responsibility consistent with the following principles and procedures, consistent with such principles of law:

a: The trust responsibility to American Indians is an established legal obligation.

b: In matters involving trust resources, the United States be held to the highest standards of care and good faith principles of common law trust. Legal and equitable remedies be available in federal courts for breach of standards.

c: The United States hold legal title to Indian trust property, but full equitable title rests with the Indian owners.

2: Before any agency takes action which may abrogate or in any way infringe any Indian treaty rights, or nontreaty rights protected by the trust responsibility, it prepare and submit to the appropriate committee in both Houses of Congress an Indian trust rights impact statement, to include, but not be limited to the following information:

a: Nature of the proposed action.

b: Nature of Indian rights which may be abrogated.

c: Whether consent of the affected Indians has been sought and obtained.

d: If the proposed action involves taking or otherwise infringing Indian trust lands, there must be notification whether or not lieu lands have been offered to the affected Indian or Indians.

3: Principles are established, when congress is considering legislation which may have an adverse impact upon treaty or nontreaty rights.

4: To diminish the conflict of interest prevalent when the Department of Justice and the Department of the Interior provide legal services to Indians, to provide for more efficient rendering of legal services to Indians and to otherwise improve the representation which Indians receive, congress enact legislation establishing within a newly created Department of Indian Affairs, an Office of Trust Rights Protection.

On Tribal Government, recommendations are:

1: The long term objective of federal-Indian policy be the development of tribal governments into fully operational governments exercising the same powers and shouldering the same responsibilities as other local governments.

2: No legislative action be undertaken by congress relating to tribal jurisdiction over nonIndians at this time.

3: Congress appropriate significant additional moneys for the maintenance of tribal judicial systems, and funding be direct to tribes.

4: Congress provide by appropriate legislation that the benefits received from those programs designed to aid in the economic development of Indians shall not be subject to federal taxation.

5: Congress provide by appropriate legislation that the benefits received from those programs designed to aid in the economic development of Indians shall not be subject to federal taxation, and congress amend the Internal Revenue Code to provide that provisions of the Code applying to nonIndian governments are to be applied in a like manner and to the same extent to Indian tribal governments.

6: Congress amend or repeal those statutes which authorize state taxation which are in conflict with federal-Indian policy to foster economic development of reservation Indians and enhance tribal self-government. That state taxation within reservations be invalidated as applied to nonIndians when the burden of such taxation falls directly or indirectly upon the Indian.

7: Congress enact legislation providing that where an Indian tribal government enacts a tax in furtherance of federal-Indian policy, designed to enhance the tribes' self-governing capacity or to protect or foster tribal economic development of Indian people or the tribe, such tax will have the effect of preempting any competing state tax which would be applicable to the same person or activity.

8: That the Department of Interior aid tribes in developing management plans. That the executive branch undertake action to stimulate the tribes and states towards cooperative agreements on off-reservation fishing activities by both Indians and nonIndians. Congress appropriate funds to aid individual tribes and intertribal organizations in development and management of fishery programs.

9: Congress enact legislation authorizing the Department of the Interior (Parks and Wildlife Division) with standby authority to allocate fish resources and enforce such allocations as to Indians or nonIndians or both, whenever the states or the tribes fail to regulate those persons under their respective jurisdiction.

10: Section 18 of the IRA (25 U.S.C. #478) which provides that no part of that act shall apply to any reservation wherein a majority of the adult Indians vote against its application, be repealed. In its place, congress enact a savings clause providing that the rights of any tribe which has organized under the terms of Section 16 or formed a corporation under Section 17 of the act will not be adversely affected. (Further comprehensive amendments to the IRA are proposed in the recommendations.)

11: Legislation be passed providing for retrocession, at tribal option with a plan.

12: That jurisdictional provisions of the 1968 Indian Civil Rights Act be re-examined. The part of the act providing for a right to trial by jury be amended to specify that the right only be applicable to offenses which if charged in a federal court would be subject to a right to trial by jury. The provisions of the act limiting the penal authority of a tribe to fines of $500 or six months imprisonment or both, be amended to increase these figures to fines of $1,000 or one year imprisonment or both.

13: That section 1738 of title 28 U.S.C. be amended to specifically include Indian tribes among those governments to whom full faith and credit be given. That congress amend title II of the Indian Civil Rights Act to provide a mechanism for limited appeals to the United States district courts after exhaustion of all available tribal remedies.

14: Legislation is proposed guaranteeing the permanency of Indian tribal governments in various assistance and service programs of the federal government.

On Federal Administration:

1: Congress enact affirmative legislation to reaffirm and guarantee the permanence and viability of tribal governments within the federal system.

2: Congress enact legislation establishing tribal governments as equal to state governments in federal domestic assistance programs.

3: Congress amend the Intergovernmental Cooperation Act to include tribal governments, and enact the Federal Program Information Act to include Indian tribes.

4: Congress enact Senate Bill S. 2175, Public Participation in Government Proceedings Act of 1976.

5: That Indian Preference in hiring, as provided in the IRA, be implemented, apart from the requirements of civil service laws in the BIA and Indian Health Service, and that such amendment be applicable to all federal agencies administering programs directed to Indian affairs.

194

6: Provisions that the executive branch implement certain provisions of various statutes, coordinate and consolidate technical assistance efforts in a single agency, establish a national professional and technical Indian skills bank administered by Indians, establish a National Indian Technical Assistance Center as a model.

7: The President submit to Congress a reorganization plan creating a department of Indian Affairs or independent agency to be comprised of appropriate functions now mainly administered by the Bureau of Indian Affairs, Indian Health Service and agencies within the Interior and Justice Departments. Rights protection to be consolidated.

Finally, specific recommendations are made for economic development, community services, on off-reservation Indians, terminated Indians, unrecognized Indians, and "special circumstances" such as the cases of Oklahoma, Alaska and California natives. It is not possible, in this study, to include all the recommendations made by the American Indian Policy Review Commission.

Those desiring to have a copy of the recommendations as they have been offered by the Commission, and published in the report, may receive one or more copies by writing to *Wassaja,* 1451 Masonic Avenue, San Francisco, Ca. 94116. Bundle orders only will be handled, at least ten and not more than one hundred in each bundle. The cost is 50c a copy, plus postage costs.

Without a doubt, the recommendations offered by the American Indian Policy Review Commission will be discussed in the tribes and Indian organizations for a number of years to come. Some recommendations will be found to be redundant. Others are distinctly a concession to the demand for states' rights, such as the recommendation on fishing allocations. Only the utmost vigilance will cause the proposals that are bound to be ineffective and those that perpetuate infringement on Indian treaty rights by virtue of the very fact that legislation is being required to assert such rights, to be opposed effectively.

At this very moment, however, (December, 1977) there are no less than six bills in the congress that are detrimental to Indian rights, proposing the abrogation of Indian treaties, and otherwise condemning the tribes to ultimate extinction. A congressional offensive has been launched against the Indian people. Whether it succeeds or not depends upon the effectiveness of an Indian support movement. Such a movement is bound to be set in motion.

It is a notable fact, at the same time, that Indians are seeking a coalition with indigenous peoples all over the world. Recent international treaty councils have been held in South Dakota and Canada. A meeting under the auspices of the United Nations Human Rights Commission took place in Geneva Switzerland late in 1977. Indians of the Americas are seeking ways to exchange views, develop a common platform and prepare for common action. This is a new development in native affairs. It appears to be gaining momentum, and is due entirely to the centuries of dishonor practiced by the various dominant governments in countries where indigenous peoples live. In the United States, the effort is to prevent a third century of dishonor practiced by the federal government and its agencies.

The Indian Nations and Tribes have endured for all these centuries. In regions and states of this nation, where it was believed the natives were extinct, they have come forward of late to assert their continued existence and to demand their rights as original owners of this land.

CHAPTER 6
References

1. American Indian Policy Review Commission Report, page 247. (Hereafter to be referred to as Report.)
2. Report, page 267.
3. Solicitor's Opinion, Oct. 25, 1934, 55 I.D. 14 at 30-32.
4. Solicitor's Opinion 17-36810, Aug. 10, 1970.
5. Report, page 199.
6. Title II, Act of Apr.11, 1968, 82 Stat. 77 (25 U.S.C. 1302,1303.
7. Report, page 213,214.
8. Report, page 224.

APPENDICES

Establishment of the American Indian Policy Review
Commission by Congressional Joint Resolution .... Page 198

A Chronology of Indian Treaties .... Page 208

Major Laws Which Apply to Indians of All Tribes ... Page 219

A Moment of Truth for the American Indian .... Page 229

The Council of State Governments Supporting the Meeds
Dissent on the American Indian Policy Review Commission
Report .... Page 235

Sources of Information .... Page 238

197

Public Law 93-580
93rd Congress, S.J. Res. 133
January 2, 1975

JOINT RESOLUTION

To provide for the establishment of the American Indian Policy Review
Commission.

Congressional Findings

The Congress, after careful review of the Federal Government's historical and special legal relationship with American Indian people, finds that—

(a) the policy implementing this relationship has shifted and changed
with changing administrations and passing years, without apparent rational design and without a consistent goal to achieve Indian self-
sufficiency;

(b) there has been no general comprehensive review of conduct of
Indian affairs by the United States nor a coherent investigation of the
many problems and issues involved in the conduct of Indian affairs since
the 1928 Meriam Report conducted by the Institute for Government
Research; and

(c) in carrying out its responsibilities under its plenary power over
Indian affairs, it is imperative that the Congress now cause such a comprehensive review of Indian affairs to be conducted.

Declaration of Purpose

Congress declares that it is timely and essential to conduct a comprehensive review of the historical and legal developments underlying the Indians'
unique relationship with the Federal Government in order to determine the
nature and scope of necessary revisions in the formulation of policies and
programs for the benefit of Indians.

*Resolved by the Senate and House of Representatives of the United
States of America in Congress assembled,* That—

(a) In order to carry out the purposes described in the preamble hereof
and as further set out herein, there is hereby created the American Indian
Policy Review Commission, hereinafter referred to as the "Commission".

(b) The Commission shall be composed of eleven members, as follows:

(1) three Members of the Senate appointed by the President pro tempore of the Senate, two from the majority party and one from the minority party;

(2) three Members of the House of Representatives appointed by the
Speaker of the House of Representatives, two from the majority party
and one from the minority party; and

(3) five Indian members as provided in subsection (c) of this section.

(c) At its organization meeting, the members of the Commission ap-

198

pointed pursuant to section (b)(1) and (b)(2) of this section shall elect from among their members a Chairman and a Vice Chairman. Immediately thereafter, such members shall select, by majority vote, five Indian members of the Commission from the Indian community, as follows:

(1) three members shall be selected from Indian tribes that are recognized by the Federal Government;

(2) one member shall be selected to represent urban Indians; and

(3) one member shall be selected who is a member of an Indian group not recognized by the Federal Government.

None of the Indian members shall be employees of the Federal Government concurrently with their term of service on the Commission nor shall there be more than one member from any one Indian tribe.

(d) Vacancies in the membership of the Commission shall not affect the power of the remaining members to execute the functions of the Commission and shall be filled in the same manner as in the case of the original appointment.

(e) Six members of the Commission shall constitute a quorum, but a smaller number, as determined by the Commission, may conduct hearings: *Provided,* That at least one congressional member must be present at any Commission hearing.

(f) Members of the Congress who are members of the Commission shall serve without any compensation other than that received for their services as Members of Congress, but they may be reimbursed for travel, subsistence, and other necessary expenses incurred by them in the performance of duties vested in the Commission.

(g) The Indian members of the Commission shall receive compensation for each day such members are engaged in the actual performance of duties vested in the Commission at a daily rate not to exceed the daily equivalent of the maximum annual compensation that may be paid to employees of the United States Senate generally. Each such member may be reimbursed for travel expenses, including per diem in lieu of subsistence.

Sec. 2. It shall be the duty of the Commission to make a comprehensive investigation and study of Indian affairs and the scope of such duty shall include, but shall not be limited to—

(1) a study and analysis of the Constitution, treaties, statutes, judicial interpretations, and Executive orders to determine the attributes of the unique relationship between the Federal Government and Indian tribes and the land and other resources they possess;

(2) a review of the policies, practices, and structure of the Federal agencies charged with protecting Indian resources and providing services to Indians: *Provided,* That such review shall include a management study of the Bureau of Indian Affairs utilizing experts from the public and private sector;

(3) an examination of the statutes and procedures for granting Federal recognition and extending services to Indian communities and individuals;

(4) the collection and compilation of data necessary to understand the extent of Indian needs which presently exist or will exist in the near future;

(5) an exploration of the feasibility of alternative elective bodies which could fully represent Indians at the national level of Government to provide Indians with maximum participation in policy formation and

program development;

(6) a consideration of alternative methods to strengthen tribal government so that the tribes might fully represent their members and, at the same time, guarantee the fundamental rights of individual Indians; and

(7) the recommendation of such modification of existing laws, procedures, regulations, policies, and practices as will, in the judgment of the Commission, best serve to carry out the policy and declaration of purposes as set out above

Powers of the Commission

SEC. 3. (a) The Commission or, on authorization of the Commission, any committee of two or more members is authorized, for the purposes of carrying out the provisions of this resolution, to sit and act at such places and times during the sessions, recesses, and adjourned periods of Congress, to require by subpena or otherwise the attendance of such witnesses and the production of such books, papers, and documents, to administer such oaths and affirmations, to take such testimony, to procure such printing and binding, and to make such expenditures, as it deems advisable. The Commission may make such rules respecting its organization and procedures as it deems necessary, except that no recommendation shall be reported from the Commission unless a majority of the Commission assent. Upon the authorization of the Commission subpenas may be issued over the signature of the Chairman of the Commission or of any member designated by him or the Commission, and may be served by such person or persons as may be designated by such Chairman or member. The Chairman of the Commission or any member thereof may administer oaths or affirmations to witnesses.

(b) The provisions of section 192 through 194, inclusive, of title 2, United States Code, shall apply in the case of any failure of any witness to comply with any subpena when summoned under this section.

(c) The Commission is authorized to secure from any department, agency, or instrumentality of the executive branch of the Government any information it deems necessary to carry out its functions under this resolution and each such department, agency, or instrumentality is authorized and directed to furnish such information to the Commission and to conduct such studies and surveys as may be requested by the Chairman or the Vice Chairman when acting as Chairman.

(d) If the Commission requires of any witness or of any Government agency the production of any materials which have theretofore been submitted to a Government agency on a confidential basis, and the confidentiality of those materials is protected by statute, the material so produced shall be held in confidence by the Commission.

Investigating Task Forces

SEC. 4. (a) As soon as practicable after the organization of the Commission, the Commission shall, for the purpose of gathering facts and other information necessary to carry out its responsibilities pursuant to section 2 of this resolution, appoint investigating task forces to be composed of three persons, a majority of whom shall be of Indian descent. Such task forces shall be appointed and directed to make preliminary investigations and studies in the various areas of Indian affairs, including, but not limited to—

200

(1) trust responsibility and Federal-Indian relationship, including treaty review;

(2) tribal government;

(3) Federal administration and structure of Indian affairs;

(4) Federal, State, and tribal jurisdiction;

(5) Indian education;

(6) Indian health;

(7) reservation development;

(8) urban, rural nonreservation, terminated, and nonfederally recognized Indians; and

(9) Indian law revision, consolidation, and codification.

(b)(i) Such task forces shall have such powers and authorities, in carrying out their responsibilities, as shall be conferred upon them by the Commission, except that they shall have no power to issue subpenas or to administer oaths or affirmations: *Provided,* That they may call upon the Commission or any committee thereof, in the Commission's discretion, to assist them in securing any testimony, materials, documents, or other information necessary for their investigation and study.

(ii) The Commission shall require each task force to provide written quarterly reports to the Commission on the progress of the task force and, in the discretion of the Commission, an oral presentation of such report. In order to insure the correlation of data in the final report and recommendations of the Commission, the Director of the Commission shall coordinate the independent efforts of the task force groups.

(c) The Commission may fix the compensation of the members of such task forces at a rate not to exceed the daily equivalent of the highest rate of annual compensation that may be paid to employees of the United States Senate generally.

(d) The Commission shall, pursuant to section 6, insure that the task forces are provided with adequate staff support in addition to that authorized under section 6(a), to carry out the projects assigned to them.

(e) Each task force appointed by the Commission shall, within one year from the date of the appointment of its members, submit to the Commission its final report of investigation and study together with recommendations thereon.

Report of the Commission

SEC. 5. (a) Upon the report of the task forces made pursuant to section 4 hereof, the Commission shall review and compile such reports, together with its independent findings, into a final report. Within six months after the reports of the investigating task forces, the Commission shall submit its final report, together with recommendations thereon, to the President of the Senate and the Speaker of the House of Representatives. The Commission shall cease to exist six months after submission of said final report but not later than June 30, 1977. All records and papers of the Commission shall thereupon be delivered to the Administrator of the General Services Administration for deposit in the Archives of the United States.

(b) Any recommendation of the Commission involving the enactment of legislation shall be referred by the President of the Senate or the Speaker of the House of Representatives to the appropriate standing committee of the Senate and House of Representatives, respectively, and such committees shall make a report thereon to the respective house within two years of such referral.

Commission Staff

SEC. 6. (a) The Commission may by record vote of a majority of the Commission members, appoint a Director of the Commission, a General Counsel, one professional staff member, and three clerical assistants. The Commission shall prescribe the duties and responsibilities of such staff members and fix their compensation at per annum gross rates not in excess of the per annum rates of compensation prescribed for employees of standing committees of the Senate.

(b) In carrying out any of its functions under this resolution, the Commission is authorized to utilize the services, information, facilities, and personnel of the Executive departments and agencies of the Government, and to procure the temporary or intermittent services of experts or consultants or organizations thereof by contract at rates of compensation not in excess of the daily equivalent of the highest per annum rate of compensation that may be paid to employees of the Senate generally.

SEC. 7. There is hereby authorized to be appropriated a sum not to exceed $2,500,000 to carry out the provisions of this resolution. Until such time as funds are appropriated pursuant to this section, salaries and expenses of the Commission shall be paid from the contingent fund of the Senate upon vouchers approved by the Chairman. To the extent that any payments are made from the contingent fund of the Senate prior to the time appropriation is made, such payments shall be chargeable against the maximum amount authorized herein.

Approved January 2, 1975.

Legislative History:

HOUSE REPORT No. 93-1420 accompanying H.J.Res. 1117 (Comm. on Interior and Insular Affairs).
SENATE REPORT No. 93-594 (Comm. on Interior and Insular Affairs).
CONGRESSIONAL RECORD:
    Vol. 119 (1973): Dec. 5, considered and passed Senate.
    Vol. 120 (1974): Nov. 19, considered and passed House, amended, in lieu of H.J.Res. 1117.
            Dec. 16, Senate concurred in House amendment with an amendment.
            Dec. 18, House concurred in Senate amendments to House amendments.

American Indian Policy Review Commission
COMMISSION MEMBERS

James Abourezk, Senator from South Dakota, Democrat. Chairman of the Commission. Born and raised on the Rosebud Indian Reservation. Has been chairman of the Senate Indian Affairs Subcommittee. Currently (1977), chairman of the Senate Select Committee on Indian Affairs.

Lee Metcalf, Senator from Montana, Democrat. Has served in both House of Representatives (1952-1960), and in the Senate (since 1962). Member of the House Indian Affairs Subcommittee.

Mark Hatfield, Senator from Oregon. Republican. Served as governor of Oregon for two terms before being elected to the Senate in 1966.

Lloyd Meeds, House of Representatives from State of Washington, Democrat. Vice chairman of the Commission. Served in the House since 1964. Chairman of the House Indian Affairs Subcommittee. Involved in the passage of the Alaska Native Claims Act, Indian Education Act of 1972, and the Menominee Restoration Act, all of which he supported. Received the National Congress of American Indians Congressional award for his work on the Menominee bill. Wrote a Dissent to the Report of the Commission, and has been opposed to the principal recommendations of the Commission.

Sam Steiger, House of Representatives from Arizona, Republican. Elected 1966 and has served since then. Member of the Interior and Insular Committee. Active in the Hopi-Navajo land dispute.

Sidney R. Yates, House of Representatives from Illinois. Democrat. Served in the House since 1948 except for a two-year period when he was U.S. Representative to the Trusteeship Council of the United Nations. Chairman of the Interior Subcommittee of the House Appropriations Committee, member of the Transportation and Legislative Subcommittee.

Ada Deer, Menominee. Chairwoman of the Menominee Restoration Committee until 1977. Withdrew from law school to lobby for the tribe's restoration to federal recognition. Returned to school upon completion of the work of the Commission. Chosen to serve on the Commission as one who is representative of federally recognized tribes.

Jake Whitecrow, Quapaw/Seneca/Cayuga. Formerly Quapaw tribal chairman, served on their business committee since 1953, director of the Inter-tribal Council of Northeastern Oklahoma, which represents the Eastern Shawnee, Seneca-Cayuga, Wyandot, Quapaw, Ottawa, Peoria, Miami, and Modoc.

John Borbridge, Tlingit of Alaska. He is the head of Sealaska, one of thirteen regional Native corporations established under the Native Alaskan Claims Act. Lobbied for passage of the act while he was president of the Tlingit-Haida Central Committee. Member of the executive committee of the Rural Affairs Commission of Alaska, member of the financial advisory board of the American Indian National Bank.

Louis R. Bruce, Mohawk/Sioux, selected as representative of urban Indians. Served as commissioner of the Bureau of Indian Affairs from 1969 to 1972. Was active in President Truman's Advisory Indian Committee in 1947, the National Tribal Chairmen's Association, and the American Indian National Bank. Has been senior fellow for Antioch Law School. Aided in the formation of the Coalition of Eastern Native Americans. Formerly engaged in the advertising business.

Adolph Dial, Lumbee of North Carolina. Chairman of the American Indian Studies Department of Pembroke State University, member of the American Indian Advisory Council of the Office of Civil Rights, Department of Health, Education and Welfare, and member of the Board of Directors, American Indian Historical Society. Author of *The Only Land I Know: A History of the Lumbee Indians*, published by The Indian Historian Press.

THE CENTRAL STAFF

Ernest L. Stevens, Oneida Tribe of Wisconsin, director. Former president of American Indian Consultants, a business management firm. Formerly director of economic development and community services in the Bureau of Indian Affairs central office, past director of the Inter-Tribal Council of California. Past first vice president of the National Congress of American Indians.

K. Kirke Kickingbird, Kiowa Tribe of Oklahoma, general counsel. Formerly a member of the executive staff, Commissioner of Indian Affairs. Took a leave from his position as executive director of the Institute for the Development of Indian Law to serve on the

Commission's staff. Following the completion of the work, returned to the Institute. Co-author of a study of current American Indian land problems *100 Million Acres*. He is chairman of the American Indian Law Committee of the Federal Bar Association and a member of the board of directors of the American Indian Lawyer's Association. Member of the Oklahoma and American Bar Associations.

Max I. Richtman, professional staff member for the American Indian Policy Review Commission, graduate of Harvard College and the Georgetown University Law Center. Has been an investigator for the Public Defender Service and co-director of the Neighborhood Corps Center, Department of Recreation, Washington, D.C. Has been legislative assistant to Congressman Sidney R. Yates. Member of the District of Columbia Bar Association.

Ray Goetting, Caddo Tribe. Active in National Congress of American Indians, treasurer of that organization at the time of his activity with the Commission. Member of the task force on Federal Administration and Structure of Indian Affairs. Was drawn into the central staff work of the Commission during the time of its tenure. Owner of a business management consulting firm assisting small businesses in New Mexico. Served as a Regional Procedures Analyst, Regional Management Analyst and Regional Administrative officer in the Bureau of Reclamation.

TASK FORCE MEMBERS

#1. Federal Indian Relationships. Hank Adams, 31, chairman (Assiniboine-Sioux). John Echohawk (Pawnee), Douglas Nash (Nez Perce).

#2. Tribal Government. Wilbur Atcitty, 32, chairman (Navajo), Alan Parker (Chippewa-Cree), Jerry Flute (Sisseton-Wahpeton).

#3. Federal Administration: Structure of Indian Affairs. Sam Deloria, 33, chairman (Standing Rock Sioux), Mel Tonasket, (Colville), Raymond Goetting (Caddo).

#4. Federal, State and Tribal Jurisdiction. Sherwin Broadhead, 44, chairman. Judge William Roy Rhodes (Gila River), Matthew Calac (Rincon).

#5. Indian Education. Helen Scheirbeck, 39, chairwoman (Lumbee), Abe Plummer (Navajo), Earl Barlow (Blackfeet).

#6. Indian Health. Dr. Everett Rhoades, chairman (Kiowa), Luana Reyes (Colville), Lillian McGarvey (Aleut).

#7. Reservation and Resource Development and Protection. Peter MacDonald, 46, chairman (Navajo). Ken Smith (Warm Springs), Phillip Martin (Mississippi Choctaw).

#8. Urban and Rural Non-Reservation Indians. Al Elgin, 43, chairman (Pomo). Gail Thorpe (Sac and Fox), Edward Mouss (Creek-Cherokee).

#9. Indian Law Revision, Consolidation and Codification. Peter Taylor, 37, chairman. Yvonne Knight (Ponca), Browning Pipestem (Otoe-Missoura, Osage).

#10. Terminated and Non-Federally Recognized Indians. Jo Jo Hunt, 25 chairwoman (Lumbee). John Stevens (Passamaquoddy), Robert Bojorcas (Klamath).

#11. Alcohol and Drug Abuse. Reuben Snake, 38, chairman (Winnebago-Sioux). Robert Moore (Seneca), George Hawkins (Southern Cheyenne).

Members of the Task Forces were chosen by the full Commission. A reading of the Commission's minutes reveals that there was considerable jockeying back and forth in the naming of individuals and chairmen of the task forces. Commission members who were congressmen usually had their favorite nominees, and often fought for them insistently. Commission members who were Indian also had their favorite choices, each proposing members of his/her tribe or state.

While it cannot be said that the choices were made on a plainly objective basis, in cases where a task force member failed to fulfill his/her obligations, the work was done despite these difficulties. In such cases the central office took over the work assigned to the individuals. Like all task forces in such projects, some performed well; others performed poorly.

It should be observed that it is due solely to the organizational skill of Mr. Ernest Stevens and his staff that the work was finally completed. Stevens, hard headed and desperate in the end, for completion of the task force reports, chose people who could be depended upon to complete the work. While this may be true in cases of other similar projects, it was and will be used as an example for future investigations in which nominations and selections come as the result of a political process. There are many highly skilled people in the Indian world who could have made remarkable contributions to the Commission. Political considerations overruled their selection.

Task force members served for one year; either from July, 1975 to July, 1976, or from August, 1975 to August, 1976.

The time period allowed for the completion of the mandate given to the Commission by the Congress was incredibly short. In such a short time (two years for the entire project), much was accomplished, and a massive quantity of data was gathered which will be the source for activities, both scholarly and pragmatic, for many years to come.

CHRONOLOGY OF INDIAN TREATIES

1778: Treaty with the Delawares
1784: Treaty with the Six Nations
1785: Treaty with the Wyandot, Delaware, Chippewa and Ottawa
      Treaty with the Cherokee
1786: Treaty with the Choctaw
      Treaty with the Chickasaw
      Treaty with the Shawnee
1789: Treaty with the Wyandot, Delaware, Ottawa, Chippewa, Potta-
      watomi, and Sac Nations
      Treaty with the Six Nations
1790: Treaty with the Creeks
1791: Treaty with the Cherokee
1794: Treaty with the Cherokee
      Treaty with the Six Nations
      Treaty with the Oneida, Tuscarora, and Stockbridge
1795: Treaty with the Wyandot, Delawares, Shawanoes, Ottawas, Chip-
      pewa, Pottawatomi, Miami, Eel-River, Weea, Kickapoo, Pian-
      kashaw, and Kaskaskia
1796: Treaty with the Seven Nations of Canada
      Treaty with the Creeks
1797: Treaty with the Mohawk
1798: Treaty with the Cherokee
1801: Treaty with the Chickasaw
      Treaty with the Choctaw
1802: Treaty with the Creek
      Treaty with the Seneca
      Treaty with the Seneca
      Treaty with the Choctaw
1803: Treaty with the Delaware, Shawanoes, Pottawatomi, Miamis, Eel
      River, Weea, Kickapoo, Piankashaw, and Kaskaskia
      Treaty with the Eel River, Wyandot, Piankashaw, Kaskaskia,
      Kickapoo
      Treaty with the Kaskaskia
      Treaty with the Choctaw
1804: Treaty with the Delaware
      Treaty with the Piankashaw
      Treaty with the Cherokee
      Treaty with the Sauk and Foxes
1805: Treaty with the Wyandot, Ottawa, Chippewa, Munsee and Dela-
      ware, Shawanee, Pottawatomi
      Treaty with the Chickasaw
      Treaty with the Delaware, Pottawatomi, Miami, Eel River, Weea
      Treaty with the Cherokee
      Treaty with the Cherokee
      Treaty with the Creeks
      Treaty with the Choctaw

Treaty with the Piankashaw
1806: Treaty with the Cherokee
1807: Treaty with the Ottawa, Chippewa, Wyandot, Pottawatomi
1808: Treaty with the Osage
Treaty with the Chippewa, Ottawa, Pottawatomi, Wyandot, Shawano
1809: Treaty with the Delaware, Pottawatomi, Miami, and Eel River
Supplementary treaty with the Miami and Eel River
Treaty with the Weea
Treaty with the Kickapoo
1814: Treaty with the Wyandot, Delaware, Shawano, Seneca, and Miami
Treaty with the Creeks
1815: Treaty with the Pottawatomi
Treaty with the Piankashaw
Treaty with the Teton
Treaty with the Sioux of the Lakes
Treaty with the Sioux of St. Peter's River
Treaty with the Yankton Sioux
Treaty with the Makah
Treaty with the Kickapoo
Treaty with the Wyandot, Delaware, Seneca, Shawano, Miami, Chippewa, Ottawa, and Pottawatomi
Treaty with the Osage
Treaty with the Sauk
Treaty with the Fox
Treaty with the Iowa
Treaty with the Kansa
1816: Treaty with the Cherokee
Treaty with the Cherokee
Treaty with the Sauk
Treaty with the Sioux ("representing eight bands of the Sioux, composing the three tribes called the Sioux of the Leaf, the Sioux of the Broad Leaf and the Sioux who shoot in the Pine Tops")
Treaty with the Winnebago
Treaty with the Weea and Kickapoo
Treaty with the Ottawa, Chippewa, Pottawatomi
Treaty with the Cherokee
Treaty with the Chickasaw
Treaty with the Choctaw
1817: Treaty with the Menominee
Treaty with the Oto
Treaty with the Ponca
Treaty with the Cherokee
Treaty with the Wyandot, Seneca, Delaware, Shawano, Pottawatomi, Ottawa, and Chippewa
1818: Treaty with the Creeks
Treaty with the Grand Pawnee
Treaty with the Noisy Pawnee
Treaty with the Pawnee Republic
Treaty with the Pawnee Marhar
Treaty with the Quapaw
Treaty with the Wyandot, Seneca, Shawnee, and Ottawa, "being

209

supplementary to the treaty concluded by the said tribes, and the
Delaware, Pottawatomi, and Chippewa.''
Treaty with the Wyandot
Treaty with the Peoria, Kaskaskia, Mitchigamia, Cahokia, and
Tamarois "tribes of the Illinois nation of Indians.''
Treaty with the Osage
Treaty with the Pottawatomi
Treaty with the Weea
Treaty with the Delawares
Treaty with the Miami
Treaty with the Chickasaw
1819: Treaty with the Cherokee
Treaty with the Kickapoo
Treaty with the Kickapoo
Treaty with the Chippewa
1820: Treaty with the Chippewa
Treaty with the Ottawa and Chippewa
Treaty with the Kickapoo
Treaty with the Weea
Treaty with the Kickapoo of the Vermillion
Treaty with the Choctaw
1821: Treaty with the Creeks
Treaty with the Creeks
Treaty with the Ottawa, Chippewa, and Pottawatomi
1822: Treaty with the Osage
Treaty with the Sauk and Foxes
1823: Treaty with the Florida Tribes of Indians
1824: Treaty with the Sauk and Foxes
Treaty with the Iowa
Treaty with the Quapaw
1825: Treaty with the Choctaw
Treaty with the Creeks
Treaty with the Osage
Treaty with the Kansa
Treaty with the Ponca
Treaty with the Teton, Yancton, Yanctonies of the Sioux tribe
Treaty with the Sioux and Oglalla bands "of Sioux Indians"
Treaty with the Cheyenne
Treaty with the Hunkpapa Band of the Sioux Tribe
Treaty with the Arikara
Treaty with the Belantse-Etoa or Minitaree Tribe
Treaty with the Mandan
Treaty with the Crow
Treaty with the Great and Little Osage
Treaty with the Kansa
Treaty with the Sioux, Chippewa, Sac and Fox, Menominee, Iowa,
Winnebago, "and a portion of the Ottawa, Chippewa and Pot-
tawatomi tribes"
Treaty with the Oto and Missouri
Treaty with the Pawnee
Treaty with the Makah
Treaty with the Shawnee

1826: Treaty with the Creeks
Treaty with the Chippewa
Treaty with the Pottawatomi
Treaty with the Miami
1827: Treaty with the Chippewa, Menominee and Winnebago
Treaty with the Pottawatomi
Treaty with the Creeks
1828: Treaty with the Miami
Treaty with the Western Cherokee (west of the Mississippi)
Treaty with the Winnebago, Pottawatomi, Chippewa, Ottawa
Treaty with the Pottawatomi
1829: Treaty with the Chippewa, Ottawa, Pottawatomi
Treaty with the Winnebago
Treaty with the Delawares
Treaty with the Delawares
1830: Treaty with the Confederated tribes of the Sauk and Fox, Medawah-Kanton, Wahpakoota, Wahpeton and Sissetong Bands or tribes of the Sioux; Omaha, Iowa, Ottoe, and Missouria

Treaty with the Choctaw
1831: Treaty with the Menominee
Treaty with the Menominee
Treaty with the Seneca
Treaty with the Seneca, and Shawnee
Treaty with the Shawnee
Treaty with the Ottawa
1832: Treaty with the Wyandot
Treaty with the Creeks
Treaty with the Seminole
Treaty with the Winnebago
Treaty with the Sauk and Foxes
Treaty with the Appalachicola Band
Treaty with the Pottawatomi
Treaty with the Chickasaw
Treaty with the Chickasaw
Treaty with the Kickapoo
Treaty with the Pottawatomi
Treaty with the Shawnee and Delawares
Treaty with the Pottawatome
Treaty with the Kaskaskia and Peoria tribes, "which, with the Michigamia, Cahokia and Tamarois bands, now united with the two first named tribes, formerly composed the Illinois Nation of Indians"
Treaty with the Menominee
Treaty with the Piankashae and Wea
Treaty with the Seneca and Shawnee
1833: Treaty with the Western Cherokee
Treaty with the Creeks
Treaty with the Ottawa
Treaty with the Seminole
Treaty with the Quapaw
Treaty with the Appalachia Band

Treaty with the Oto and Missouri
Treaty with the Chippewa, Ottawa and Pottawatomi
Treaty with the Pawnee
1834: Treaty with the Chickasaw
Treaty with the Miami
Treaty with the Pottawatomi
Treaty with the Pottawatomi
Treaty with the Pottawatomi
Treaty with the Pottawatomi
1835: Treaty with the Caddo
Treaty with the Comanche and Witchetaw "and their associated bands" and between "these nations or tribes, and the Cherokee Muscogee, Choctaw, Osage, Seneca and Quapaw nations or tribes of Indians"
Treaty with the Cherokee at New Echota, Georgia
1836: Treaty with the Pottawatomi
Treaty with the Ottawa and Chippewa
Treaty with the Pottawatomi
Treaty with the Pottawatomi
Treaty with the Pottawatomi
Treaty with the Pottawatomi
Treaty with the Wyandot
Treaty with the Chippewa
Treaty with the Pottawatomi
Treaty with the Menominee
Treaty with the Sioux of Wahashaw's tribe of Indians.
Treaty with the Iowa, and bands of Sauks and Foxes of the Missouri "residing west of the state of Missouri"
Treaty with the Pottawatomi
Treaty with the Pottawatomi
Treaty with the Pottawatomi
Treaty with the Sauk and Fox
Treaty with the Sauk and Fox
Treaty with the Sauk and Fox
Treaty with the Oto, Missouri, Omaha, Yankton and Santee bands of Sioux
Treaty with the Sioux
1837: Treaty with the Chippewa
Treaty with the Choctaw and Chickasaw
Treaty with the Pottawatomi
Treaty with the Kiowa, Katoka and Tawakaro
Treaty with the Chippewa
Treaty with the Sioux
Treaty with the Sauk and Fox
Treaty with the Yankton Sioux
Treaty with the Sauk and Fox
Treaty with the Winnebago
Treaty with the Iowa
Treaty with the Chippewa
Treaty with the New York Indians (Six Nations)
1838: Treaty with the Chippewa

212

Treaty with the Oneida
Treaty with the Iowa
Treaty with the Miami
Treaty with the Creeks
1839: Treaty with the Osage
Treaty with the Chippewa
Treaty with the Stockbridge and Munsee
1840: Treaty with the Miami
1842: Treaty with the Wyandot
Treaty with the Seneca
Treaty with the Chippewa
Treaty with the Sauk and Fox
1845: Treaty with the Creeks and Seminole
1846: Treaty with the Kansa
Treaty with the Comanche, Aionai, Anadarko, Caddo, Lepan, Longwha, Keechy, Tahwacarro, Wichita, and Waco "and their associate bands."
Treaty with the Pottawatomi Nation
Treaty with the Cherokee
Treaty with the Winnebago
1847: Treaty with the Chippewa of the Mississippi and Lake Superior
Treaty with the Pillager Band of Chippewa Indians
1848: Treaty with the Pawnee Four Confederated Bands: Grand Pawnee, Pawnee Loups, Pawnee Republicans, and Pawnee Tappage
Treaty with the Menominee
Treaty with the Stockbridge
1849: Treaty with the Navaho
Treaty with the Utah
1850: Treaty with the Wyandot
1851: Treaty with the Sioux, Sisseton and Wahpeton Bands
Treaty with the Sioux, Mdewakanton and Wahpakoota Bands
1851: Treaty of Fort Laramie With the "Indian nations, residing south of the Missouri River, east of the Rocky Mountains, and north of the lines of Texas and New Mexico, viz., the Sioux or Dakotahs, Cheyennes, Arrapahoes, Crows, Assinaboines Gros Ventre Mandans, and Arrickaras.
1852: Treaty with the Chickasaw
Treaty with the Apache
1853: Treaty with the Comanche, Kiowa and Apache
Treaty with the Rogue River
Treaty with the Umpqua-Cow Creek Band
1854: Treaty with the Oto and Missouri
Treaty with the Omaha
Treaty with the Delawares
Treaty with the Shawnee
Treaty with the Menominee
Treaty with the Iowa
Treaty with the Sauk and Fox of Missouri
Treaty with the Kickapoo
Treaty with the Kaskaskia, Peoria, Piankashaw and Wea
Treaty with the Miami

Treaty with the Creeks (supplementary to treaty at Fort Gibson on Nov. 23, 1838).

Treaty with the Chippewa

Treaty with the Choctaw and Chickasaw

Treaty with the Rogue River

Treaty with bands of the Chasta, the Scotons, and the Umpquas

Treaty with the Umpqua and Kalapuya

Treaty with the Confederated Oto and Missouri

Treaty with the Nisqualli, Puyallup, Steilacoom, Squawskin, S'Homamish, Stehchass, T'Peeksin, Squiaitl, and Sahehwamish

1855: Treaty with the Kalapuya, Yam Hill Band, Chelukimauke Band, Chepenepho or Marysville Band, Chemepho or Maddy Band, Chlamela or Long Tom Band (all of the Kalapuyas), Molalla Band, Winnefelly and Mohawk Bands, Tekopa Band, Chafan Band, Wahlalla Band of Tumwaters, Clackamas Band, Clowwewalla or Willamette Tumwater Bank, and the Santiam Band

1855: Treaty with the Dwamish, Suquamish, Sktahlmish, Sahmamish, Smalhkamish, Skopeahmish, Stkahmish, Snoqualmoo, Skaiwhamish, N'Quentlmamish, Sktahlejum, Staluckwhamish, Snohomish, Skagit, Kikiallus, Swinamish, Squinahmish, Sahkumehu, Noowhaha, Nookwachahmish, Meeseequaquilch, Chobahahbish, "and other allied and subordinante tribes and bands of Indians occupying certain lands situated in said Territory of Washington."

Treaty with the S'Klallam

Treaty with the Wyandot

Treaty with the Makah

Treaty with the Chippewa

Treaty with the Winnebago

Treaty with the Walla Walla, Cayuse, and Umatilla tribes, "and bands of Indians, occupying lands partly in Washington and partly in Oregon Territories, and who, for the purposes of this treaty, are to be regarded as one nation acting for and in behalf of their respective bands and tribes . . ."

Treaty with the Yakima and delegates of the "Palouse, Pisquouse, Wenatchapam, K'likitat, K'linquit, Kowwassayee, Liaywas, Skinpah, Wisham, Shyiks, Ochechotes, Kahmiltpah, and Seapcut, "confederated tribes and bands of Indians, occupying lands hereinafter bounded and described and lying in Washington Territory, who for the purposes of this treaty are to be considered as one nation, under the name of Yakama."

Treaty with the Nez Perces, "occupying lands lying partly in Oregon and partly in Washington Territories."

Treaty with the Choctaw and Chickasaw

Treaty with the tribes of Middle Oregon (mainly Walla Walla and Wascoe Bands).

Treaty with the Quinault and Quileute

Treaty with the Flatheads, Kootenay, and Upper Pend d'Oreilles "It being understood and agreed that the said confederated tribes do hereby constitute a nation, under the name of the Flathead Nation.

Treaty with the Ottawa and Chippewa of Michigan

Treaty with the Chippewa of Saginaw and "that portion of the band of Chippewa Indians of Swan Creek and Black River parties to the Treaty of May 9, 1836 and now remaining in the State of Michigan."

Treaty with the Blackfeet

Treaty with the Molala

1856: Treaty with the Stockbridge and Munsee

Treaty with the Menominee

Treaty with the Creeks, and Seminoles

1857: Treaty with the Pawnee

Treaty with the Seneca, Tonawanda Band

1858: Treaty with the Ponca

Treaty with the Yankton Sioux

Treaty with the Sioux "made and concluded at the city of Washington."

Treaty with the Sioux "made and concluded at the city of Washington."

1859: Treaty with the Winnebago

Treaty with the Chippewa (Swan Creek and Black River), and the Munsee "or Christian Indians."

Treaty with the Sauk and Fox.

Treaty with the Kansa.

1860: Treaty with the Delawares, ("at Sarcoxieville, Delaware Reservation).

1861: Treaty with the Arapaho and Cheyenne.

Treaty with the Sauk and Fox of Missouri.

1861: Treaty with the Delawares, "concluded at Leavenworth City, Kansas."

Treaty with the Pottawatomi

1862: Treaty with the Kansa.

Treaty with the Ottawa of Blanchard's Fork and Roche de Boeuf.

Treaty with the Kickapoo.

1863: Treaty with the Chippewa of the Mississippi and the Pillager and Lake Winnibigoshish Bands.

Treaty with the Nez Perces.

Treaty with the Eastern Shoshoni.

Treaty with the Northern Bands of Shoshoni.

Treaty with the Western Shoshoni.

Treaty with the Chippewa, Red Lake and Pembina Bands.

Treaty with the Utah, Tabeguache Band.

Treaty with the Shoshoni-Goship.

1864: Treaty with the Chippewa, Red Lake and Pembina Bands.

Treaty with the Chippewa, Mississippi, and Pillager and Lake Winnibigoshish Bands.

Treaty with the Klamath, Modoc, and Snake Tribes.

Treaty with the Chippewa of Saginaw, Swan Creek and Black River.

1865: Treaty with the Omaha.

Treaty with the Winnebago

Treaty with the Ponca.

Treaty with the Snake.

Treaty with the Osage.

Treaty with the Sioux, Miniconjou Band.
Treaty with the Sioux, Lower Brule Band.
Treaty with the Cheyenne and Arapaho.
Treaty with the Apache, Cheyenne, and Arapaho.
Treaty with the Comanche and Kiowa.
Treaty with the Sioux, Two Kettle Band.
Treaty with the Blackfeet Sioux.
Treaty with the Sioux, Sans Arcs Band.
Treaty with the Sioux, Hunkpapa Band.
Treaty with the Sioux, Yanktonai Band.
Treaty with the Sioux, Upper Yanktonai Band.
Treaty with the Sioux, Oglala Band.
Treaty with the Middle Oregon Tribes.
1866: Treaty with the Seminole.
Treaty with the Pottawatomi.
Treaty with the Chippewa, Bois Fort Band.
Treaty with the Choctaw and Chickasaw.
Treaty with the Creeks.
Treaty with the Delawares.
Treaty with the Cherokee.
1867: Treaty with the Sauk and Fox.
Treaty with the Sioux, Sisseton and Wahpeton Bands.
Treaty with the Seneca, Mixed Seneca and Shawnee, Quapaw, Con-
federated Peoria, Kaskaskia, Weas and Piankashaw, Ottawas of
Blanchard's Fork and Roche de Boeuf, and "certain Wyandots."
Treaty with the Pottawatomi.
Treaty with the Chippewa of the Mississippi.
Treaty with the Kiowa and Comanche.
Treaty with the Kiowa, Comanche and Apache.
Treaty with the Cheyenne and Arapaho.
1868: Treaty with the Ute.
Treaty with the Cherokee.
Treaty with the Sioux: Brule, Oglala, Miniconjoy, Yanktonai,
Hunkpapa, Blackfeet, Cuthead, Two Kettle, Sans Arcs, and San-
tee; and with the Arapaho.
Treaty with the Crows.
Treaty with the Northern Cheyenne and Northern Arapaho.
Treaty with the Navaho.
Treaty with the Eastern Band Shoshoni and Bannock.
Treaty with the Nez Perces.

AGREEMENTS

These agreements have a strange history. Some are contracts between the tribes and individuals. Some are unratified treaties which, for some reason, have attained the status of "agreements." And some have been ratified, but never proclaimed by the president.

1792: An Agreement with the Five Nations of Indians, April 23. (American State Papers, Indian Affairs, Vol 1. p. 232.) (To expend, annually for the Seneca, $1,500, in purchasing for them clothing, domestic animals and implements of husbandry, and for encouraging useful artificers to reside in their villages.)

1797: Agreement with the Seneca. A contract entered into, under sanction of the United States of America, between Robert Morris and the Seneca Nation of Indians. (Sept. 15, 1797, 7 Stat. 601.) For the sum of $100,000. the Senecas "sold to Robert Morris, and to his heirs and assigns forever, all their right to all that tract of land . . .) described in the agreement. This gave Robert Morris the beginnings of a huge fortune.

1805: Treaty with the Sioux. Ratified by the Senate Apr. 16, 1808, but never proclaimed by the president. (Laws Relating to Indian Affairs, 1883, p. 316.) While the President did not proclaim the treaty, more than 25 years later the War Department speaks of the cessions of land described in the treaty as an accomplished fact. Under this treaty, which was honored by the Sioux (under duress) but dishonored by the United States, the "Sioux Nation grants unto the United States for the purpose of establishment of military posts, nine miles square at the mouth of the river St. Croix, also from below the confluence of the Mississippi and St. Peters, up the Mississippi, to include the falls of St. Anthony, extending nine miles on each side of the river. That the Sioux Nation grants to the United States, the full sovereignty and power over said districts forever, without any let or hindrance whatsoever." In consideration of the grants, the United States agreed to pay to the Sioux $2,000. The United States promised, however, "to permit the Sioux to pass, repass, hunt or make other uses of the said districts as they have formerly done, without any other exception, but those specified in article first."

1818: Agreement with the Piankeshaw. A contracted between Governor Thomas Posey, superintendent of Indian affairs, and Chekommia or Big River, principal chief of the Piankeshaws. Unratified. (Indian Office Compilation of Treaties, 1837, p. 230.) By this Agreement, the chief ceded to the United States a tract of land two miles square, but the Agreement granted to the tribe a tract of land two square miles, "the fee of which is to remain with them forever."

1823: Agreement with the Seneca. Unratified. (Indian Office Compilation of Treaties, 1837, p. 305.) By this Agreement, the Senecas are said to have ceded to John Greig and Henry B. Gibson, "forever," a tract of land "commonly called and known by the name of the Gordeaux Reservation, in the counties of Livingston and Genesee in the State of New York, for $4,286.

1825: Agreement with the Creeks, at Broken Arrow, Creek Nation. This Agreement attempted to pardon "all of the late General McIntosh's party who have opposed the Laws of the Nation," returning their property to them, and property lost, was to have been restored when available. This Agreement was not ratified; (Indian Office, General Files, Creek, 1825-26, E.P. Gaines).

1830: Treaty with the Chickasaw. Unratified. (Indian Office, box 1, Treaties, 1802-1853.)

1835: Agreement with the Cherokee. Unratified. (Indian office, box 1, Treaties, 1802-1853.)

1843: Agreement with the Delawares and Wyandot. Ratified July 25, 1848. Granted and quitclaimed "forever" to the Wyandot Nation, three sections of land, containing six hundred and forty acres each."

1853: Agreement with the Rogue River. Unratified. (Indian office, Oregon, 1844-1858, Ore. Supt. L. 323.)

1865: Agreement with the Cherokee and other tribes in the Indian Territory. Unratified. (With the Cherokee, Creeks, Choctaws, Chickasaws, Osages, Seminoles, Senecas, Senecas and Shawnees, and Quapaws. Found in the Report of the Commissioner of Indian Affairs for 1865, pp 312-353 for full report.

1866: Agreement at Fort Berthold. Unratified. (Indian office, Treaties, Box 3, 1864-1866.)

1872: Agreement with the Sisseton and Wahpeton Bands of Sioux Indians. Unratified. (Indian office, Sisseton, 8,247, 1872.)

1873: Amended Agreement with certain Sioux Indians. Ratified by acts of Feb. 14, 1873 (17 Stat. 456, and June 24, 1874, 18 Stat. 167.) Provides for the payment of $10,000 per annum for a period of ten years, to the tribes, in payment for lands previously ceded.

1880: Agreement with the Crows. Unratified. (Indian office Montana C. 839, 1880)

1882-1883: Agreement with the Sioux of Various Tribes. Unratified. (See H.R. Ex. Doc. 68, 47th Congress, 2nd session.)

1883: Agreement with the Columbia and Colville. Ratified July 4, 1884 (23 Stat. 79, Vol. 1, p. 224). Also see Report of Commissioner of Indian Affairs for 1882, p. 1xx. Tonasket of the Colville asked for a saw and grist mill, a boarding school for 100 pupils, and a physician, and $100 for himself each year. Sarsarpkin of the Columbia Reservation asked to be allowed to remain on the Columbia Reservation with his people, and to be protected in their rights as settlers, and more land for farming, or to be allowed to move on to the Colville Reservation. Chief Moses of the Columbia to receive a sufficient number of cows to furnish each member of his band with two cows, and to give Moses $1,000 to erect a home for himself. Also asked for farming equipment.

MAJOR LAWS WHICH
APPLY TO INDIANS
OF ALL TRIBES

(From Felix Cohen, *Handbook of Federal Indian Law*, and the Report of Assistant Secretary of Interior for Indian Affairs Forrest Gerard, May, 1977.)

August 7, 1789 (1 Stat. 49). Established Department of War with responsibility for such other matters . . . as the President of the United States shall assign to the said department . . . relative to Indian affairs.''

July 22, 1790 (1 Stat. 137). Indian Trade and Intercourse Act. First in a series of four such acts, regulating "trade and intercourse with Indian tribes." Amendments to this act on March 1, 1793 (1 Stat. 329); May 19, 1796 (1 Stat. 469); and March 3, 1799 (1 Stat. 743).

April 18, 1796 (1 Stat. 452). Established government trading houses with Indians, under control of the President.

May 18, 1796 (1 Stat. 469 (see above). Contained first provision regarding punishment of tribal Indians living in peace with the U.S. for crimes committed on nonIndian lands.

March 30, 1802 (2 Stat. 139). Permanent Trade and Intercourse Act. Incorporated the first four temporary Intercourse acts (see above) and restricted liquor consumption among tribes.

March 3, 1817 (3 Stat. 383). Gave Federal courts jurisdiction over Indians and nonIndians in Indian territory, specifically excluding crimes committed by one Indian against another.

March 3, 1819 (3 Stat. 516). Made "provision for the civilization of the Indian tribes adjoining the frontier settlements," including appropriation of funds to this end.

May 28, 1830 (4 Stat. 411). Indian Removal Act. Established policy of exchanging federal lands west of the Mississippi for other lands occupied by Indian tribes in the eastern portion of the U.S.

July 9, 1832 (4 Stat. 564). Established Commissioner of Indian Affairs position under the Secretary of War.

June 30, 1834 (4 Stat. 735). Provided for organization of the Department of Indian Affairs within the Department of War.

June 30, 1834 (4 Stat. 729). Indian Trade and Intercourse Act. Redefined boundaries of Indian lands; ended passport requirements for nonIndian Americans; summarized previous criminal and trader laws; proclaimed that crimes of Indians against Indians on Indian land were not within federal jurisdiction.

March 3, 1849 (9 Stat. 395). Established the Department of Interior and placed the Commissioner of Indian Affairs position thereunder, as head of the Bureau of Indian Affairs.

March 27, 1854 (10 Stat. 269) Extended tribal jurisdiction over crimes committed by Indians against Indians on Indian lands.

1862, the Homestead Act brings vast numbers of settlers into Public Domain land, to claim 160 acres of land for each head of the family. Many settled on land belonging to Indian tribes, and were certified after the required conditions were met, as owners in fee simple to the illegally taken land. In 1875, the Homestead Act was amended to allow Indians the same rights, but very few Indians availed themselves of the opportunity, believing the land was theirs in the first place.

March 2, 1871 (16 Stat. 544, 566). Ended treaty-making by declaring that Indian nations and tribes within U.S. Territory would no longer be recognized as those with whom treaties could be made, at the same time declaring that treaties made until then would be recognized and would remain in effect.

March 3, 1883 (22 Stat. 582, 585). First general statute regarding Indian funds; released through the Treasury all pasturage, mining and other "proceeds of labor " funds, to be used by the tribes, with approval of the Interior Department.

March 3, 1885 (23 Stat. 362, 385). Extended federal court jurisdiction over Indian lands to seven major crimes.

February 8, 1887 (24 Stat. 388). General Allotment Act (Dawes Act). Authorized the individual allotment of reservation lands to tribal members and conveyed citizenship upon the allottee upon termination of the trust status of the land, or to any Indian who voluntarily established residence apart from his tribe and adopted the "habits of civilized life." Rationale behind this policy was that by encouraging individual Indians to farm, instead of following the ancient communal ways of the tribe, they would more easily assimilate into American society. (Backed by land seekers and reformers.)

March 3, 1891 (26 Stat. 851). Depredations claims for damages sustained by acts of Indian individuals or bands of tribes living at peace with the U.S., sent to the Claims Courts and settled.

July 13, 1892 (27 Stat. 120). Authorized Commissioner of Indian Affairs to make and enforce regulations to secure the attendance of Indian children "at schools established and maintained for their benefit."

August 13, 1894 (28 Stat. 286, 313). Required Interior Department to hire Indians in the Indian service "as practicable."

November 2, 1921 (42 Stat. 208). Snyder Act. Authorized permanent appropriations and expenditures for the administration of Indian affairs.

June 2, 1924 (43 Stat. 253). Conferred U.S. citizenship on all non-citizen Indians born within the territorial limits of the U.S.

February 29, 1929 (45 Stat. 1185). Directed the Secretary of Interior to permit agents and employees of any State to enter on Indian lands to inspect health and educational conditions, to enforce sanitation and quarantine regulations, or to enforce compulsory school attendance of Indian pupils as provided by State law.

April 16, 1934 (48 Stat. 596). Johnson O'Malley Act. Provided for Federal-State cooperation in Indian affairs (education in particular) by means of Federal contracts with State governments, or political subdivisions thereof, for the operation of Federal Indian programs.

June 18, 1934 (48 Stat. 984). Indian Reorganization Act. Ended allotments; ended practice of terminating trust periods of restricted alienability of Indian lands; appropriated two million dollars a year for the purpose of lands for tribes in order to augment the diminished Indian land base; directed the Secretary of the Interior to issue conservation regulations to prevent erosion, deforestation and over-grazing of Indian lands; authorized annual appropriations not to exceed $25,000 for educational loans; provided that qualified Indians are accorded employment preferences in the Bureau of Indian Affairs, et. al. This in effect laid the foundation of a new policy toward Indians, much of which is still in effect.

August 13, 1946 (60 Stat. 1049). Established Indian Claims Commission to hear and settle remaining Indian land claims (The Act was extended through 1977).

August 1, 1953. House Concurrent Resolution 108. Set forth the sense of Congress that specified tribes should be freed from "Federal supervision and control" in accord with the policy of making "as rapidly as possible," Indians "within the territorial limits of the United States subject to the same laws and entitled to the same privileges and responsibilities as are applicable to other citizens of the United States . . . ." This became known as the policy of "termination."

August 15, 1953 (67 Stat. 588) ("Public Law 280"). Transferred specified jurisdiction (criminal and civil) to five States and gave other the option of assuming such jurisdiction over Federal Indian reservations within their borders.

221

June 17, 1954 (68 Stat. 250). Menominee tribe terminated. Other tribes terminated by other statutes. While these are specific statutes applying to specific tribes, they reflected the national policy of termination as expressed in H. Con. Res. 108.

August 5, 1954 (68 Stat. 674). Transferred Federal responsibility for Indian health from BIA to HEW.

April 11, 1968 (82 Stat. 77). Applied certain of the rights outlined in the Bill of Rights, or similar rights, to tribal self-government; authorized a model code of justice for Indian offenses on Indian reservations, and conferred jurisdiction over criminal and civil actions to States only with the consent of the tribe (thus amending Public Law 280, above, which did not require such consent).

June 23, 1972 (86 Stat. 334). Indian Education Act (Title IV of Higher Education Act). Authorized expanded Elementary and Secondary Education Act and impact aid programs to assure that the portions of these funds affecting Indians be administered with community control or in Indian-controlled schools.

December 22, 1973 (87 Stat. 770). Menominee Restoration Act. Effectively repudiated termination as a national policy.

January 4, 1975 (88 Stat. 2203). Indian Self-Determination and Educational Assistance Act. Clarified and expanded the authority of the Secretary of the Interior and the Secretary of Health, Education and Welfare (in the matters of Indian health service) to contract with Indian tribes and tribal organizations to operate Federally-funded programs on reservations.

January 2, 1975. The American Indian Policy Review Commission is established, with a mandate to review past performance of the U.S. Government in Indian affairs and to recommend changes.

* * *

There are 389 treaties made by the Indian nations and the United States, and an estimated 200 Agreements. Statutes affecting all Indian tribes may be found up to the year 1938, in *Handbook of Federal Indian Law*, appendix.

Felix Cohen, in the *Handbook* (Page iii of Appendix) estimated that, from the time of the first treaty with the Delawares in 1787, to the year 1939, there were 3,264 statutes passed, 389 treaties, 1,725 reported cases at court, 523 Opinions of the Attorney General, 838 Interior Department Rulings, 141 Tribal constitutions, 112 Tribal charters, and 301 Congressional Reports. Adding some 629 legal texts and articles, the total amount of items used in reference in the Handbook, amounted to 8,922.

Added to this, would be similar types of items dating from the year 1939, to the date of this publication, 1977, a span of 38 years, in which an educated guess would add at least as many thousands of Interior Department rulings, cases at court, Bureau of Indian Affairs regulations, and tribal constitutions and charters.

This is a formidable body of regulatory documentation. Viewing the broad panorama of regulations, statutes and judicial decisions by which Indian tribes have been and are now ruled in every aspect of their lives, it illustrates the confusion inherent in Federal-Indian relations as reflected in this body of regulatory material.

Quite often, the basic doctrine of the Federal-Indian relationship appears to be lost within a jungle of regulations and statutes. That such a basic doctrine does indeed exist and must persist is without question.

* * *

For purposes of reference, below is a sampling of laws and statutes referring to specific tribes and groups whose status is exceptional, owing to historical circumstances. These include, among others, the Pueblos of New Mexico, the Natives of Alaska, the Indians of New York, and the Indians of Oklahoma. Some of the laws relating to these Indian groups and tribes are listed below.

Pueblos of New Mexico: The special body of laws dealing with the Pueblos derives from the historical fact that these Indians became U.S. citizens following cession of New Mexico to the U.S. by provision of the Treaty of Guadalupe Hidalgo and had special land claims predating that treaty which derived from the Spanish and Mexican governments. The Pueblos never made a treaty with any foreign country. Their position has been challenged, but they retain their sovereignty and stature as nations with recognized governments to this day.

July 22, 1854 (10 Stat. 308). Provided for appointment of a surveyor general for New Mexico who was to ascertain the origin, nature, character and extent of all claims to lands under the laws and customs of Spain and Mexico, before the annexation of that territory by the United States.

December 27, 1858 (11Stat. 374). Acted favorably upon report of the surveyor general for Territory of New Mexico, confirming pueblo land claims of specified pueblos.

July 15, 1870 (16 Stat. 335, 357). Appropriated a sum of money "to be expended in establishing schools among Pueblo Indians."

May 17, 1882 (22 Stat. 68). Contained provision embodying first assumption of federal responsibility for "civilizing" the Pueblo Indians. Included funds to pay teachers, purchase of seeds and agricultural implements, and construction of irrigation ditches.

July 1, 1898. (30 Stat. 571, 594). Established the post of special attorney for Pueblo Indians.

March 3, 1905 (33 Stat. 1048). Exempted lands held by pueblo villages or individuals within Pueblo reservations from "taxation of any kind whatsoever . . . until Congress shall otherwise provide." Included in this exemption were cattle, sheep and any personal property furnished by the United States or used in the cultivation of lands.

June 20, 1910 (36 Stat. 557). New Mexico Enabling Act. Contained a specific provision that the terms "Indian" and "Indian country" shall include the Pueblo Indians of New Mexico and the lands now owned or occupied by them." Background to this statute and the special status of the Pueblos at that time is given in *Handbook*, (Page 902):

"It may be said that during the period from the accession of New Mexico to the granting of statehood, the Pueblos had a legal status sharply distinguished from that of most other Indian tribes and comprehended under Indian legislation only where Congress had expressly so provided, as in the matter of agency maintenance, 'civilization' appropriations, and tax exemption. In all other respects, each Pueblo had a status substantially similar to that of any other municipal corporation of the Territory . . .

"With the admission of New Mexico to statehood, however, a sharp reversal occurred . . . The termination of the Territorial government created a clear distinction between State and Federal authority and the center of control over the Pueblos shifted from Santa Fe to Washington. Thus the Pueblos came to be treated more and more as other Indian tribes.

"The first important step in this direction was taken in the New Mexico Enabling Act, which contained a specific provision that the terms 'Indian' and 'Indian country' shall include the Pueblo Indians of New Mexico and the lands now owned or occupied by them.' "

June 7, 1924 (43 Stat. 636). Pueblo Lands Act. Established a "Pueblo Lands Board" to investigate Pueblo land titles and provided the means by which a final solution was made regarding the many nonIndian claims with the lands of the Pueblo Indians.

The Alaskan Natives. The Natives of Alaska occupy a unique status among aboriginal peoples in the United States, in that the 1867 Treaty of Cession (15 Stat. 539) virtually gave Congress a blank check regarding what the Russians had considered "uncivilized" tribes by providing that such tribes "will be subject to such laws and regulations as the United States may from time to time adopt in regard to the aboriginal tribes of that country."

However, the Treaty of Cession provided for the collective naturalization of the members of the "civilized" native tribes in Alaska. Congress consented by implication to this contract, obligating it to incorporate the inhabitants, except "uncivilized" tribes, as citizens of the United States, by extending certain laws to the Territory and by passing the Organic Acts of 1884 and 1912. Thus, the difficulty of defining "civilization" made the legal status of the Alaskan Natives a matter of official conjecture.

Now, however, "the legal position of the individual Alaskan Natives has been generally combined with that of the Indians in the United States." (*Handbook*, page 934.)

Among the laws specifically relating to Alaskan Natives are numerous acts pertaining to hunting and fishing rights, reindeer ownership, and similar regulatory measures. In addition, there are numerous laws relating to the possessory rights of the Natives in the land used and occupied by them.

In 1971 the Alaska Native Claims Settlement Act provided for the conveyance of both property title and monetary award to Alaska Natives in settlement of their aboriginal land claims. (December 18, 1971, 85 Stat. 688.)

Finally, the Alaska Reorganization Act of May 1, 1936 (49 Stat. 1250) extended the incorporation and credit privileges of the Indian Reorganization Act to the organizations in Alaska, providing for a type of organization more suited to the existing Native groups and activities than organizations authorized for Indians in the Lower 48 States.

The Indians of New York. Because of the persistence of traditional forms of tribal organization, and treaty arrangements with New York which preceded the Federal Constitution, and special dealings with the State since that time, the various New York tribes have a unique status.

The State of New York has legislated for and dealt with the Indians within its borders for many years. The Revised Statutes of the State of New York of 1882 (pp. 272-336) show the extent and purpose of this legislation.

Since the State of New York has legislated so extensively regarding the Indian tribes living within its borders, there is a smaller body of federal law concerned with these Indians than with certain other tribes. Nonetheless, certain federal laws specifically regarding the Indians of New York have been enacted. These include restrictions upon the alienation of Indian lands, treaties involving removal of some tribes of the state to the West, and other matters primarily involving recognition by the federal government of specific tribes or establishment of reservations.

Indians of Oklahoma. The *Handbook* notes that "the laws governing the Indians of Oklahoma and the applicable decisions are so
voluminous that analysis of them would require a treatise in itself."
(Page 985.)

However, Cohen states: "In many respects the statutes and legal
principles generally applicable to Indians of the United States also
apply to Oklahoma Indians, while in other respects Oklahoma Indians, or certain groups thereof, are excluded from the scope of such
statutes and legal principles . . .

"Some of the important fields in which Oklahoma Indians have
received distinctive treatment and which present distinctive legal
problems . . . include enrollment, property laws affecting the Five
Civilized Tribes, taxation, and, among the Osages, questions of
head rights, competency, wills, and leasing. In each field, effort is
made to note how far principles generally applicable to Indians are
applicable or inapplicable in Oklahoma, rather than to explore the
distinctive problems of the various Oklahoma tribes, many of which
are still unsettled by the courts." (Handbook, pp. 985-6.)

Initially, laws dealing with Oklahoma tribes were concerned with
locating these Indians in that Territory—since few of these tribes
were indigenous to the area. "By treaty and the use of a degree of
force in instances, the tribes agreed to take up their abode farther
west, out of the way of the white man, on the land that was after-
ward designated as Indian Territory." (*Handbook*, Page 988.)

In 1893 Congress inaugurated a policy of terminating the tribal
existence and government of the Five Civilized Tribes (This term
refers to the five tribes removed to Oklahoma from the southeastern
United States: Cherokees, Chickasaws, Choctaws, Creeks and
Seminoles.) Their lands were allotted to individual Indians (Act of
March 3, 1893, Sec. 16, 27 Stat. 612, 645.) Agreements with the
tribes were negotiated by a Commission created for the purpose, as
directed by Congress, in order to carry out these objectives. This
was in conjunction with a number of other laws designed to further
the extinction of the tribes of Oklahoma and open up the Territory to
homesteading and settlement.

March 1, 1889. (25 Stat. 783). Established a special court for Indian Territory which was given jurisdiction of many offenses against
the United States, and of certain civil cases not wholly between
persons of Indian blood.

May 2, 1890. (26 Stat. 81,91.) Created a portion of Indian Territory into the Territory of Oklahoma. Enlarged the jurisdiction of the

226

special court created by Act of March 1, 1889 and put in force several general statutes of the State of Arkansas.

June 7, 1897. (30 Stat. 83-84.) Gave to the special court exclusive jurisdiction of all future cases, civil and criminal, and made the laws of the United States and the State of Arkansas in force in the Territory applicable to "all persons therein, irrespective of race," but with the qualification that any agreement negotiated by the Commission with any of the Five Civilized Tribes, when ratified, should supercede as to each tribe any conflicting provision of the Act.

June 26, 1898. (30 Stat. 495.) Forbid the enforcement of tribal laws in the special court and abolished tribal courts.

April 28, 1904. (33 Stat. 573.) Extended and continued all the laws of Arkansas heretofore put in force in the Indian Territory, so as to embrace all persons and estates therein, "whether Indian, freedmen, or otherwise," and conferred "full and complete jurisdiction" upon the district courts in the Territory regarding "all estates of decedents, the guardianships of minors and incompetents, whether Indians, freedmen, or otherwise."

June 16, 1906. (34 Stat. 267.) Enabling Act; providing for admission into the Union of both Indian Territory and Oklahoma Territory as the State of Oklahoma. Provided that "the laws in force in the Territory of Oklahoma shall extend over and apply to said State until changed by the legislature thereof."

Other special laws affecting Oklahoma Indians include those regarding preparation of tribal rolls to bring about allotment of tribal lands to individual Indians, alienation and taxation of allotted lands, leasing of allotted lands, inheritance, and various other special laws relating specifically to the Osage Indians.

A MOMENT OF TRUTH FOR THE
AMERICAN INDIAN

Keynote Address to the

First Convocation of American Indian Scholars
Princeton University
1970

BY RUPERT COSTO

This is a moment of truth for the American Indian—a moment when we stand on the threshold of great change. We have it in our power now to overcome the disasters of centuries, and to perform a miracle of change in favor of a better life for our people.

Our history in this land has a force of thousands of years' duration, and cannot be overlooked. Our profound concern for this land and for our people has a force so ancient and all-absorbing that it cannot be ignored. Yet we are indeed ignored and we are overlooked, in all the practical elements of life as it affects our people. Somehow, despite the many promises, and despite the many evidences of concern, the Native American lives in poverty, receives a complete and fruitful education only by the exercise of the greatest personal sacrifices, and dies in squalor.

At this moment in our history, our American Indian Historical Society conceived the idea of calling a Convocation of American Indian Scholars. Our purpose is to set in motion a responsive leadership that can give effective help in performing that miracle of change so desperately needed for our people. We entered upon the planning and organization of this Convocation with a sense of great pride in our people. In spite of centuries of being cheated out of our land, defrauded of our rights, and denied every privilege accorded all others in this nation, we have survived as a people. We have among us distinguished Native Americans who possess magnificent leadership qualities. Among us there are scholars who have contributed to knowledge, as well as those who, without formal education, have managed to help their people, and with utmost dedication. Above all, there is an upsurge of student population in higher education. Indeed it is in these young people that the hope of our race resides.

It is not the purpose nor the intention of this Convocation to dictate policies or to make decisions which will affect all of our people, or to impose upon the sovereignty of the tribes. It is our purpose only to point out a direction, to provide the help needed to reach certain necessary goals, and to support our own people wherever and whenever they need us.

Among us, traditionally, the scholars are the servants of the people. The *People* reign supreme, by virtue of their right to approve or disapprove actions in all areas of life, and by reason of their prerogative to protect individual and tribal rights. And so we say—let the people come for help to their own scholars. And let the scholars spend *their very lives* and energies in the service of their people.

To perform this miracle of change, we must, however, deal with our own problems and our own situations. The problems that disturb us—the issues that we need to talk about openly—the *facts of life* that beg for a meeting of our minds, these are the things we must deal with in our tribal meetings, and in our organizations, if we are to achieve our goals. We need to ask questions of ourselves, and of one another. We need to explore areas of concern, and come to mutual and unified decisions. It is not true that Indians cannot unite. We have united for years in our immense effort for sheer survival. In matters of practical need, it is enough if we can unite on a point no larger than the head of a pin, in order to make gains. In matters of the larger concern, it becomes a matter of exploration of thought and ideology—of ideas . . . and the use of creative intelligence. Let us ask ourselves some of these questions . . . questions of profound concern for ourselves as a people.

Is there, truly and honestly, anything left of our Indian cultures, traditions, and lifeways? I know there is, and you know it too. Therefore, let us pinpoint these areas of remaining Indian heritage, preserve the remaining cultures, traditions, philosophy, and the languages of our people. Indeed we have a duty to our historical heritage. I don't believe there is anybody here who would disagree.

Just the same, there is a tendency to vulgarize our cultures and history, even among our own people. For example, there is a class being conducted in Native history, at California State College at Hayward, in which the white students are given "cute" Indian names, are assigned to imaginary Indian tribes, and who then conduct themselves as though they are "real Indians," war whoop and all. We all know about some of the things that are taught by white teachers that are degrading to our people. But when an Indian pursues this type of vulgarization, then we must stop and view the whole situation, and begin to teach the true history of our people, teach it with respect and scholarly interpretation both to our own people and to the American public at large. I am not forgetting that the class just described was taught by an Indian, a Chippewa named Adam Nordwall. We have been remiss with respect to our children.

We should have had, long ago, practical schools for our children, to keep the languages alive, to keep the beauty of our heritage alive. It is not too late to do this even now.

Another question: Shall we allow tribal society and leadership, tribal autonomy and rights, to be wiped out? Or, shall we fight to preserve our ancient sovereign rights. The present situation, I grant you, is bad, and the present leadership in many tribes has been criticized, especially by our young people. Is it not time to make a stand, and change this situation, to change this leadership if change is needed?

If we do not improve our tribal leadership, by action of the people themselves, we are faced with total destruction of Indian life and cultures. What is left of Indian culture, when the tribal entity is gone? I ask this question of our young people who are so active on the urban front, and who have forsaken their own Indian people in favor of a struggle with windmills and shadows. This is our political entity. This is what remains of our social structure and lifeways. This is where it is *at*—within, by and through the tribe. Tribal society has been deformed and degraded by the Bureau of Indian Affairs. I believe this should be changed. I know it can be changed. But only with the greatest courage and single-mindedness, and only by our young people.

Let me pose another question. Shall we continue to allow our scholars, artists, and leaders to be overlooked and overshadowed, and even completely ignored by educational institutions, cultural programs, and institutional projects? Is it not time that we refuse to allow ourselves to be exploited for the sake of the self-interest of an ambitious intellectual, an ambitious city or state, or a Chamber of Commerce seeking to develop tourist attractions?

I say that we must insist, that wherever Indian programs are considered, Indian scholars and tribal people shall be dealt with, and shall constitute the leadership of such programs. We are continually confronted with ready-made programs that are carbon copies of programs for blacks, Chicanos and other ethnic groups. These programs have no relationship to our history and culture, nor to our situation today, either for teaching about Indians, or for teaching Indians themselves.

I would like to deal more directly with some of the profound questions with which we are faced in this moment of truth, at this time of change. And these questions can find answers only if the Indian scholars work well with the Indian people, and if the Indian people will turn to their own scholars for help.

The Bureau of Indian Affairs has dominated the Indian world for nearly a hundred and fifty years. It has stultified our intiative, corrupted our society, and caused a creeping paralysis to set in among our people—economically, and socially as well. Notwithstanding this fact, I don't know any Indians who want termination to take place. It would automatically abrogate our treaties, which are valid under international law, and valid in the Constitution of the United States of America. Despite the seriousness of this question, there is no unanimity of opinion as to the course of action that should be taken to rid ourselves of this Bureau domination. I submit to you, that the method of *supplanting* Bureau controls of programs, by *Indian tribes* and organized groups, is one good way to accomplish this.

The greatest and most important problem for us is the development of support for one another, as tribes, as organized groups, and as individuals. Some practical consideration as to the method of developing such support should be given. It is not enough simply to support one another, regardless of the quality of any program, or its administration. Support should be given after one is permitted the right to be consulted, to be informed, to be assured that there is a responsible intelligence at work. We must have a standard of leadership, and we must insist upon the highest standards. We should make it clear, to ourselves, to our own people, and to the general public, that leaders are chosen by the people, and that no one has a right to this status unless he is so chosen. This is an internal problem, and how we shall solve it is for ourselves to determine, and nobody else.

I would like to say that most of our so-called internal problems are not part of our heritage, nor are they part of our philosophy of human relations. To take one example—that of factionalism among Indian peoples and tribal groups. This is a condition that has been elevated as part of the "Indian syndrome" by some anthropologists. Factionalism, as it is understood in the western sense, is not an Indian tradition. It was not a normal way of life for the Native American. It is a European influence, a result of the disruption of Indian life, standards, and of the total destruction of distinctive Indian tribal land bases. Our tradition, ordained that man lived in peace with his brothers. Only when tribe after tribe was pushed off their land into the land of another tribe, did inter-tribal conflict occur. The ideology of this type of European or western civilization and its influence must be wiped out of our Indian society if we are to survive and prosper in any area of our lives.

I say, let us be aware of these influences. Let us put a stop to it. Let us defend one another, protect and help one another in our relationships, both individually and as a race. This is not to say that Indian people who are wrongdoers should be covered up for their evils. But surely we can handle these things ourselves. Not all Indians are noble. Not all Indians are little red angels.

I think the time has come when we must consider the question of land usage, land development, and land reclamation, as a whole. It seems rather foolish to fight for the reclamation of land in purely general terms. It seems foolish, too, when one considers that many Indians are being forced to sell their land at lowest prices, currently held by tribes or individuals. A glance at the Pine Ridge or Rosebud situation is an example. These people have only a small fraction of their land left to them, and an effort should be made, to help them out of their poverty, to develop them economically, so that they are not confromted with the loss of their land. Indeed it seems logical and even absolutely necessary, to buy the land back from nonIndians wherever that can be done, so that the tribal land base may be stabilized. This too, is one of the questions which scholars, students, and tribal people should be able to discuss and develop programs about.

The Native American population is small, compared to that of the whole country. It would appear that efforts should be combined, expended wisely and with the greatest promise of effectiveness. I know there are some who have become stupefied with the public interest, the publicity, the headlines. By itself, however, it will not solve anything. Together with a sound program of change, it will help enormously.

Where shall we look for help, to cause a miracle of change to happen? Certainly not from the federal government. Neither the Eisenhower, the Johnson, or the Nixon administration has developed a single effective and successful program leading to the practical improvement of our situation. We ourselves will have to take positive and effective action to make this change possible.

In this great effort, those who are scholars, those who are students, and those of us who are tribal activists, must unite all our energies and talents, so that the people may once again be the leading force in our lives and destiny.

Today's society is being torn apart by internal struggle. There is destruction ahead. Already there are forces in motion questioning the whole fabric of American society, questioning the form of government here in this country, struggling and fighting, but truly they don't know for what, and often they don't know why. This land is rotting to death. It is corrupt in so many ways and in so many places that water pollution is secondary to spiritual pollution.

Poverty is rampant in this nation, and the Indian is suffering most from this disease. I don't see any way to help, other than by our own people helping one another. We must be aware of the current tumult in this land. Every value is being questioned, and many are already discarded like a dirty rag. The government that exists in peace today, may be confronted with questions of mere survival tomorrow. The society that has been happy with its porcelain bathtubs, its television sets, automobiles, and all the supposed comforts of life, is no longer happy to own an automobile and a television set, while also being owned by a finance company or a bank. In the intellectual world, the same turmoil is taking place, and perhaps even more deeply. Because all the beliefs of western civilization are now being challenged. The honors that men receive with such gladness today, may well be the shame of tomorrow.

I think that the true Indian values, however, persist. And I am proud to know this, and to know that my people still hold to their spiritual life and their love of their land. I believe in the deep and profound integrity of our people. I believe that we Indians have more to offer this world than any other section of society today.

The Council of State Governments

RESOLUTION
ON THE
AMERICAN INDIAN POLICY
REVIEW COMMISSION

WHEREAS, the American Indian Policy Review Commission has recently completed its report to Congress; and

WHEREAS, the Commission Report has assumed as first principles that all policy and legal issues in contemporary Indian law should be resolved in favor of the Indians; and

WHEREAS, the Western Conference of The Council of State Governments believes that the Commission Report fails to recognize the following facts:

1. That the Constitution of the United States provides for only two sovereign powers—the United States and the several states within their spheres of influence.

2. Indian tribes are political subdivisions of the United States and are not sovereign in their own sphere.

3. Powers not specifically denied by treaty are not reserved to the tribes.

4. The intent of the Federal Congress in establishing Indian self-government was purposive in nature, to maintain tribal integrity and identity. Therefore, Congress did not intend Indian government to be general or territorial in nature.

5. There is no legal doctrine whereby one entering the land of another consents to general lawmaking and enforcing authority of the landowner.

6. The Commission Report fails to recognize that Indian tribes are no longer isolated communities; and

WHEREAS, the granting of sovereignty to Indian tribes and the necessary inclusion of non-Indians under their jurisdiction will destroy the ability of Indian peoples to make their own laws and be governed by them.

THEREFORE, BE IT RESOLVED, by the Western Conference of The Council of State Governments, that it agrees with the Minority Report of Congressman Lloyd Meeds, Vice Chairman of the American Indian Policy Review Commission, that Americans are justified in believing that 400 years have been sufficient to quiet title to the continent; and

BE IT FURTHER RESOLVED that the Western Conference also agrees with the following recommendations and opinions of the Minority Report:

1. That Congress should enact comprehensive legislation defining the scope and nature of tribal self-government, making clear that tribal governmental powers are limited.

2. Legislation should be enacted directly prohibiting Indian courts from exercising criminal jurisdiction or civil jurisdiction over any non-Indian or Indian who is not a member of the tribe which operates the court.

3. Congress should enact legislation allowing civil jurisdiction in state courts against Indian defendants in all cases where states would have jurisdiction were it not for Indian status of the defendant, and tribal government does not provide a judicial forum. Tribal interests could be protected by providing that rules of decision must be given appropriate weight in state courts.

4. Congress should bar actions by Indians against non-Indians for claims arising on reservations where tribes have not provided forums for similar actions by non-Indians against Indians.

5. Congress should enact legislation confirming that states have the same power to levy taxes, the legal incidence of which falls upon non-Indian activities or property, on Indian reservations as they have off Indian reservations. The exemptions to this blanket state authority should come in instances where federal regulation of special subject matter would preempt state regulation.

6. Congress should expressly proscribe the authorization for tribal taxation of nonmembers or property of nonmembers.

7. With regard to the Indian Civil Rights Act of 1968, if Indian governments are to exercise governmental powers as licensees of the United

States, it is imperative that they be fully answerable for the improper exercise of those powers.

8. To the extent that chosen national Indian policy entails financial burdens on persons other than Indians, it is neither fair nor rational for those burdens to be cast disproportionately on the taxpayers of the states in which Indian reservations are situated.

9. Congress should undertake to define "Indian Country" for the various purposes for which the term is used.

10. In regard to the operation of Public Law 280, if withdrawal from state jurisdiction is to be done on grounds of federal policy, the policy choices should be made by Congress, which can weigh fairly the cost of balkanizing state jurisdictions as well as the advantages to Indians.

11. In the Absence of ultimate authority over Indian land use planning lying with federal officials, the fairest system would be to place final authority in state planning agencies in which Indians would participate equally with other affected citizens; and

BE IT FURTHER RESOLVED, that copies of this resolution be delivered to the President of the United States, the President Pro Tempore of the United States Senate, the Speaker of the United States House of Representatives, the Secretaries of Agriculture and the Interior and to the Congressional Delegation of each of the member states of the Western Conference of the Council of State Governments and each of the six easterly adjoining states.

As Approved by the Western
Conference of The Council
of State Governments,
September 28, 1977

SOURCES OF INFORMATION

NEWSPAPERS:

The Navajo Times, P.O. Box 310, Window Rock, Az., 86515. Weekly, by Navajo Indian Tribe.

The Rawhide Press, Box 393, Wellpinit, Washington 99040, by the Spokane Tribal Council. Published monthly.

Ni-Mi-Kwa-Zoo-Min, P.O. Box 217, Cass Lake, Minnesota, 56633. By the Minnesota Chippewa Tribe in Leech Lake, published monthly.

The Chickasaw Times, 6033 Glencove Place, Oklahoma City, Oklahoma 73132. Published monthly by the Chickasaw Tribe.

Fort Belknap Camp Crier, Extension Office, Box 74, RR 1, Harlem, Montana, 59526. Published weekly by the Bureau of Indian Affairs.

Muskogee Nation News, P.O. Box 1114, Okmulgee, Oklahoma, 74447. Monthly newspaper, published by the Creek Nation.

Choctaw Community News, Philadelphia, Mississippi, 39350. Monthly tribal newspaper.

Hualapai Times, P.O. Box 68, Peach Springs, Arizona, 86434. Published monthly by the Hualapai Tribe.

Southern Ute Drum, Tribal Affairs Building, Ignacio, Colorado 81137. Published bi-weekly by the Southern Ute tribe.

Yakima Nation News, P.O. Box 386, Toppenish, Washington, 98948. Published bi-weekly by the Yakima Indian Nation.

Confederated Umatilla Journal, Route 1, P.O. Box 638, Pendleton, Oregon, 97801. Monthly, published by the Confederated tribes of the Umatilla Reservation (Cayuse, Umatilla, Walla Walla).

Pima Maricopa Echo, Gila River Indian Community, P.O. Box 185, Sacaton, Arizona 85247. Monthly, published by the Pima and Maricopa Tribes of the Gila River Indian Community.

Qua' Toqti, Box 266, New Oraibi, Arizona, 86039. Published bi-weekly, by the Hopi Publishers, "serving the Hopi Nation."

Talking Leaf, 1111 W. Washington Blvd, Los Angeles, California 90015. Published by the Los Angeles Indian Center, monthly.

Carolina Indian Voice, P.O. Box 1075, Pembroke, North Carolina 28372. Independent, published weekly.

The Tundra Times, Box 1287, Fairbanks, Alaska 99801. Published weekly by an all-Native corporation.

Fort Apache Scout, P.O. Box 898, Whiteriver, Arizona. Published monthly, by the Fort Apache tribe.

Alligator Times, 6073 Sterling Road, Hollywood, Florida, 33024. Monthly, by the Seminole Tribe.

Nishnabe News, University Center, Northern Michigan University, Marquette, Michigan 49855. Monthly, by the Indian students. (An excellent example of a student newspaper, actually more than just a student paper.)

Ni-Mi-Kwe-Zoo-Min, P.O. Box 697, Cass Lake, Minnesota, 56633. Published monthly, by the Chippewa Tribe.

The Native Nevadan, 98 Colony Road, Reno, Nevada 89502. Published monthly by the Nevada Intertribal Council.

Jicarilla Chieftain, P.O. Box 147, Dulce, New Mexico 87528. Published monthly by the Jicarilla Apache Indian Tribe.

Crazy Horse News, P.O. Box 1788, Rapid City, South Dakota 57779. Published monthly by an individual Oglala Sioux.

United Sioux Tribes News, Star Route 3, Pierre, South Dakota. Published by the United Sioux Tribes Development Association.

Wassaja, a national newspaper of Indian America, 1451 Masonic Avenue, San Francisco, California 94117. Published as an All-Tribes newspaper, monthly, by the American Indian Historical Society.

BOOKS:

This listing of books contains only a few of the vast numbers that are available. The listing includes those that can be used as information, both background and current, applicable to events now taking shape in Indian affairs.

Indian Land Tenure, by Imre Sutton. Published by Clearwater Publishing Company, New York, 1975, 290 pages.

The Corporation and the Indian, by H. Craig Miner. Published by University of Missouri Press, Columbia, Missouri, 1976, 236 pages.

Uncommon Controversy, Fishing Rights of the Muckleshoot, Puyallup and Nisqually Indians, a Report. University of Washington Press, 1970, 232 pages.

100 Million Acres, by Kirke Kickingbird and Karen Ducheneaux. Published by the Institute for the Development of Indian Law, Washington, D.C. (How the Indians lost their land.)

Textbooks and the American Indian, by R. Costo & J. Henry. Published by The Indian Historian Press, 1970.

The American Indian Reader: History. Published by The American Indian Historical Society, 1972.

The Indian in America, by Wilcomb E. Washburn. Published by Harper & Row, New York, 292 pages.

Mass Media: Forces in Our Society, by Francis -H. Voelker & Ludmila A. Voelker. Published by Harcourt, Brace, Jovanovich, 431 pages.

Native American Tribalism, by D'Arcy McNickle. Published by Oxford University Press, 190 pages.

Documents of United States Indian Policy, by Francis Paul Prucha. University of Nebraska Press, Lincoln, 278 pages.

The Pueblo Indians, by Joe Sando. Indian Historian Press, 276 pages.

A Century of Dishonor, by Helen Hunt Jackson. Originally published in 1881, it has been reprinted by Harper Torchbooks, New York. Reveals conditions and discrimination suffered by the Indians in the 19th century. It deserves to be re-read.

Indian Americans: Unity and Diversity, by Murray L. Wax. Prentice Hall, Englewood Cliffs.

The Only Land I Know, by Dial & Eliades. Published by the Indian Historian Press. (Unusual story of the Lumbee Indians of North Carolina.)

PERIODICALS:

American Indian Law Review, twice a year. Published by the University of Oklahoma Press, Norman. Contains more than 100 pages of basic articles on Indian law and law history.

The Indian Historian, published by the American Indian Historical Society since 1964, quarterly, 64 pages of history, cultures, literature, book reviews, commentary and education.

The Weewish Tree, a national magazine of Indian America for young people. This is the only youth magazine published by any ethnic group, regularly 32 pages, large type, published by the American Indian Historical Society, 6 times a year.

The American Indian Journal, monthly, usually 24-28 pages, Published by the Institute for the Development of Indian Law, Washington, D.C. Up-to-date information as well as basic articles on issues.

It is emphasized that there are other magazines and periodicals. These are the four most highly recommended by readers and educators.

240

FEDERAL INFORMATION SOURCES:

The Congressional Record, published as a daily record of deliberations of both the U.S. Senate and House of Representatives. Pending legislation is recorded here, the discussions of the legislators are published, and issues coming before the Congress may be found in the pages of this closely printed record. The *Record* has been criticized because congressmen have found it possible to insert material and have speeches printed in that publication which they have not made personally. It costs approximately $85 a year.

The Federal Register, published as an official record of bills and regulations, laws that go into effect, and hearings that are scheduled on pending legislation. This publication is usually too late to be of any use to the Indian tribes and members. As a rule, a certain time is allocated for response to pending regulations. By the time the Indian people receive notice through the Register, it is too late to respond. Criticism and objection to this procedure has been filed officially, and this may change. The Federal Register is published twice a week, and costs $50 per annum.

Bureau of Indian Affairs Information Department, 1951 Constitution Avenue, N.W. Washington,D.C. 20245. During the last two or three years this office has been very helpful to Indian tribes and organizations. They publish a small newsletter, as well as information concerning issues and events.

Most of the various federal agencies now have "Indian desks." An inquiry will bring you the name and address of the person who is responsible for such agencies as Health, Education, and Welfare, Manpower, and the like.

Any federal information bulletin listing agencies will provide addresses and telephone numbers.

Tribal Education and Communication Departments. Most of the larger tribes have such departments. A listing of the tribes may be found in the Department of Commerce book mentioned above.

Universities also have information services which are capable of providing sources and personnel. Among these is the University of New Mexico, Albuquerque, N.M.; and University of Minnesota, Minneapolis. Both universities have Indian programs. The University of California at Berkeley and Los Angeles, are examples of only two educational institutions that may be tapped for information in the field of education.

The Native American Rights Fund, at Boulder, Colorado, has a fine legal library, a staff of attorneys (most of whom are Indian), and supplies information upon request.

BASIC REFERENCES:

Handbook of Federal Indian Law, by Felix Cohen. Reprint by AMS Press, New York.

Indian Affairs: Treaties, Kappler. Reprinted by AMS Press, New York.

Federal and State Indian Reservations and Indian Trust Areas, U.S. Department of Commerce, Washington, D.C., 592 pages.

American Indian Policy Review Commission, Final Report. U.S. Government Printing Office, Washington, D.C.

Law and the American Indian: Readings, Notes and Cases, by Monroe E. Price. Bobbs-Merrill, New York. 807 pages.

Hearings on various Indian investigations and legislation are held periodically by the Senate and House Subcommittees on Indian Affairs. Your senators and congressmen can send them upon request.

ORGANIZATIONS:

National Congress of American Indians, 1430 K Street, N.W. Washington, D.C. 20005.

National Indian Education Association, 1115 Second Ave. South, Minneapolis, Minnesota 55403.

American Indian Historical Society, 1451 Masonic Avenue, San Francisco, California 94117.

The National Tribal Chairmen's Association, 1701 Pennsylvania Avenue, Room 207, Washington, D.C. 20006. No regular information service, and no newsletter. Information concerning the tribes upon request.

National Indian Youth Council, 201 Hermosa N.E. Albuquerque, New Mexico 87108. Publishes *Americans Before Columbus* irregular and a good source of information concerning current Indian affairs.

There are approximately 200 Indian organized groups, as well as Indian centers in the cities and towns of the country numbering at least 250. Most Indian centers publish newsletters. Many Indian organized groups send informational documents periodically. But the above three organizations publish regularly, information and documents concerning the American Indian.

THE AUTHORS

Rupert Costo, a Cahuilla Indian of southern California. Active in Indian affairs for more than half a century. Served his people as tribal spokesman for eight years. Founded and is president of the American Indian Historical Society. Editor of *Wassaja*, a national newspaper of Indian affairs. Professions: engineering, surveying, agriculture, cattle raising. Special studies: economics, minerology, education, government.

Jeannette Henry, Eastern Cherokee of North Carolina. Active in Indian affairs for thirty-five years. Publications editor of The Indian Historian Press, editor of *The Indian Historian,* a scholarly quarterly devoted to Indian history, culture, literature. Profession: author, editor, journalist. Special studies: literature, education, economics, philosophy.

The Indian Historian Press has published more than twenty books in Native American history, education, literature and current affairs.

A catalog of books and periodicals published by this all-Indian professional publishing house will be sent upon request to:

The Indian Historian Press
1451 Masonic Ave.
San Francisco, Calif. 94117

INDIAN TREATIES:
Two Centuries
of Dishonor ══════

(Volume 5 in the American Indian
Reader Series: Current Affairs)

One copy: $6.95
Five or more copies: $4.00 each

All five volumes of the American Indian Reader: $20.00

The volumes are: Anthropology, Education, History, Literature,
Current Affairs

● ORDER FORM ●

Please send_____ #copies
    of Indian Treaties

_____ # sets
    of the American Indian Reader series

Name:_____

Address:_____

City & State:_____

Zip# _____ Amount enclosed_____

Purchase Order Accepted_____ #

Please allow two weeks for delivery from the time order is received.

    Send order to: The Indian Historian Press
    1451 Masonic Avenue, San Francisco, Ca. 94117